Sustainability

A Biological Perspective

Encouraging students to engage in the challenges and complexity of sustainability, this text considers not only the theories underlying sustainability, but, more importantly, how theories are translated into practice and the difficulties of achieving this in the world in which we live. This pragmatic focus gives students a greater understanding of the practice of sustainability and highlights the challenges involved. Models and theories are illustrated throughout with real-world examples to help students move away from the abstract and connect with genuine issues.

The text begins by focusing on sustainable production and consumption and how they are related. The role of tools such as modelling and sustainability indicators are explored, and extended into the fields of stakeholder participation, livelihoods and evidence-based policy. The final chapter explores the interconnections between apparently disparate subjects, including ecology, environmental science and economics, and the importance of taking an interdisciplinary perspective.

STEVE MORSE has been involved in sustainable development projects and research for 30 years. His research interests focus on the practical achievement of sustainability in development and natural resource management and he has been involved with such projects across the world. He is a Fellow of the Royal Geographical Society, the Higher Education Academy and the Institute of Biology, and a member of the Development Studies Association.

Sustainability

A Biological Perspective

STEPHEN MORSE
Department of Geography
University of Reading

CAMBRIDGE UNIVERSITY PRESS
Cambridge, New York, Melbourne, Madrid, Cape Town, Singapore,
São Paulo, Delhi, Dubai, Tokyo

Cambridge University Press
The Edinburgh Building, Cambridge CB2 8RU, UK

Published in the United States of America by Cambridge University Press,
New York

www.cambridge.org
Information on this title: www.cambridge.org/9780521835336

First published 2010

Printed in the United Kingdom at the University Press, Cambridge

A catalogue record for this publication is available from the British Library

ISBN 978-0-521-83533-6 Hardback
ISBN 978-0-521-54300-2 Paperback

Contents

Preface

At the time of writing this book, towards the end of the first decade of the twenty-first century, the human race is facing many challenges. It can almost be said that we are facing a 'Perfect Storm'. On the one hand we have a growing population. The United Nations estimates that global populations will continue to increase, as shown in the following graph.

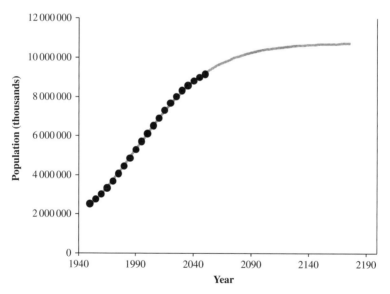

Latest global population trend as predicted by the United Nations (black dots) and a fitted logistic curve. (Source of data: esa.un.org/unpp.)

There is a levelling of population around 11 billion towards the turn of the twenty-first century, but not enough data as yet to suggest whether this will eventually decline. Hence the fitting of a logistic curve which delivers a levelling rather than an eventual decline. More on that form of population curve later in the book, but what we do know is that those people need food and water to live. Yet the UN is concerned about global increases in food prices and in 2009 it has been estimated that the world's hungry have surpassed one billion, with 265 million of them in sub-Saharan Africa, an increase of almost 12% relative to 2008 (www.un.org/issues/food/taskforce). If we are struggling now then how will it be possible to feed the population 30 years from now? With water supply the situation is little better. The World Water Council estimates that 'water stress' (the balance between withdrawal and replenishment) is 'very high' in many parts of the world and we already face a water crisis and an increase in tensions as populations compete for the resource (www.worldwatercouncil.org). This is not only a matter of water supply for human consumption and sanitation. It has been estimated that it takes the following 'water footprints' to produce these goods:

- *16 000 litres to produce 1 kilo of beef*
- *140 litres to produce 1 cup of coffee*
- *120 litres to produce 1 glass of wine*
- *23 000 litres to produce a leather bag*
- *900 litres to produce 1 kilo of corn*
- *3000 litres to produce 1 kilo of rice*
- *1000 litres to produce 1 litre of milk*
- *1350 litres to produce 1 kilo of wheat*

> (Water at a crossroads, Dialogue and Debate at the Fifth World Water Forum, Istanbul 2009; available at www.worldwatercouncil.org)

If the increasing demands for food and water while we are struggling to meet these demands now is not enough to worry about, we also have to put human-induced climate change into the mix. The following graph has been based on Figure 10–4 in Chapter 10 of the *Fourth Assessment Report of the Intergovernmental Panel on Climate Change* (Meehl *et al.*, 2007). It shows the predicted trends in global surface warming (change over average) until the year 2100. The three scenarios (A1B, A2 and B1) are based upon assumptions as to how the human race will respond to the challenge in the coming years.

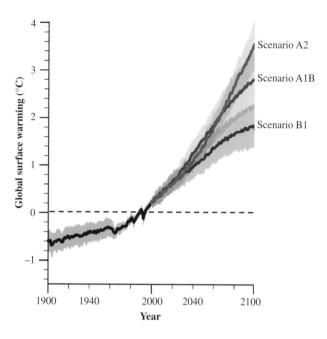

The trends are ominous. All three scenarios suggest that global temperatures will steadily increase. The 'fuzziness' around each of the lines is intended to provide a range of estimates for each year. The A2 scenario provides the 'worse case' of the three in the graph, and is characterised by a fragmented world of independently acting, self-reliant nations and increasing population. Scenario A1B is that of a more integrated world, with a balanced emphasis on a range of energy sources rather than a continued reliance on fossil fuels. It also assumes that the population will reach 9 billion in 2050 and then decline rather than remain stable, as suggested by the logistic curve presented earlier. Scenario B1 is the 'best case' of the three in the graph and assumes an integrated and ecologically friendly world with the same population trend as A1B (i.e. eventual decline), but a major emphasis on promotion of cleaner technologies and global, rather than regional, solutions to global warming. But even here we will still witness an increase in global temperature over the next 100 years. Thus I'm afraid the bad news is that even if we do act now we are still faced with not only limiting the damage we do for future generations, but having to cope with the damage that has already been wrought. No one can say with any certainty what the repercussions will be in different places of the globe, but there is no doubt that changes will occur, including sea-level rise (resulting in the salinisation of soil), changes in agricultural patterns and redistribution of fresh-water sources.

Hence the phrase 'Perfect Storm'; an increasing population in parallel with an increase in global temperatures and the need to provide food and water for all these people when we are struggling to do that now. As a result there has never been a greater need for us to understand the changes we are bringing about and how we can best cope with them. That is the Holy Grail of sustainable development.

But while the above is often the way in which the importance of sustainable development (or sustainability) is portrayed as a means of allowing future generations to have access to adequate resources, we do have to bear in mind the positives. Food and water are vital for life, but humans also speak of the quality of that life; the need for a reasonable income, education, health care and recreation. We all want a long and healthy life and we all want to enjoy that life. Sustainability is about making these things a reality and thus inevitably we have to take a broad view spanning the social sciences and economics. Unfortunately, sustainability can have a bad press, as it is all too often equated with the rhetoric of doom and gloom, as I've used at the start of the Preface, and to some extent this is understandable, as it has to reflect a warning of the dilemmas we face, but this can go hand in hand with a feeling of joylessness and severity. It seems that sustainability is only associated with bad news and preaching about what we can't do rather than what we can. I hope this book, while not having all the answers, can at least map the territory and help point to a positive way forward.

The aim of this book is to help make the often messy and imprecise visions of sustainability accessible to natural scientists. Sustainability is more than just science, but science, and in particular biology, does nonetheless have a vital role to play. Thus the intended readership for the book comprises undergraduate students in biology, particularly ecology, environmental science, natural resource management (e.g. agriculture and forestry) and also the physical sciences (particularly chemistry and engineering). While the focus is upon a biological perspective towards sustainability, it is simply not possible to exclude social and economic concerns, and sustainability is about the overlap between all these perspectives. Thus, while the book is not intended primarily for students of the social sciences, they may find it useful as an introductory supplement alongside other texts. Also, in line with the very ethos of sustainability, the book takes a global perspective, drawing upon examples from many countries – developed and developing. Sustainability is not about 'us and them' but 'all'.

If the book encourages young scientists at the start of their careers to partake in the human race's striving for sustainability, then I will have deemed it to be a success. We will sorely need them.

ACKNOWLEDGEMENTS

I would like to thank my family (Maura, Llewellyn and Rhianna) for putting up with the many hours I had to devote to writing this book. I would also like to thank Reverend Sister Nora McNamara for giving me my very first opportunity of engaging with sustainable development, even if we didn't call it by that name at the time.

1

Sustainability: a word of our time

Sustainability, often employed as a short-hand term for sustainable development, is truly a word of our time. In the early twenty-first century we inhabit a world which is witnessing a dramatic change in climate, the rise of new economic powers, a crisis in the global financial system and technological breakthroughs that happen almost on a daily basis. All of this can only enhance what we all intuitively know – that the planet is in a state of flux when assessed in environmental, economic or social terms. What we see around us today may not be what we see in the future – the world will be different. But what will that world be like, or perhaps more to the point, what do we wish it to be like? Do we want our children and our children's children to be able to enjoy the environment we have today or do we want them to have better than that? These are important questions, but in the busy lives we lead trying to do better for our families in this generation, it can be tough thinking that far ahead.

Sustainability is all about people and time; the past, present and the future. The past because it teaches us a great deal about human existence and how we have responded to stresses, the present because we have a moral duty to make sure that those alive today have the best quality of life that can be provided and the future because what has been done in our past and present should not damage the ability of future generations to enjoy a good quality of life. Thus, for example, we have a duty not only to limit any damage we do to the environment, but to ameliorate any damage done by past generations.

This book is about sustainability, but it is specifically about how the science of biology is a vital component of sustainability. The classic diagram of sustainability as the intersection of three

1

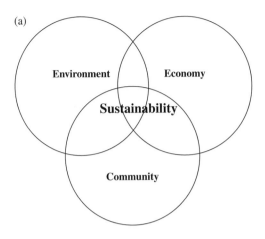

(a)

Environment   Economy

Sustainability

Community

(b)

Economy

Growth, business (banks),
globalisation, competitive
advantage, infrastructure, transport

Development
trade-offs,
protests

Environment

Sustainability?

Tourism

Tax, employment

Community

Votes! Security

Figure 1.1 The three interlocking circles of sustainability: (a) three equal
circles implying an equal consideration to each; (b) dominance of
economics and community.

circles (Figure 1.1a) bearing the labels 'environment', 'economics' and 'community' (or variations of those terms) does not usually mention biology as one of the key elements. Instead we tend to think of biology as being somehow wrapped up within the 'environment'. After all, ecology is a sub-branch of biology and surely 'environment' is at least in part about ecology? Sustainability occupies the overlap of the three ircles; implying that we need all of these fields to be considered on an equal basis. We cannot have sustainability solely by protecting the environment and ignoring people. Unfortunately, sustainability is so often seen by politicians as more a sub-branch of economics than anything else; the circles unfortunately don't have the same size (Figure 1.1b) and the issues become rather one dimensional. Figure 1.1b might be a rather jaundiced view of a society dominated by concerns of economic development, the need to win elections and environment as a place to be used by us rather than something which demands a moral need for protection, but I wonder whether there is at least some resonance with what we see around us? In this book an effort will be made to redress that balance and make those circles more equal. The case will be made for the importance that biological science and biologists can play in sustainability. But in doing so, it is important to stress how biologists need to interface with other fields, especially with the social sciences. In other words, this book is about the overlaps in Figure 1.1.

1.2 SCIENCE AND SUBJECTIVITY

The notion of 'sustainability' seen in its most basic sense as an acknowledgement by people that what they do now could have consequences for the future is arguably as old as the human race. Neither is it a prerogative of 'Western', 'Eastern' or any other civilisation. The adjective 'sustainable' can be applied to a host of human activities and structures to imply that they can continue into the future without detriment to either people or their environment. It has been used for activities such as agriculture, water supply, resource management and development, as well as the institutions charged with supporting them. We often forget that it is the activities which are the important elements (and generally well defined) and 'sustainable' is added to convey the importance of the activities continuing into the future without detriment. As a result there is some plasticity as to the meaning of 'sustainable'. How far into the future are we talking about, and what exactly does detriment mean and to whom does it apply? Unsurprisingly, the evolution of sustainability has been long and complex, with rich intersections to economics and politics. Given that agriculture, water supply and so on are described in terms of what people do, then sustainable is a human-centric adjective; it is defined by people to be applied to people.

So where does biology fit into this landscape? Given that human beings are biological, then biology is arguably fundamental to sustainability. After all, can there be such a thing as sustainability without sentient beings to care about their future? Life on Earth is thought to have originated some 3.5 billion years ago, at least that is our best guess based upon what appear to be microbe-like objects we can find in ancient rocks, and this is only one billion years after the Earth itself came into existence. Since that time, life has evolved into a myriad of different species, many of which have become extinct. Employing our human-centric definition, then these extinct species were certainly not sustainable! Many extinctions have occurred during the 3.5-billion-year history of life on Earth and there have been periods where the rate accelerated (Raup and Sepkoski, 1982; Rohde and Muller, 2005). Figure 1.2a is a graph showing changes in marine biodiversity up to 540 million years ago, while Figure 1.2b shows the extinction rate over that same period. It may surprise the reader to see that marine biodiversity now is much higher than it has been. In Figure 1.2b it can be seen that there have been a number of major extinction events, with the one at the border of the Permian-Triassic (250 million years ago) being especially noteworthy when up to 96% of marine species disappeared. It is the only known mass extinction event for insects. As a result this event is called the 'great dying'. What are the causes for the extinction events we see in Figure 1.2b? Well, there are many suggestions, including increased volcanism and the impact of an asteroid or comet, but it is as well to remember that people have not been involved in any of them; they were 'natural' events. Thus, while extinctions have occurred, and it has been estimated that 99% of all species that ever lived have become extinct, life has proved itself to be very durable. Indeed it is now known that some prokaryotic species are durable enough to survive in the hostile environment of space and could potentially seed other planets. Thus the evidence of life on Earth is that it is highly 'sustainable' – it is a great survivor. If humans disappeared from the Earth, if we were shown to be unsustainable as a species, then life would go on adapting and perhaps survive almost to the very death of the planet.

Biologists are used to studying change, and replacement of some species in the fossil record by others has no value judgement associated with it. Indeed, in biology we don't normally use the term 'sustainable'

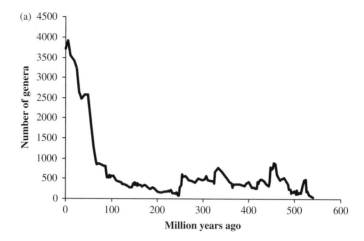

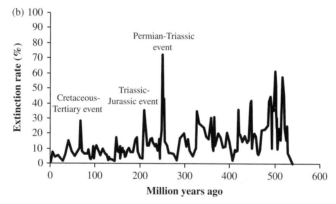

Figure 1.2 Extinction events and change in biodiversity: (a) biodiversity (assessed here as number of marine genera); (b) extinction rate (assessed as % of marine genera), estimated as the percentage of genera entering a period, but not surviving to the end of it.

Data taken from strata.geology.wisc.edu/jack/. Based upon the work of Sepkoski (2002).

for life. After all, life is a catchall phrase that covers species which feed and reproduce in many ways, including some that depend upon exotic sources of energy such as deep-sea volcanic vents. But the phrase 'life is sustainable' is not one that is used much, if at all, in biology. Instead we talk of the 'durability' or 'resilience' of life; it's ability to continue after shocks and protuberances, of which there have been many since the birth of the planet. Sustainable is a human-centric term; it is applied to people and the interactions we have with our environment. Thus when we are talking of the role of biology within sustainability, we mean the role that biology plays vis-à-vis people, and we are talking of very short timescales relative to those in Figure 1.2. The most commonly used definition of sustainable development is:

> *development that meets the needs of the present without compromising the ability of future generations to meet their own needs.* (WCED (1987, page 8))

The generations being referred to in this definition are those of *Homo sapiens*; of us. Thus the timescale is perceived in terms of human lifespans and we are in the realm of decades, not millions of years. But if a disaster occurred (man-made or otherwise) and human beings were almost wiped off the planet, as the evidence suggests we nearly were following the volcanic eruption of Lake Toba in what is now Sumatra, Indonesia, some 75 000 years ago, we don't regard the survival of a remnant population of humans hanging on for survival in caves as being 'sustainable', although technically they would be 'future generations'. The key word in the WCED definition is actually the most plastic – 'needs'. This is a highly subjective term and will vary a great deal depending on personal tastes and ambitions, but whatever the starting point, the desired change in this context is almost always for the better. So what are these 'needs'?

People are, of course, biological and some of our basic needs include adequate supplies of food, water and air, as well as freedom from disease, parasites and harmful chemicals. These can be expressed in clear terms. For example, it is estimated that a human male adult needs to consume on average some 2500 calories each day, along with associated minerals and vitamins and 3 litres of water. The average male adult takes 12 to 15 breaths in a minute while at rest and each of these involves the intake of 0.5 litres of air. This approximates to 9000 to 11 000 litres of air being breathed in a day or 1800 to 2200 litres of oxygen. All of these requirements can change, of course, depending upon factors such as environment, age and activity, but they are relatively stable and the figures are not plucked out of nothing, but have arisen from research. We know that consuming less or indeed more of these requirements can imply or lead to problems with health. We can formulate policies which provide these needs for food, water and air free of disease and contaminants, and also to encourage people to avoid over-consumption of food, which can be harmful to health. Thus at a biological level the 'needs' talked about in the WCED definition can be identified.

But the WCED were talking of 'needs' not only at this fundamental level of biology, but also in terms of the need for adequate income, education, clothing, leisure etc. and here matters are far more subjective and far less scientific. For example, the oft-quoted income figures of $1/day and $2/day to be achieved through the Millennium Development Goals (MDGs; www.un.org/millennium-goals) are remarkable examples of durability in themselves, but what do they mean? Well $1/day can be easily translated into local currencies via the exchange rates we are used to seeing in banks and tourist centres, and they fluctuate on a daily and even hourly basis in ways which are difficult to predict. Sometimes the exchange rate value of the US dollar goes up relative to another currency (you get less local currency for each dollar) and sometimes it goes down (you get more local currency for each dollar). But not only do we have these currency fluctuations, but also the local purchasing power of $1/day can vary a great deal across nation states and even places within the same nation state. One famous and light-hearted method of illustrating the differing 'purchasing power' of an international currency such as the US dollar was invented by *The Economist* magazine. They came up with 'burger-nomics' based upon the local retail price of a 'Big Mac' hamburger as sold by McDonalds, a large international restaurant chain. The 'Big Mac' hamburger is much the same wherever it is sold, and thus we can use it to compare the purchasing power of a US dollar. In Figure 1.3 we have the prices of the 'Big Mac' in three places (based upon a survey carried out in 2009 by *The Economist*); China, USA and the 'Euro Zone'. The local prices are, of course, different. In China a 'Big Mac' costs Yuan 12.50, in the USA it costs $3.57 and in the Euro Zone it costs €3.31. However, once converted to the US dollar (based upon currency exchange rates) we see very large differences. The 'Big Mac' in Chwina looks like excellent value at $1.83, while in the Euro Zone the price is $4.60. Thus $2 will buy you one hamburger in China (with change), but won't even buy you half a hamburger in the Euro Zone. Why the large difference? It must be noted that hamburgers are not produced in the USA and shipped across the world. If that were the case then hamburgers everywhere would probably be more expensive than in the USA because of the added cost of global transportation. The hamburgers are, for the most part, produced from locally sourced materials in each of the countries where the chain has a restaurant. Therefore the large disparity when converted to US dollars is due to a host of factors, including local wage rates and differing costs of locally sourced materials such as beef, as well as local transportation. Thus the meaning of $1/day in real purchasing terms can vary enormously from place to place, yet it serves

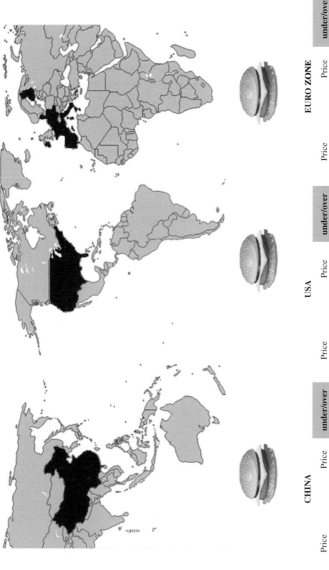

CHINA				USA				EURO ZONE			
Price (local currency)	ER	Price (US$)	under/over valuation	Price (local currency)	ER	Price (US$)	under/over valuation	Price (local currency)	ER	Price (US$)	under/over valuation
Yuan 12.50	6.83	1.83	−49%	US$ 3.57	1	3.57	0	Euro 3.31	0.72	4.60	+29%

Figure 1.3 Burger-omics: purchasing power parity calculated on the basis of a cost of a 'Big Mac' hamburger (*The Economist*, 16 July 2009). Prices are those of the 'Big Mac' hamburger sold in the McDonalds chain of restaurants. Exchange rate (ER) of local currency to the US dollar (as of 13 July 2009).

as a convenient banner or clarion call, which if realised will make a difference to the lives of millions of people, and economists have no choice but to factor in the 'purchasing power' of currencies when making international comparisons.

Indeed, going a step further, income is not the be-all and end-all of quality of life. There are other factors which matter, and these may well be quite different from person to person. There are the obvious ones like education, clothing and health care, but water provision, power supply, sanitation, quality of housing and infrastructure, availability of amenities such as shops, climate, pollution, traffic, neighbours, mobile phones, access to the internet and so on can also be important. Some of these are 'measurable' in the same sense that we can measure biological needs and 'purchasing power', while others are not, and even if we could 'measure' them it is likely that what one person perceives as 'good' could be different from someone else's perspective. Here we are moving far away from the biological or even economic needs and into a realm which is far more subjective and value laden. As a scientist, this innate immeasurability, except in rather simplest forms such as 'scoring' or 'ranking', may be frustrating, but I'm afraid that is the nature of the beast we call sustainability. Any attempt to reduce that complexity of 'need' to say economics will inevitably provide us with a very partial picture and could fail to recognise changes that may be occurring in another dimension which are also important. Therefore in this book the reader will come across many faces of sustainability which are not 'science'.

1.3   ROOTS OF SUSTAINABILITY

There are many roots to sustainable development, and here it is really only possible to provide a few of the highlights in that complex history. If the reader wishes to delve deeper into this story then I can recommend Pepper (1987), as well as Kidd (1992), Goodland (1995), Mitcham (1995), Mebratu (1998), Adams (2001) and Costanza *et al.* (2007). Indeed, if we pick apart this phrase into its two components we can gain an understanding as to why this is such a complex term with a long history. In biology the verb 'develop' means to grow or to change (as in the development of an embryo), but here we are using 'develop' to broadly mean to improve or to make something better. Thus we talk of 'human development' not so much as development of a human being from an embryo through a child to an adult, with associated anatomical, physiological and psychological changes, but an improvement in people's lives. As the United Nations Development Programme (UNDP) puts it:

> *Human development is a process of enlarging people's choices. In principle, these choices can be infinite and change over time. But at all levels of development, the three essential ones are for people to lead a long and healthy life, to acquire knowledge and to have access to resources needed for a decent standard of living. If these essential choices are not available, many other opportunities remain inaccessible.* (UNDP HDR (1990, page 10))

Human development in the sense of us improving our lot is as old as the human race, and the pace and extent of change has often been spurred by changes in the environment. The first sedentarisation (or semi-sedentarisation) of people is said to have occurred as early as 12 000 BC in the Mediterranean region; occupying what is now Israel, Lebanon and Jordan. The Natufian culture existed even before the development of agriculture and its people lived through hunting and gathering just as their ancestors had done, but the carrying capacity of the environment was high enough to remove the need for a nomadic lifestyle. Thus people no longer had to keep moving to find food and water. Sedentarisation in turn helped facilitate the development of agriculture in that part of the world between 10 800 and 9500 BC. The latter was perhaps aided by a change in the climate towards one which was cooler and dryer, thereby reducing the hunting/gathering-based carrying capacity (Munro, 2003, 2004). Interactions of cultures, either positively through trade or negatively through colonialisation and even war, have also acted as catalysts for change. Even during the years of European expansionism in the nineteenth and early twentieth centuries, the colonial powers continued to stress the positive changes which they were bringing about through creation of physical infrastructure such as roads, railroads and ports, but also through education. The latter was particularly so for the Christian missionary movements, which founded schools and hospitals wherever they went. Thus sustainability is not the same as stasis, and change can often be spurred by stress. We are facing such stress now with the current theories on human-mediated global warming and the impacts that could have on our societies. Indeed it is perhaps no accident that the rise in popularity of sustainability in the latter years of the twentieth century corresponded with a time when we realised that there is nowhere else for us to go; this planet is our home and despoliation of its carrying capacity will negatively impact upon us all.

Rightly or wrongly, the birth of what we today regard as modern development is often taken to be President Truman's programme for peace and freedom (1949), stressing four major courses of action that his presidency would pursue during his tenure, which began soon after the end of the Second World War. The fourth course of action states:

> *We must embark on a bold new program for making the benefits of our scientific advances and industrial progress available for the improvement and growth of underdeveloped areas.*
>
> *More than half the people of the world are living in conditions approaching misery. Their food is inadequate. They are victims of disease. Their economic life is primitive and stagnant. Their poverty is a handicap and a threat both to them and to more prosperous areas.*
>
> *For the first time in history, humanity possesses the knowledge and skill to relieve the suffering of these people.*
>
> *The United States is pre-eminent among nations in the development of industrial and scientific techniques. The material resources which we can afford to use for assistance of other peoples are limited. But our imponderable resources in technical knowledge are constantly growing and are inexhaustible.*
>
> *I believe that we should make available to peace-loving peoples the benefits of our store of technical knowledge in order to help them realize their aspirations for a better life. And, in cooperation with other nations, we should foster capital investment in areas needing development.*

Here there is a strong sense of trusteeship expressed in the phrase 'help them realize their aspirations' as well as a clear emphasis on the application of technical knowledge and capital investment as means of meeting people's aspirations 'for a better life'. The latter became known as 'modernisation'. In the nearly 60 years that have elapsed since 1949 this sense of trusteeship for the 'developed' to help the 'developing', as well as the emphasis on modernisation, has been attacked from a number of directions. The sense of trusteeship can be interpreted as a 'new colonialism' (neo-colonialism), given that it is based on the assumption that richer countries such as the USA have power and resources, and the under-developed world is expected to follow the pattern of development that the richer countries set out for them (i.e. the modernising route). Even so, it is probably fair to say that development today still follows a modernisation agenda. We have a tendency to think in terms of technology solving our problems, and indeed there are good reasons for this, given what we have achieved in terms of boosting food production and improving health care, to name but two sectors. This is a theme we will return to throughout this book.

In parallel with the rise of modernising development since the late 1940s the fact that humans can have a negative impact on the environment is also an old one. For example, Thomas Malthus, an economist, was one of the first to link population growth to food supply, and other checks and balances such as disease. He asserted that food supply grows linearly (arithmetically), while populations increase geometrically. Hence there comes a time when food production is not able to sustain a population. His ideas were published in 1798 as *An Essay on the Principle of Population* and were influential in establishing the 10-year census in Britain, which we have to this day. However, while the roots are old, it is generally accepted that the origins of sustainable development can be found in the environmental movements of the 1950s and 1960s. This movement had various manifestations. In the literature there are seminal texts such as William Vogt's *Road to Survival* (1949), Rachel Carson's *Silent Spring* (1962), Garret Hardin's *The tragedy of the commons* (1968) and Paul Ehrlich's *The Population Bomb* (1968). These works are non-fiction in that they present the facts of what was known about people and their interaction with the environment. Some like *Road to Survival* and *Silent Spring* were aimed at a wide audience, not only scientists or academics, and became best sellers. *Silent Spring* had its roots in the negative effects brought about by the intensification of agriculture after the Second World War and the growing use of organic pesticides such as DDT. These pesticides caused mortality amongst non-target organisms such as the predators and parasites that helped reduce pest numbers, but also upon the eggshells of birds. The result was thinning of eggshells and enhanced mortality amongst birds, and Carson projected this in the future as ultimately a 'Silent Spring'; no more birds left to add their song to that time of the year. The book has been highly influential and helped bring about a ban on DDT in the USA during the early 1970s. One passage from Carson's book refers to the widespread use of pesticides as a part of the intensification of agriculture and calls for the human race to take a new road (page 277), which today we call sustainability:

> We stand now where two roads diverge. But unlike the roads in Robert Frost's familiar poem, they are not equally fair. The road we have long been travelling is deceptively easy, a smooth superhighway on which we progress with great speed, but at its end lies disaster. The other fork of the road – the one less travelled by – offers our last, our only chance to reach a destination that assures the preservation of the earth.

Garret Hardin, an ecologist, published his paper *The tragedy of the commons* in the prestigious journal *Science* in 1968. In the paper he points out the problems of trying to manage resources (land, fisheries, forests etc.) which no one person or indeed group of people owns; the 'commons' referred to in the title. In effect, everyone has a perceived right to exploit that resource and they will often do so, even if it means that collectively these actions ultimately destroy that very resource. He was by no means the first to point this out, but his work highlighted the problems that can occur without controls. The paper has been interpreted by some as implying that resources need to be in the hands of individuals or companies which can exert such control, but Hardin did call for effective regulation to avoid this happening.

Indeed one feature of sustainability has been the portrayal of its central ethos – the inescapable connectivity between humankind and their environment – within popular culture, as well as the scientific literature. There have been fictional accounts such as the *Grapes of Wrath*, a novel written by John Steinbeck and first published in 1939 which describes the devastating impacts of the 'Dust Bowl' in the USA and its impact from the point of view of one family. A severe drought in the 1930s coupled with inappropriate land management over thousands of hectares, which often resulted in soil being left bare for months, led to substantial wind erosion of the soil and the loss of livelihood for thousands of farmer and their families. People had no other choice but to emigrate to the cities where life was often little better in those days of the Great Depression. Those that remained and tried to continue farming had to endure years of near starvation and high mortality as lungs choked with dust or became infected. The message of the 'Dust Bowl' disaster was a clear one; farming had to be more in tune with the environment. *The Grapes of Wrath* and the highly acclaimed film of the same name released in 1940 and starring Henry Fonda helped bring this message of human-mediated environmental catastrophe to a wider audience than more academic-orientated publications could ever hope to reach. Other films, such as Alfred Hitchcock's *The Birds* (1963), where birds take revenge upon the human race for damage that had been done to the environment, have echoes of *Silent Spring* which was published at about the same time as the film's release. *The Birds* is a fictional movie, but it is said to have been influenced by real events. According to an article in the journal *Nature* published on 27 October 2008, the behaviour of the birds in the film may have been based on a real incident caused by poisoning of seabirds with domoic acid in California in 1961. Demoic acid is a neurotoxin which can alter behaviour in animals, and is produced by phytoplankton, which pass through food chains. Release of nitrogen found in fertilisers and sewage into waterways can result in enhanced growth of phytoplankton and this is thought to have caused the poisoning of the seabirds in California. A non-fiction and more recent movie which has had a significant impact is *An Inconvenient Truth* (2006) written and presented by Al Gore, the ex-Vice President of the USA. The documentary won Academy Awards for Best Documentary Feature and for Best Original Song. The movie specifically deals with global warming, and the theory and existing body of evidence which points towards the primary cause being the release of greenhouse gases (carbon dioxide, methane and others) into the atmosphere by humans.

The sustainability theme has also reverberated in popular music. As Neil Young so eloquently put it in his famous song *After the Gold Rush*: 'Look at Mother Nature on the run in the nineteen-seventies.' There is no space to describe all of this here, but one of the most played songs of all time is Led Zeppelin's *Stairway to Heaven*, recorded in 1970 and released in 1971. Many have sought to interpret the meaning of the lyrics of the song and the influences that may have been involved, but as an aside let me add one of my own ideas for one of the verses:

> *If there's a bustle in your hedgerow*
> *Don't be alarmed now,*
> *It's just a spring clean for the May Queen.*
> *Yes, there are two paths you can go by*
> *But in the long run*
> *There's still time to change the road you're on.*
>
> Led Zeppelin, *Stairway to Heaven* (1970)

I personally think this is an allusion to the 'two roads' ('two paths') message in Carson's book with 'spring clean' referring to pesticides and the damage it can cause to non-pest insect populations in hedgerows. If so, then Rachel Carson's call for sustainability is a vibrant one to this day, although many may not realise it. But maybe I'm biased and can see sustainability everywhere!

Perhaps the most influential hybridisation of music with development can be seen in the 'Live Aid' event of July 1985, which had been inspired by the 1984–5 famine in Ethiopia, caused by a civil war, but exacerbated by a series of droughts. The famine had a death toll of over a million. Live Aid brought together some of the most popular musical artists of the day into two events, one hosted at Wembley Stadium in North London and the other in the JFK Stadium in Philadelphia.

Pressures arising from scientific findings plus voter enthusiasm for 'green' issues have resulted in a number of major international meetings to address the interactions of development and environment and these are often employed as 'milestones' for the history of sustainability. In 1972 there was a United Nations Conference on the Human Environment (UNCHE) in Stockholm; the UN's fist major international conference dedicated to environmental issues. This was preceded by a special publication of *The Ecologist* (1972) magazine entitled 'Blueprint for survival' which remains highly influential to this day and excerpts are still available on the internet. More than 10 years later, in 1983, the World Commission on Environment and Development (WCED), often referred to as the Brundtland Commission after its chair Gro Bruntland, published *Our Common Future* and derived the definition of sustainable development quoted above which, for all of its ambiguity, remains the definition of sustainability most in use today. The WCED was also commissioned by the United Nations to address concerns that the Earth's environment and natural resources were deteriorating at an increasing rate. Barely 10 years after WCED, in 1992 the United Nations Conference on Environment and Development (UNCED), more commonly known as the 'Earth Summit', was held in Rio de Janeiro between 3 and 14 June. In some ways this represents the culmination of the series of UN-sponsored meetings on the environment which began in 1972. Over 172 governments participated in UNCED and 108 heads of state attended for at least part of the meeting. The UN Commission for Sustainable Development was established with the mandate to follow up on the decisions made at Rio. The UNCED conference had a number of major outcomes, including action to address climate change (later leading to the Kyoto Protocol on limiting greenhouse-gas emissions) and an emphasis on the need for local action, stakeholder participation and sustainability indicators to allow us to gauge progress (or lack of it). Ten years later, in 2002, a follow-up 'Rio+10' conference was held in Johannesburg, where the emphasis was understandably on the linkages between poverty and environmental damage.

So where do we go from here? What is the future of sustainable development? Given what has been said in this chapter and indeed the Preface to the book, one would have thought that sustainability would be embraced unanimously by all of us living on the planet, but that is not so. The concept is certainly not without its critics, spanning those who feel that it provides a brake on development and economic growth to those who argue that this is yet another cynical attempt by the rich developed world to impose its version of change on the world. The latter, the so-called post-developmentalists, see sustainable development as little more than an attempt to disguise a business-as-usual position with comforting rhetoric; a deception of the poor led by the rich. Unfortunately we have often seen fashions come and go in environmentalism, partly reflecting changes in our knowledge, but also the realities of a world divided into competing nation states. After all, it wasn't that long ago, the 1970s in fact, when some scientists came to the conclusion that we were not facing a problem with global warming, but global cooling! That theory arose out of incomplete knowledge which suggested that the Earth's climate had cooled since the 1940s. Knowledge moves on, of course, and we now know that the global cooling evidence is incorrect, but a perceived swing from one scientific conclusion (global cooling) to an exact opposite (global warming) in the space of but a few years can readily be seized upon by those eager to show how unwise it would be to make major changes to wealth creation in nation states. As a result there will inevitably be critics who may well accept a generalised definition of sustainable development, but will resist any attempt to put it into practice while they think it will negatively impact upon their lifestyle.

Acceptance of the broad philosophy at the heart of sustainability is easy; making it work is a lot harder. Much of the latter is not only about science, but it is about us as a species and how we interact with our environment. That is where biologists have a major role to play and that is precisely why this book is entitled *Sustainability: A Biological Perspective*.

1.4   CONCLUSION AND STRUCTURE OF THE BOOK

Life on Earth is durable and the demise of people will not mean the end of life. Thus sustainability is about people; it is our construct of how we wish to live in such a way as to make sure that we and future generations can make a living and enjoy the planet. The ideas encapsulated within sustainability are as old as the human race. It is impossible to imagine any time or indeed place where people did not want to make their lives better and where they were also concerned for the lives of their children or indeed their children's children. These are not new ideas. Neither are we the only generation to realise that what we do can impact upon the environment or indeed that changes in the environment will impact upon us and we have to alter our behaviour. The Dust Bowl was a rapid degradation which occurred within a few years and only too apparent to all those who unfortunately were affected, but longer-term changes may be less apparent to a single generation. The climatic changes that occurred in what we now call the Middle East may have helped spawn the development of agriculture, but no doubt the adaptation from hunter/gatherer was a gradual one in Natufian society. There was time and space to make that change and the transition from collecting grains to actively planting and cultivating the same plants is in many ways a small one. But what we are faced with now is a global-scale change which can impact at local scales. That is the new challenge which we face and why sustainability is so important. After all, Natufian people could migrate to another 'world' outside of the one they knew. Indeed the human race has been remarkable in its ability to colonise almost every place on the surface of the Earth, and people and their machines have been to the depths of the oceans and to other planets. But we cannot, as yet, migrate to another world once this one is no longer able to sustain us, and frankly our neighbouring planets Mars and Venus are hardly hospitable! No one will come from over the horizon with new ideas and technical 'fixes' to help us survive a collapse of the planets carrying capacity. Sustainability is about us; it is personal. Indeed the fact that life will go on if the human race were to die out is frankly of little – if any – consolation if we are not there to see it.

There are many paths that could be taken in any exploration of sustainability and the role played by biologists, and no doubt each reader will have their own view. Given that this book is meant to be an introduction to the topic, as well as a spur to engagement, there is a mix of angles spanning extrapolation from some basic biological concepts to more complex fields at the frontiers of research. I have also sought to approach the subject from two main directions: production and consumption. Chapters 2, 3 and 4 will dissect production in three sectors; agriculture (notably primary production), fisheries and industry. As well as the three sectors being distinct, each of the three chapters will also take a different perspective on production and introduce the reader to some of the approaches which have been taken (or not as the case may be) in making the philosophy of sustainability a reality. Chapters 2, 3 and 4 have a biological focus, but there are overlaps with socio-economic concerns. Chapter 5 brings this out more strongly by starting with socio-economic matters of importance to sustainability and showing the linkages with biology. Chapter 5 will also present a mix of perspectives spanning both production and consumption.

Chapter 6 will explore sustainability, not so much in terms of production but consumption. Consumption is obviously linked to production (what is produced has to be consumed or discarded), but all too often the focus in sustainability has been upon reducing the negative impacts that production has on the environment while concerns over consumption have remained in the background. But production is driven by demand and both have to be part of the sustainability equation.

Chapter 7 will pull the story together and tease out the main lessons we have learnt so far in making sustainability a reality and what more needs to be done. The short answer to the latter is, unfortunately, a lot! I don't pretend to have an answer, but I will at least try to make some suggestions which I hope the reader will dissect and ponder for themselves.

2

Sustainable agriculture: more and more production

2.1 INTRODUCTION

While the industrial revolution which began in Britain but rapidly spread elsewhere began to raise concerns of pollution and living standards, it is perhaps in agriculture that the first recorded concerns began to arise. Some of the earliest known texts relate to the so-called 'Arab Agricultural Revolution' (Watson, 1974, 1981, 1983), part of the Islamic Golden Age from the eighth to the thirteenth centuries. Given that agriculture is thought to have begun in the Middle East this geographical focus is understandable. The revolution included much research on technologies such as irrigation, crop rotation and introduction of new crops and varieties, and coincided with the rise of the market economy. But writers such as Alkindus, Costa ben Luca, Rhazes, Ibn Al-Jazzar, al-Tamimi, al-Masihi, Avicenna, Ali ibn Ridwan, Isaac Israeli ben Solomon, Abd-el-latif and Ibn al-Nafis expressed concerns regarding air contamination, water contamination, soil contamination and solid waste mishandling as a result of this revolution (Gari, 2002). Indeed, as we have already seen in Chapter 1 it can be argued that agriculture as an industry has had a significant role in the formulation of what we currently refer to as sustainable development (sustainability). This is perhaps not too surprising given that:

(1)　The end product of agriculture is often food, and as such agriculture is one of the foundations of human society.

(2)　Agricultural systems occupy large areas of land, far more than any other industry, with the possible exception of forestry.

(3)　Agriculture on a global scale has undergone substantial change over the past century, and in a number of developed countries has moved from subsistence to agribusiness, which has had a visible impact on the environment, as well as the problems mentioned in Chapter 1.

(4)   Agriculture is an important source of livelihood, either directly for producers or indirectly for traders, processors and retailers.

At the most basic level it has to be reiterated that cultivation of crops and pasture obviously means a change to what was growing on the land before. Even the most 'environmentally sensitive' practice of agriculture by definition means the management of a plant and animal community to some degree and thus a move away from what would be regarded as a natural community: one that would exist on that land without the intervention of humans. Thus, agriculture is synonymous with environmental change, and much of the literature on agricultural sustainability has tended to revolve around technical issues of maximising what growers, or indeed consumers, want, while at the same time minimising as far as possible the extent of any change to the natural community and/or the impacts of the change. The desire to produce more, increase quality and decrease cost of production has resulted in a series of adaptations – fewer farms, larger fields and a replacement of human energy with that derived from fossil fuels. The scale and rapidity of the change in some richer countries inevitably meant that negative effects on the environment (human and physical) were unavoidable. The changes happened before we understood what they were let alone what was causing them. The Dust Bowl catastrophe in the USA is an example of that. But how have people defined sustainable agriculture? Well, this has been contentious to say the least, and without wishing to labour the point here are a few examples spanning a period of 20 years:

Profitability, consumer safety, resource protection and viability of rural America. (Kelling and Klemme (1989, page 32))

Sustainable agriculture is one which achieves production combined with conservation of the resources on which that production depends, thereby maintaining the maintenance of productivity. (Young (1989, page 10))

Sustainable agriculture is one that, over the long term, enhances environmental quality and the resource base on which agriculture depends, provides for basic human food and fiber needs, is economically viable, and enhances the quality of life of farmers and society as a whole. (American Society of Agronomy (cited in Stockle et al. 1994, page 45))

A sustainable agriculture is one that equitability balances concerns of environmental soundness, economic viability and social justice among all sectors of society. (Allen et al. (1991, page 37))

Sustainable agricultural systems are those:

> *that are economically viable, and met society's needs for safe nutritious food, while conserving or enhancing natural resources and the quality of the environment.* (Science Council of Canada (1992))

> *Sustainable agriculture consists of agricultural processes, that is, processes involving biological activities of growth or reproduction intended to produce crops, which do not undermine our further capacity to successfully practice agriculture.* (Lehman et al. (1993, page 139))

> *A cropping system is sustainable if it has an acceptable level of production of harvestable yield which shows a non-declining trend from cropping cycle to cropping cycle over the long term.* (Izac and Swift (1994, page 107))

> *Sustainable agriculture refers to the use of resources to produce food and fiber in such a way that the natural resource base is not damaged and that the basic needs of producers and consumers can be met over the long term.* (Yunlong and Smit (1994, page 299))

> *A sustainable agriculture must be economically viable, environmentally sound, and socially acceptable . . . it must also be politically achievable.* (Zimdahl (2005))

Given the diversity in the above list, it is perhaps not surprising that a precise and absolute definition that pleases everyone has not been possible. However, there are common themes that emerge. Most apparent in these definitions is a sense of maintaining production of 'food and fiber' for the good of society and doing this in a way which at the very least does not damage the economic wellbeing of farmers. Thus, we also have phrases along the lines of maintaining and enhancing profitability. In one case there is an explicit reference to yield. All of these are related:

$$\text{yield} = \frac{\text{production}}{\text{area}}$$
$$\text{production} = \text{yield} \times \text{area}$$

profitability (or more pecisely the gross margin) = revenue obtained by selling products − cost of production

But they are also different. Profitability can be enhanced by producing less, provided prices obtained by the farmer go up (not necessarily good news for consumers) or the costs of production go down (not necessarily good news for those companies and their workers making those inputs). Production can be enhanced by increasing yield (production for each unit area) and/or bringing more land into agriculture. These two strategies have different consequences. An increase in yield is referred to as intensification and could mean the use of more inputs such as fertiliser and pesticide, perhaps allied with plant or animal breeding programmes designed to generate varieties or breeds best suited to using those inputs. Increasing agricultural land area is called extensification and could mean the use of marginal land not best suited for agriculture or even land of high conservation value such as rainforest. Some definitions also stress the need to avoid damaging the environment, for example by not depleting the resource base, and the need for the quality of products to be maintained or enhanced. Obviously there is the need to ensure that food is safe to eat.

Agricultural production has re-emerged as a priority in the first years of the twenty-first century. The United Nations has set a target of increasing global production by 70% by 2050 to feed a growing population:

> Contrary to popular perception that the food crisis is 'over', food insecurity stalks the globe, with over a billion people going to bed hungry every night. This is unacceptable, and unsustainable. We must take a comprehensive approach to the problem as outlined by the United Nations System High-Level Task Force on Global Food Security Crisis. This means not only addressing the needs of people who are hungry today, but also making the investments in agriculture that will allow us to avoid this situation in the future. (Press Release from the Secretary-General of the UN (ENV/DEV/1060, 9 July 2009))

Note how the failure to produce and distribute enough food to avoid this hardship is seen as both unacceptable and unsustainable. But balancing what an agricultural system produces, and indeed its profitability, against what change the practice brings about in the environment and society are also key considerations. While the definitions above have plenty of caveats, all too often the focus has been on maintaining an 'acceptable' level of production and profitability, and this requires that the resource base is not diminished. If it were to be damaged, then maintaining production would not be possible and profitability is also likely to suffer. Hence it is here, with production, that we will begin the story of sustainability. We will briefly explore the central process that underpins all agricultural production – photosynthesis. From here we will explore the range of agricultural systems to show how some of them are closer to a natural environment than others, and how this can work. For example, how can a cropping system be highly diverse yet provide the production the farmer is looking for? What are the biological principles than underpin this? Secondly we will look at the balance between what the farmer receives and what they have to put into the system to achieve these outputs. We will explore this through the concept of Total Factor Productivity. Finally we will look at a modern yet highly contentious development in agriculture – genetic modification (or genetic engineering) – and how it is seen within the sustainability discourse. I admit that these topics provide a very constrained view of the interaction between agriculture and environment, but they do allow for some central issues to be aired.

2.2   GREEN IS THE COLOUR OF SUSTAINABILITY

The colour green is strongly associated with sustainability. We often speak of 'green politics' or a 'green economy' or the 'greening' of industry. The 'Green Party' of the UK gives its philosophical stance as:

> Life on Earth is under immense pressure. It is human activity, more than anything else, which is threatening the well-being of the environment on which we depend. Conventional politics has failed us because its values are fundamentally flawed.
> (Green party UK (www.greenparty.org.uk/about.html; accessed 15 August 2009))

The last sentence of this statement explains the involvement of the party in 'traditional' political systems as well as campaigning and 'direct action' (politically motivated activity outside normal political channels). But why green? Well green is, of course, the predominant colour of plants and is perhaps the most apparent colour of life on Earth. Thus green is the colour of life and the adjective is used to signify a 'pro-life' (environmentalist) position. The choice of the dominant colour of plants as a signifier of life in general is apt. The major primary energy input into most ecosystems is, of course, sunlight. I say most because, of course, we now know that some ecosystems can utilise energy from other sources such as deep-sea vents and the heat and chemicals which emerge at such great depths. The primary energy is 'fixed' by the plants in the system via photosynthesis (Figure 2.1). There are two distinct components to photosynthesis: the light and dark reactions. The light reaction is the liberation of chemical energy from the splitting of water into hydrogen and oxygen (Figure 2.2). Sunlight and chlorophyll are essential for this process, along with water. It involves the release of oxygen from water. Light energy is converted to chemical energy in the form of adenosine triphosphate and nicotinamide adenine dinucleotide phosphate (ATP and NADPH, respectively). This complex process takes place in organelles called chloroplasts, which are located mostly in leaf cells. Note that the process is not 100% efficient, as there is much waste of the light energy

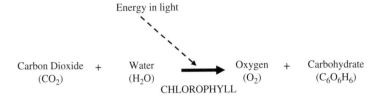

This contrasts with respiration where carbohydrate is burnt to release energy

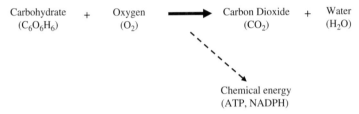

Figure 2.1 Photosynthesis: the fixing of energy from light into carbohydrate.

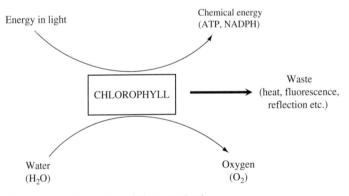

Figure 2.2 Light reaction of photosynthesis.

through heat, radiation, fluorescence and reflection, and not all of the wavelengths present in sunlight are utilised by chlorophyll. Figure 2.3 is a graph showing the absorption of wavelengths by chlorophyll b, along with the visible colours that correspond with certain wavelengths. The utilised band is referred to as photosynthetically active radiation (PAR). Only wavelengths between 400 and 650 nm, approximately corresponding to the colours blue to red of the spectrum, are

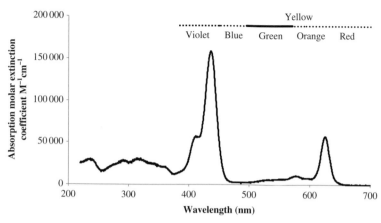

Figure 2.3 Absorption of wavelengths in the visible part of the spectrum by chlorophyll. Graph is for chlorophyll b (in ether). Also shown are the colours corresponding to certain wavelength bands. Note that absorption in the green part of the spectrum is low, hence that light is reflected and plants often appear green.

'used' in photosynthesis and even within this band, light with a wavelength of between 480 and 600 nm is not utilised. The latter corresponds to the green part of the spectrum and that light is reflected; hence plants appear to us as green. The chemical energy generated from the light reaction is used to fuel the dark reaction, whereby carbon dioxide is combined with water to generate carbohydrate. We also use the general term 'photosynthate' (literally 'made from light') to describe the products of photosynthesis.

There are two main photosynthetic pathways; C3 (the Calvin–Benson cycle) and C4 (the Hatch–Slack cycle; Hatch, 1992). The C3 cycle was the first to be studied in detail, and is found mainly in plants of temperate origin (wheat, barley, beans, potato, rice, groundnut). The C4 pathway is found in tropical plants (maize, sorghum, millet, sugar cane). Generally, the rate of photosynthesis increases with increasing amounts of light energy (Aikman, 1989) and concentrations of CO_2 (Lawlor and Mitchell, 1991), but C3 plants are more easily saturated by light than are C4 plants. Figure 2.4 illustrates the typical form of the response to increasing light intensity amongst C3 and C4 plants. Both curves in the graph are of the 'diminishing return' type, which we will come across throughout this book in a range of contexts. The rate of photosynthesis does not keep increasing with more light, but levels off at some point and we call this 'saturation'. At this point

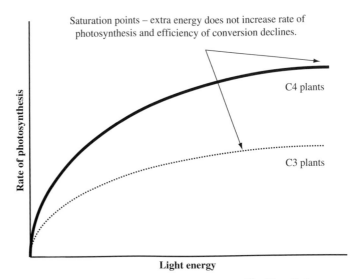

Figure 2.4 Rate of photosynthesis as a function of incident light energy.

and beyond, the cellular machinery which engages in photosynthesis is working at its maximum efficiency and no more incident energy can be converted to chemical energy. Indeed, if light intensity continues to increase, the plants will die as the tissues will heat up. In effect, the plant will burn. But the key point here is that C4 plants become saturated at higher levels of light intensity than do C3 plants. Indeed it has been estimated that C4 plants account for some 30% of global carbon fixation and are especially efficient in conditions of low CO_2 concentration and high temperatures, and have been referred to as 'nature's green revolution' (Osborne and Beerling, 2006). So why isn't the world covered in C4 plants if they are so good at 'grabbing' CO_2 and thus could presumably out-compete C3 plants? The answer is simple: while C4 plants do well under tropical conditions in environments where temperature and light intensity are lower (i.e. the temperate regions), C3 plants are more efficient at photosynthesis than are C4 plants.

Photosynthetic efficiency, the percentage conversion of incident light energy to chemical energy, is approximately 3 to 6% (Zhu *et al*, 2008), with a theoretical maximum estimated to be 13% (Bolton and Hall, 1991). A theoretical example, but based upon figures from a range of experiments, of the losses which occur from incident energy (in this case PAR) to final gain in photosynthate is shown in Figure 2.5. Of the 100 units of incident PAR energy, there is a gain of only 6.3 units of photosynthate; an efficiency of 6.3%. Under natural conditions of

Table 2.1 *Use of incident light energy by a community of plants in Silver Springs, Florida (after Odum, 1957).*

	Energy (kcal/ m²/year)	Percentage of incoming energy
Insolation (light energy input from the sun)	1 700 000	100
Absorption by plants	410 000	24
Gross photosynthesis	20 810	1.2
Net photosynthesis (gross photosynthesis – carbohydrate used during respiration)	8833	0.52

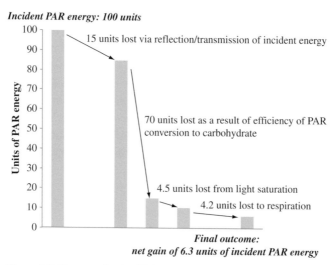

Figure 2.5 Photosynthetic efficiency: a theoretical example based upon incident PAR energy of 100 units.

variable temperature, light conditions, water availability and so on, the efficiency could be much lower, often well under 1%. Table 2.1 provides a summary of one of the classic studies of energy utilisation in natural plant communities carried out by Odum (1957). Of the incident radiation barely 0.6% ends up as net photosynthate. By way of contrast, commercially available solar panels have an energy conversion rate of between 5 and 18%, although this does vary with light and is improving as technology advances.

However, while photosynthetic efficiencies may be relatively low, the carbohydrate which is generated provides the primary food source not only for the plant, but also for other components of the system through herbivores. Thus, it is no exaggeration to say that survival of human beings and a large proportion of life on Earth is completely dependent upon photosynthesis and chlorophyll. Not only would we sorely miss the oxygen by-product, but all of our agricultural and forest systems are founded upon photosynthesis. Therefore it is fair to say that photosynthesis is the prime mechanism on Earth upon which sustainability is founded and this is often forgotten by those that see sustainability purely in economic terms. So is there potential for improving upon the efficiency of photosynthesis and thereby increase crop yields? There is certainly scope for doing this and some have estimated that yields could increase by up to 50% as a result, but there is much complexity involved in making the necessary adjustments within such a complex process (Long *et al.*, 2006). Genetic engineering may provide some tools to aid in this, but the task is certainly daunting and there are other issues to consider with the use of such a controversial technology, as we will see later in the chapter. Are there simpler avenues that can be explored to boost crop yields? In the next section we will explore some of the cropping systems of the world and how they balance production with other concerns of importance to sustainability. As we will see, there are relatively simple and low-cost ways of boosting production and enhancing sustainability, but there are costs associated with this.

2.3   CROPPING SYSTEMS AND YIELD MAXIMISATION

Throughout the world there are many types of agricultural system and modes of classifying them; profitability, productivity and complexity being just three. The systems can be entirely crop based (arable) or include animals (pastoral), and an individual farmer may be engaged in both crop and animal production. Thus there is a spectrum, and one way of presenting this specifically for arable systems is shown in Table 2.2. Pastoral systems have largely been excluded so as to allow a sole focus on primary production. In the table there is a fundamental classification as either single or multiple depending upon how many crop species are grown on the same area of land in a growing season. 'Single' indicates one crop is grown per season, while 'multiple' means more than one crop is grown. Hence the columns in Table 2.2 indicating some separation of crop species in time and space. Single cropping tends to predominate in more developed countries, while multiple cropping is popular in the developing world. Within this broad

Table 2.2 *Spectrum of cropping systems based upon separation of species over time and space.*

		Separation in a year in terms of Time	Space
Natural ecosystems		X	X
Agricultural ecosystems	*Intercropping systems*		
	Permaculture	**X**	**X**
	Agroforestry	**X**	**X**
	Intercropping	**X**	**X**
Multiple cropping	**Relay intercropping**	**little**	**X**
	Sole crop systems		
	Sequential cropping (a) more than 1 crop/year	**√**	**X**
Single cropping	**(b) one crop/year**	**√**	**√**
	Monoculture	**√**	**√**

Biodiversity

categorisation of single and multiple there is a gradient of biodiversity. In Table 2.2 the least diverse are those systems at the bottom while the most diverse are those at the top.

Natural ecosystems, represented by the top end of Table 2.2, are generally far more diverse than cropping systems, thus agriculture almost inevitably results in a managed simplification of habitat. Remove that management and the system will revert back to what it once was. Thus, by definition all cropping and indeed agricultural systems are unsustainable (they will not remain in place) unless they are managed. The most complex cropping systems in terms of biodiversity are those based on permaculture (permacultureprinciples.com; Strange, 1983). Here, as the name implies, crops and usually trees are mixed together and kept in place on a permanent basis, sometimes with the inclusion of livestock. It is an emulation of a natural ecosystem, albeit one that is managed, and the very name implies something that can be sustained indefinitely. In other words, well-designed and managed permaculture-based systems have what ecologists call resilience (King, 2008), an ability to resist and recover from environmental perturbation.

Related to permaculture is agroforestry. This refers to the growing of crops between trees and covers a variety of approaches, with various advantages and disadvantages associated with each of them and some being more visually akin to natural forests than others (Sibbald, 1999). Agroforestry is an old technique, practised for millennia and should not be thought of as a modern invention (Miller and Nair, 2006). It is more of a re-discovery. At one extreme it could simply mean the cultivation of crops as an understory in a forest environment and thus disturbance is kept at a minimum, while at the other extreme there are more recent developments, such as alley cropping, which entails a systematic planting of crops between planted rows of trees (Ghosh et al., 2007). The latter are usually leguminous and with alley cropping the trees are pruned on a regular basis and the nitrogen-rich prunings are incorporated into the soil where the crop is grown. Thus soil quality is enhanced with organic matter and nutrients and so is biodiversity. Agroforestry does tend to result in reduced biodiversity relative to natural forests, or indeed permaculture, as annual crops are an important component of the system (Scales and Marsden, 2008). Nonetheless some forms of agroforestry have the advantage of maintaining goods and services from the forest (medicines, firewood, fruits etc.), as well as providing additional benefits from crops (Pandey, 2007). While much research effort, agronomic, ecological and socio-economic, has been invested into agroforestry, there are still many gaps in our knowledge, which is understandable given the complexity involved (Scherr, 1991; Pannell, 1999; Montambault and Alavalapati, 2005).

Next in the hierarchy of Table 2.2 are intercropping systems. Intercropping is the planting of different crop species on the same piece of land at the same time. An example for a maize and cowpea intercrop is shown as Figure 2.6a. In this case there are two cropping seasons in the year, as indeed there are in much of the tropics, and the intercrop in grown in the early season while the late season is left fallow. The result can be an apparent 'mess' of crops, perhaps a dozen or more on the same area of land, and indeed until quite recently intercropping was thought to be an inferior system practiced by unskilled farmers, mostly in the less-developed parts of the world, who did not know what they were doing. It's only since the 1960s, when scientists began to research these systems in detail, that it has been realised how productive and beneficial they can be. Intercropping is commonly found throughout the world. Indeed, in many parts of the tropics these systems dominate, especially where those engaging in

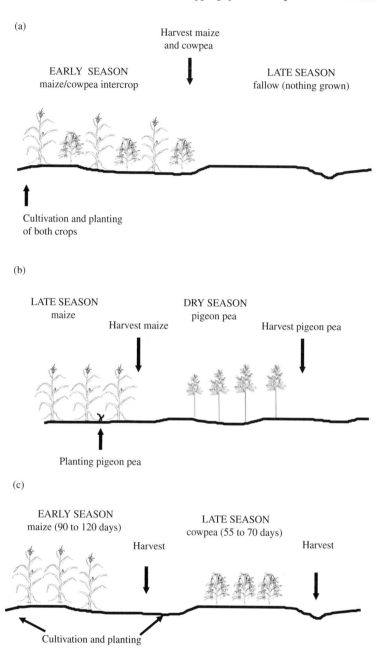

Figure 2.6 Examples of three different types of multiple-cropping system: (a) intercrop (different crops planted at the same time on the same piece of land): two crops (maize and cowpea); (b) relay intercropping: maize followed by pigeon pea; (c) sequential cropping (more than one crop/growing season): maize followed by cowpea.

the production will also be the consumers (subsistence agriculture), although excess production may well be sold in local markets. Agroforestry and intercropping systems are complex by definition, with different components having different requirements in terms of planting, fertilisation, pest and weed control, harvesting etc. This makes mechanisation difficult and certainly requires a great deal of knowledge and skill on behalf of the farmers. Production in such systems is defined in terms of the output from the mix rather than any one component (Malezieux *et al.*, 2009).

There are some intercrop systems where the overlap in time between crops is smaller than in others. In Figure 2.6b there is an example of what is called a 'relay intercrop' where pigeon pea (*Cajanus cajan*) is planted after a maize crop has been growing for some time. Once the maize has been harvested the pigeon pea can continue its growth. The two crops are present on the land at the same time for a relatively short period.

At the less diverse end of the spectrum in Table 2.2 are systems which involve growing one crop on a piece of land in one season. An example is provided as Figure 2.6c where maize is grown in the early season and cowpea in the late season. In other words the crops are grown sequentially rather than together as an intercrop. This is a sole crop system, but the farmer does benefit from having more than one crop yield from the same land in one growing season. Therefore we can classify permaculture, agroforestry, intercropping and sequential cropping, where there is more than one crop in a season, as multiple-cropping systems.

Towards the foot of Table 2.2 are cropping systems most commonly observed in more developed parts of the world, typically where farmers are producing crops almost entirely for sale. One crop is typically grown on the same piece of land in a single year, and this greatly simplifies the management regime. The farmer can apply a single planting date, fertilisation and pest-control regime and all plants are ready for harvest at the same time. This homogenisation means that yield (production per unit area) can be maximised; after all there is only one component for the farmer to consider and often all of the plants are of the same variety and thus genetically homogeneous. In order to help maintain production over time farmers engaged in single cropping will rotate the crops on a piece of land (sequential cropping), thus avoiding depletion of nutrients and avoidance of a build-up of soil pests and diseases. The classic example is the Norfolk four-course rotation, where wheat (year 1) is followed by a root crop (year 2), barley and clover mixture (year 3) and finally grass (year 4). Thus farmers will still need to have at hand a range of machinery designed for the different crops (cereals, root crops, grass etc.), as well as a mix of fertiliser types and pesticides, each designed to meet the requirements of the various crops. Even with organic systems, where farmers are not allowed to use artificial fertiliser or pesticide, these single-crop systems provide an advantage of simplification.

At the other end of the spectrum in Table 2.2 are monocultures, where the same crop species is grown on the land over a number of years. The advantage of monoculture for the farmer is that they can specialise and reduce the range of machinery and inputs they require. Monoculture lends itself to a factory-line approach to agriculture over large areas, as crops ripen at the same time, and lends itself not only to a maximisation of production, but also to a maximisation of gross margin, where:

$$\text{gross margin} = \text{revenue from production} - \text{costs of production}$$

For the most part, farmers will aim to maximise a positive gross margin (profit).

Given that single cropping, and indeed monoculture, can help farmers maximise production, an obvious question to ask is why do many farmers engage with the more complex systems of permaculture, agroforestry and intercropping? Intercropping is undoubtedly a very popular cropping system on a global scale. Table 2.3 provides estimates for a number of crops grown in two African countries (Nigeria and Uganda) of the percentage area of land in which the crop is grown as a

Table 2.3 *Estimated extent of intercropping in Nigeria and Uganda (after Papendick et al., 1976; Francis, 1986, 1989).*

Crop	Percentage of total area as an intercrop	
	Nigeria	Uganda
Cowpea (Vigna unguiculata)	99	62
Groundnut (Arachis hypogaea)	5	56
'Beans' (various)		81
Pigeon pea (*Cajanus cajan*)		76
Melon (various)	93	
Cocoyam (various)	86	
Cassava (Manihot esculenta)	7	50
Cotton (Gossypium hirsutum)	80	26
Maize (*Zea mays*)	6	84
Rice (Oryza sativa)	8	

component of an intercrop system. In Nigeria, for example, it is esti-mated that 99% of the cowpea (*Vigna unguiculata*) crop area is planted as an intercrop. There are many advantages to these multiple-cropping systems, and it boils down to farmers trying to maximise production in ways which try to minimise inputs, especially in terms of human labour, and reduce risk. Thus, it's all about efficiency founded upon diversity (Malezieux *et al.*, 2009). This is a general mantra for farmers everywhere, of course, but those engaged in these more complex systems often do so as a means of handling uncertainty, while having a limited set of options for handling that uncertainty. Thus, these more complex systems are a coping strategy (Torquebiau, 1992; Manrique, 1993). It should be noted that those farmers more usually engaged in intercropping and agroforestry are amongst the poorest farmers on the globe and thus have little or no ability to pay for machinery, fertilisers and pesticides. Thus, the spectrum in Table 2.2 can be inversely related to farmer income. Indeed it is perhaps ironical that in terms of agricul-tural sustainability, at least if thought of in more environmental terms as a means of limiting use of damaging inputs such as pesticides, the most sustainable systems are being practised by the poorest farmers. Thus it can be argued that poverty forces thinking along the lines of diversity and sustainability! But are these associations fair? In order to address this question let us begin by unpicking some of the claimed advantages for intercropping systems.

The first point to make is that intercropping is a more intensive system in terms of the resources (nutrients, water, light) consumed over a unit area and volume of soil. After all, more than one crop on a piece of land leads to greater use of water and plant nutrients as well as light. Indeed many studies have shown that intercrops provide more yield (product/area) than if the same population of the component crops were planted on separate pieces of land. For example, if full populations of crops A and B provide 1 and 0.5 tonnes/ha, respectively, then logic suggests that half populations of the two crops planted together on one hectare should provide 0.5 and 0.25 tonnes/ha, half the number of plants should provide half the yield. However, in prac-tice we typically see higher yields in intercrops than predicted based upon sole crop yields, as demonstrated in Figure 2.7. This graph presents the yields of the sole crops, the theoretical yield of an inter-crop which has half the number of plants of each of the two compo-nents and what we often see as an 'observed' yield. Such 'over-yields' associated with intercropping have been commonly observed in a wide range of crop combinations and contexts. One straightforward method

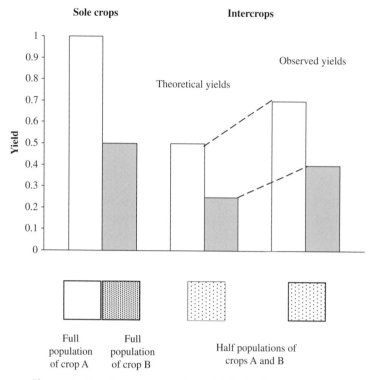

Figure 2.7 The phenomenon of 'over-yielding' in intercrops.

of comparing intercrop and sole crop yields is the land equivalent ratio (LER; Mead and Willey, 1980; Riley, 1984). This is simply a ratio between intercrop yield and sole crop yield aggregated over all the components of the intercrop.

$$\text{LER} = \frac{\text{intercrop yield of crop A}}{\text{sole crop yield of crop A}} + \frac{\text{intercrop yield of crop B}}{\text{sole crop yield of crop B}}$$

This equation is somewhat cumbersome so we can replace the repetitive text with symbols as follows:

$$\text{LER} = \frac{Y_{ab}}{Y_{aa}} + \frac{Y_{ba}}{Y_{bb}}$$

where the symbols Y_{ab} and Y_{ba} are used to denote yields of A and B respectively in the intercop, and the symbols Y_{aa} and Y_{bb} are the sole crop yields of A and B respectively.

Referring to our example above, if the product for each plant remains the same irrespective of whether they are grown as an intercrop or sole crop, then the LER should be:

$$LER = \frac{0.5}{1.0} + \frac{0.25}{0.5}$$
$$LER = 0.5 + 0.5 = 1.0$$

Thus, half the population of each crop put together as an intercrop produces half the yield. However, in practice we might typically find something like the following (still assuming that the sole crop yields are 1.0 and 0.5 for crops A and B, respectively):

$$LER = \frac{0.7}{1.0} + \frac{0.4}{0.5}$$
$$LER = 0.7 + 0.8 = 1.5$$

Thus, the observed yield from the intercrop is 50% greater than the theoretical yield, and this in fact is the situation demonstrated in Figure 2.7. 'Real' examples for a range of intercrops and countries are provided in Table 2.4, and, as can be seen, the over-yield from intercropping can be substantial, with LERs as high as 2.0 (doubling of yield). Also, it should be noted that my theoretical example for crops A and B above is based on half-populations relative to the sole crops. In practice, farmers may 'pack' more plants into the intercrop, perhaps as high as 60 to 70% of the sole-population equivalents. This over-yield has to be 'paid' for by a greater consumption of resource. Nonetheless, the bottom line is that intercropping does provide farmers with a yield advantage relative to sole cropping and for farmers who may be short on land and labour to cultivate that land, the attraction is obvious.

However, it would be a mistake to assume that higher yield is the only reason why farmers intercrop. A further important advantage is that if one crop fails for any reason, then the remaining crop can grow into the space which is left and thus provide an element of compensation. As shown in Figure 2.8, the earlier the time of failure of one of the crops then the more time which is available for the remaining crop to compensate. Such compensation is of particular importance where all the farm work is carried out with scarce (and expensive) hand labour. If only one crop had been planted then failure would result in the loss of all the time and energy spent cultivating the land let alone planting and weeding the crop. The ability of the remaining crop(s) to compensate for this loss will depend upon the innate 'agressiveness' of the remaining crop and the time it has left to compensate. For example, in Figure 2.8 early and medium times of failure of crop A allow crop B to compensate (i.e. crop B produces a higher yield than expected) while late failure of crop A does not provide an opportunity for crop B to compensate. This ability of intercrops to compensate for the loss of a

Table 2.4 *Examples of intercrop advantage measured in terms of land equivalent ratios.*

Intercrop	Country	LER	Reference
Radish (Raphanus sativus)/lettuce (Lactuca sativa)	Brazil	1.69–2.05	Graciano *et al.* (2007)
Kenaf (Hibiscus cannabinus)/cowpea (Vigna unguiculata)	Nigeria	1.5–2.0	Raji (2007)
Potato (Solanum tuberosum)/maize (Zea mays)	India	1.98	Prakash *et al.* (2004a)
Cowpea/scarlet eggplant (Solanum aethiopicum)	Ghana	1.38–1.94	Ofori and Gamedoagbao (2005)
Tomato (Lycopersicon esculenium)/ maize	India	1.86	Prakash *et al.* (2004b)
Maize/cowpea	India	1.84	Sharma *et al.* (2008)
Taro (Colocasia esculenta)/parsley (Petroselinum crispum) or coriander (Coriandrum sativum)	Brazil	1.15–1.83	Zarate *et al.* (2007a)
Taro/lettuce	Brazil	1.47–1.82	Zarate *et al.* (2007b)
Maize/blackgram (*Vigna mungo*)	India	1.68	Padhi and Panigrahi (2006)
Lentil (Lens culinaris)/linseed (Linum usitatissimum)	India	1.66	Sarkar *et al.* (2004)
Maize/soybean (*Glycine max*)	Nigeria	1.02–1.63	Muoneke *et al.* (2007)
Kenaf/sorghum (Sorghum bicolor)	Nigeria	1.6	Raji (2008)
Fodder sorghum/pigeonpea (*Cajanus cajan*)	India	1.58	Verma *et al.* (2005)
Cabbage (Brassica oleracea)/radish	India	1.57	Patil *et al.* (2004)
Groundnut (Arachis hypogaea)/ sunflower (Helianthus annuus)	India	1.44–1.52	Patil *et al.* (2007)
Castor (Ricinus communis)/ greengram (Vigna radiata), blackgram (Vigna mungo), clusterbean (Cymopsis tetragonoloba) or sesame (Sesamum indicum)	India	1.52	Porwal *et al.* (2006)
Maize/cassava (Manihot esculenta)	Benin	>1.5	Schulthess *et al.* (2004)

Table 2.4 (*cont.*)

Intercrop	Country	LER	Reference
Arracacha (*Arracacia xanthorrhiza*)/ Japanese bunching onion (*Allium fistulosum*),	Brazil	1.49	Zarate *et al.* (2008)
Pigeonpea/urdbean (Phaseolus mungo)	India	1.45	Shrivastava *et al.* (2004)
Peanut (Arachis hypogaea)/rice (Oryza sativa)	China	1.36–1.41	Chu *et al.* (2004)
Greater yam (*Dioscorea alata*)/maize	India	1.37	Nedunchezhiyan (2007)
Pearlmillet (Pennisetum glaucum)/ clusterbean	India	1.35	Sharma (2008)
Sorghum/greengram (Vigna radiata)	India	1.32	Rao *et al.* (2009)
Cotton (*Gossypium hirsutum*)/cowpea	Pakistan	1.28	Ali *et al.* (2005)
Barley (*Hordeum vulgare*)/Austrian winter pea (*Pisum sativum* ssp. arvense)	USA	1.05–1.24	Chen *et al.* (2004)
Wheat (Triticum aestivum)/faba bean (Vicia faba)	Ethiopia	1.03–1.22	Agegnehu (2008)
Eggplant (*Solanum melongena*)/lettuce	Turkey	1.18–1.21	Guvenc and Yildirim (2005)
Maize/soybean)	Malaysia	1.11–1.19	Rahimi and Yadegari (2008)
Mustard (Brassica juncea)/chickpea (Cicer arietinum)	India	1.19	Tripathi *et al.* (2005)
Groundnut/pigeonpea	India	1.18	Dutta and Bandyopadhyay (2007)
Barley/vetch (Vicia desycarpa)	Iran	1.14	Mohsenabadi *et al.* (2008)
Soybean cultivars	Iran	1.11	Biabani *et al.* (2008)
Linseed (Linum usitatissimum)/ wheat, oats (Avena sativa) or false flax (Camelina sativa)	Germany	1.1	Paulsen (2008)
Wheat/chickpea	Iran	1.01–1.1	Jahansooz *et al.* (2007)

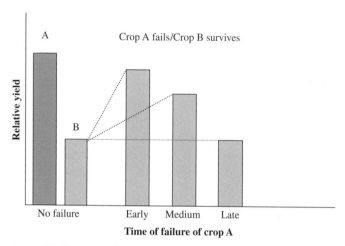

Figure 2.8 Compensation in intercrops; a mechanism for resilience.
This example has crops (A and B), with crop A dominating crop B, but
crop A fails. If crop A fails at an early stage then crop B can compensate for
this failure. The ability to compensate reduces with later failing of crop
A. This compensatory ability provides the farmer with some resilience
against adverse environmental conditions.

component provides the farmer with a degree of resilience in the
growing season and can make a contribution to sustainability – the
maintenance of production over time. However, there are other factors
that come into play with regard to sustainability, most notably the
availability of resources to maintain plant growth.

How does over-yielding in intercrops work? Underlying the benefits from some of the more complex cropping systems is the notion of
inter- and intra-specific competition. Components within a permaculture, agroforestry or intercrop-based system will compete with individuals of the other components, as well as with individuals of the same
species. Such competition can, of course, be highly detrimental and
suppress both the quantity and quality of produce harvested.
Unsurprisingly, research on agroforestry and intercrop systems has
often focused on understanding and measuring inter- and intra-specific
competition. For example, following the LER style of calculation
we can estimate 'aggressivity' using the proportional yields of the
components:

$$\text{proportional yield of crop A} = \frac{Y_{ab}}{Y_{aa} \cdot P_{ab}}$$

$$\text{proportional yield of crop B} = \frac{Y_{ba}}{Y_{bb} \cdot P_{ba}}$$

where the symbols Y_{aa}, Y_{ab} etc. denote yield set out above for LER and P_{ab} and P_{ba} are the proportions of crops A and B respectively in the total plant population of the intercrop. Therefore the denominator component of the equations is the expected yield of the component in the intercrop based upon the sole crop yield and its proportional 'presence' in the intercrop. Therefore the equations compare observed yield (numerator) in the intercrop with expected yield (denominator). For example, if the yield of a sole crop of species A is 1.0 tonne/ha and 50% of the population of species A is planted in an intercrop with species B then the expected yield is 0.5 tonnes/ha. Using our intercrop example from earlier:

$$\text{proportional yield of crop A} = \frac{0.7}{0.5} = 1.4$$
$$\text{proportional yield of crop B} = \frac{0.4}{0.25} = 1.6$$

In both cases the observed yield in the intercrop is higher than the expected yield. Once these proportional yields have been calculated, it is possible to find a measure of 'aggressivity' of the components as follows:

$$
\begin{aligned}
\text{aggressivity of crop A} &= \text{proportional yield of A} \\
&\quad - \text{proportional yield of B} \\
&= 1.4 - 1.6 \\
&= -0.2 \\
\text{aggressivity of crop B} &= \text{proportional yield of B} \\
&\quad - \text{proportional yield of A} \\
&= 1.6 - 1.4 \\
&= 0.2
\end{aligned}
$$

If aggressivity is zero then both crops are equally competitive (neither is dominant). If aggressivity is positive for one species compared with another then this species is more competitive (dominant) than the other, while if aggressivity is negative then this species is less competitive than the other. In our example above, crop B is more aggressive than is crop A, although the difference is relatively small. We can summarise the notion of yield advantage as measured with the LER and agressivity on a single graph, as shown in Figure 2.9.

Aggressivity matters in the design of intercrop systems, as the farmer needs to avoid a situation where one crop dominates the other to the extent that its yield becomes greatly diminished. For example, if we take the following situation:

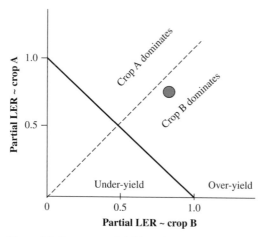

Figure 2.9 Summary of yield performance and dominance in intercrops. If the system rests below the solid line then this represents under-yielding and if it is on the line then yields of sole and intercrops are the same (no advantage from planting the crops as an intercrop). If the system is above the solid line there is over-yielding (intercropping gives a yield advantage relative to sole cropping). The graph also shows which of the two crops dominates. Points to the left of the dashed line signify that crop A dominates over crop B, while points to the right of the dashed line signify the opposite. The dot presents the results for the example discussed in the text. The system shows over-yielding, with crop B being more aggressive than crop A.

$$LER = \frac{0.1}{1.0} + \frac{0.4}{0.5} = 0.1 + 0.8 = 0.9$$

then:

$$\text{proportional yield of crop A} = \frac{0.1}{0.5} = 0.2$$

$$\text{proportional yield of crop B} = \frac{0.4}{0.25} = 1.6$$

$$\text{aggressivity of crop A} = 0.2 - 1.6$$
$$= -1.4$$
$$\text{aggressivity of crop B} = 1.6 - 0.2$$
$$= 1.4$$

Here, crop B is dominating crop A to such an extent that the yield of A is greatly suppressed and the system as a whole performs badly: there is under-yielding. Clearly the farmer has to get the combination right, but how does he/she know what crops to put together and in what population density, especially when he/she might not have access to results from research stations and the sort of calculations shown above? The equations for LER and aggressivity are certainly instructive and help provide clues, but are dependent upon planned experimentation where we can measure the yields and proportions. While farmers may not do such work for themselves, they will experiment in a purposeful way and over generations create a bank of indigenous technical knowledge (ITK) which is passed from parents to children, as well as amongst peers. The language may not be in terms of 'LER' or 'aggressivity' but it will be about what can be planted together, when and how. Thus farmers learn by doing and it is this process that has resulted in the sophisticated intercropping systems we observe today in much of the developing world. The moral of this story is that it should be remembered that biological research comes in all shapes and forms and is not the preserve of scientists working in research stations and universities. We have to be careful in our consideration of 'knowledge'. The equations and graphs shown so far in this chapter are the sort one would find in refereed journals and books on the subject of intercropping, but that does not make the knowledge of greater intrinsic 'value' than ITK (Long and Long, 1992). The question is value to whom? After all, it is ITK which is at the heart of sustainability for many trying to survive in challenging environments.

2.4   THE NICHE: COMPLETION AND CO-EXISTENCE IN CROPPING SYSTEMS

A key biological concept of relevance in intercropping is the niche; the sum of all the interactions of an organism and its abiotic (non-living) and biotic (living) environment. The term was first coined by Grinnell in 1904 and expanded upon by Elton (1927), Hutchinson (1957) and Levins (1968), amongst others. The niche concept has also been adopted within sociology and economics where it is 'the position or function of an entity, such as an organization or population of organizations, within a larger community environment' (Popielarz and Neal, 2007). In ecology, the niche can be thought of as the set of resources which are used by any organism. For example, in Figure 2.10 the two curves show the use of a resource (for example, nitrogen in soil) by two plant species. The curves represent the range of the resource which each species can theoretically exploit (referred to as the fundamental niche). In this particular example there is virtually no overlap between the two niches and hence there is no competition between the

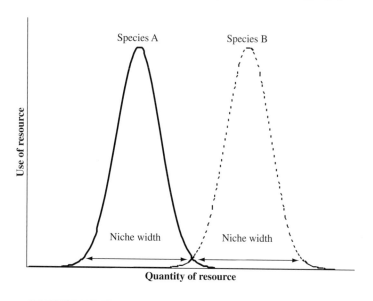

Figure 2.10 Examples of niches for two species. In this example the niches are theoretical (or fundamental).

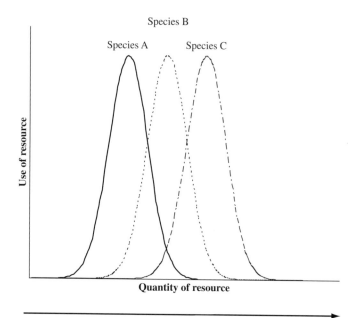

Figure 2.11 Examples of niches for three species.
In this example the niches are theoretical (or fundamental).

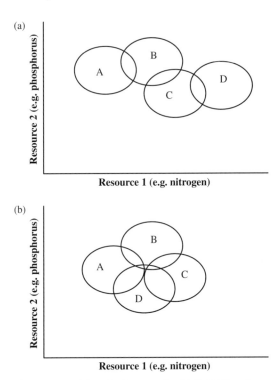

Figure 2.12 Niches for four species (A, B, C, D) and two resources (N and P): (a) some overlap between species; (b) much overlap between species.

two species for the resource (in this case nitrogen). However, there can be overlaps in resource use, as shown in Figure 2.11 for three species, and this leads to competition for the resource at the points of overlap. Diagrams such as these can become extremely complex if more than one resource is considered. For example, in Figure 2.12 there are two resources and four species. In practice we see little overlap, as competition will force species out, leaving dominant ones in place (realised niches). But these are requirement niches measured in terms of what the plants need. It is also possible to talk of an impact niche, the changes which plants bring about in an environment (Leibold, 1995).

The resources being referred to in these diagrams are typically light, mineral nutrients and water. Oxygen and carbon dioxide are also resources in the sense that they are required for respiration and photosynthesis, but they are usually not limiting, so we don't consider them. The important mineral nutrients for plant growth include the primary nutrients (nitrogen, phosphorus and potassium), secondary nutrients (calcium, magnesium and sulfur) and the micro-nutrients (includes

Table 2.5 *Maximum rooting depth and depth where main uptake of water and nutrients takes place.*

	Maximum rooting depth (cm)	
Crop	All roots	Main roots for nutrient and water uptake
Pepper (*Capsicum sp.*)	100	50–100
Rice (Oryza sativa)	100	<50
Soybean (*Glycine max*)	>180	60–130
Groundnut (Arachis hypogaea)	180	50–100
Maize (*Zea mays*)	200	80–100
Sorghum (Sorghum bicolor)	100–200	100–200
Carrot (Daucus carota)	50–100	<60
Tomato (Lycopersicon esculentum)	150	70–150

Source: Landon (1984)

iron, manganese, zinc, boron and copper). Crops differ markedly in their requirement for these nutrients, as well as for water and light. Cereals such as maize, for example, have a relatively high demand for nitrogen and need to absorb it as nitrate or ammonium ions from the soil solution. Thus, the nitrogen has to be present in adequate levels for the crop to do well. Legumes, on the other hand, can 'fix' nitrogen from the atmosphere and do not need to absorb it from the soil solution. Thus a maize–legume intercrop, as shown in Figure 2.6a, has a synergy, as the legume does not compete with maize for nitrogen. In addition, plants root at different depths within the soil and this includes the depth at which most uptake of water and nutrients takes place. Some examples are provided in Table 2.5. Groundnut (a legume) has a shallower root system compared with maize and this allows for further compatibility between the two crops.

Nutrients can become exhausted from the soil over time, of course, so farmers must either add more of these resources or allow time for them to replenish naturally (a much slower process). In sole-crop systems the management of these resources is straightforward given that all of the crop plants are the same, but in intercrop systems the demands of the crops can be quite different and while a level of one group of nutrients may be fine for one component they can be detrimental to another. To some extent this can be compensated for by 'side placement' of fertiliser next to the particular plants that need it at the correct stage of their growth, thus avoiding damaging the other components as well as creating waste, but this requires skill and yet more labour.

Light is another important resource which can be competed for within intercrops, but as we have already seen, there are significant differences between C3 and C4 crops in terms of their response to increasing light intensity, and it is no accident that many intercrops involve a tall C4 crop (maize, millet, sorghum) planted in conjunction with a C3 under-story crop such as a legume. The taller C4 crop is less easily saturated with incident light energy while the C3 crop would make the best of what light filters through the canopy. This makes for a much greater efficiency of light use by the system as a whole.

While nutrients and light are important resources in agricultural systems, water is often the resource which has the largest influence on the crops that can be grown in a particular region. As well as differences between crop species in the amount of water required, there are also different requirements at different stages of growth. A useful measure often employed by agricultural scientists is water use efficiency (WUE), the mass of water required for each unit of biomass. Interestingly, because water leaves the plant via the same route that carbon dioxide enters (i.e. the stomata), there is a link between WUE and whether the plant is C3 or C4 (Figure 2.13). Plants which are good at 'grabbing' CO_2 (C4 plants) can reduce water loss and hence be more efficient, as measured by WUE (Table 2.6).

While compatibility in terms of resource use between crop species is an important explanation for over-yielding in intercrops, there are other reasons. All crops and animals that we manage within agriculture are subject to attack from pests and diseases. Their attack can cause a direct loss in production or perhaps reduce the quality of what is produced, thereby reducing its economic value. Experiments have occasionally shown a reduced incidence of pests, diseases and weeds in intercrops relative to sole crops (Andow, 1991; Verkerk et al, 1998; Hooks and Johnson, 2003), although this is not always the case (Smith and McSorley, 2000). Various mechanisms may be acting to bring about a reduction in pest and disease attack in intercrops. For example, non-host species in the intercrop may be acting as simple mechanical barriers to the spread of pests and diseases or as a more attractive environment for predators. One of the classic studies of the barrier phenomenon is provided by Speight (1983) for mixtures of susceptible and resistant varieties of wheat and oats (Table 2.7). While this system is based on mixtures of varieties rather than crops, the same principles apply (Smithson and Lenne, 1996). In Table 2.7 yields of the susceptible

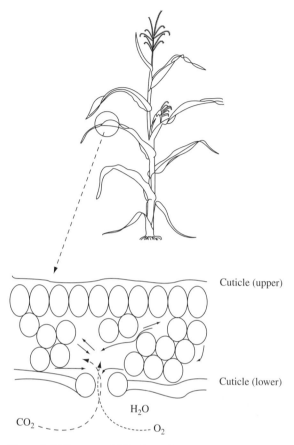

Cuticle (upper)

Cuticle (lower)

H_2O

CO_2

O_2

Figure 2.13 Passage of CO_2, O_2 and water vapour through stomata.

variety (S) and mixtures of susceptible and resistant (R) varieties are expressed as a percentage of resistant variety yield. For the three mixtures of susceptible and resistant varieties (3:1, 1:1 and 1:3) there are two figures, an observed and an expected yield. For all of the mixtures the observed yield was higher than the expected yield, and Speight explains this primarily through the R plants acting as physical barriers for the fungal pathogen. In essence, the R plants get in the way of the disease spreading amongst the S plants. As well as providing a simple barrier to pest and pathogen spread, it has also been shown in various studies that natural enemies (predators and parasitoids) of the pest may accumulate better in an intercrop relative to a sole crop, perhaps due to the presence of alternative (non-pest) prey in more diverse cropping systems or perhaps because the diverse

Table 2.6 *Comparison of C4 and C3 plants in terms of their water use efficiency.*

	Resistance to	
Type of Plants	CO_2 entry	Water loss
C4	low	high
C3	high	low

Some measurements for C4 and C3 crops are as follows:

C3 crop	WUE (g water/g biomass)	C4 crop	WUE (g water/g biomass)
Barley	518	Sorghum	304
Wheat	557	Maize	350
Potato	575	Foxtail millet	285
Oats	583		
Rye	634		
Rice	682		

plant architecture is more attractive and conducive. An example of this phenomenon with spiders is provided by Sunderland and Samu (2000). Much may depend upon whether the natural enemies are 'generalists' (have a wide prey/host range, such as spiders) or 'specialists' (only attack the pest). The 'generalist' natural enemies may do best in intercrops where a variety of prey are available, while the 'specialists' may do best in sole crops where their prey are easier to find.

Thus, intercrop systems are successful on a number of fronts, as proven by their popularity with many farmers in the tropics, and we have biological explanations for this success. They can generate over-yielding so farmers gain more for their labour input and provide an element of insurance in case one component fails to reach harvest or suffers from a decline in market price. Such systems may also reduce the need for weeding if the understory crop spreads to cover the soil. But does that actually make them any more sustainable compared with single-crop systems? Well, as always, it depends upon the meaning one ascribes to 'sustainable'. Intercrop systems may provide better yields relative to sole crops grown under the same environmental and

Table 2.7 Barrier effect on fungal pathogen spread in crops (after Speight, 1983).

Crop	Pathogen	Pure stand		Mixture of susceptible (S) and resistant (R) plants					
		Susceptible (SSSS)	Resistant (RRRR)	3:1 SSSR		1:1 SSRR		1:3 SRRR	
		Observed	Observed	Observed	Expected	Observed	Expected	Observed	Expected
Wheat	Stem rust	43	100	94	57				
Oats	Crown rust	58	100	75	69	86	79	94	89
	Stem rust	72	100			92	86		
	None (fungicide)	99	100			98	99		

Figures are percentage yields relative to a pure stand of resistant plants (equals a yield of 100%). For each mixture of susceptible (S) and resistant (R) plants there is an observed and an expected yield (based on the yields of the pure stands). For example, the expected yield of a 3:1 mixture of susceptible and resistant wheat plants (SSSR) attacked by stem rust is found by:

$$\frac{43 + 43 + 43 + 100}{4} = 57\%$$

where 43 is the relative yield for the susceptible variety of wheat (43% of resistant variety) and 100 is the relative yield of the resistant variety. For each crop and pathogen the observed yields of the mixtures are greater than the expected yields. This can be explained by the resistant plants acting as a barrier for the pathogen spread amongst susceptible plants.

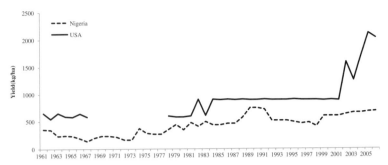

Figure 2.14 Yield of cowpea (black-eyed pea; *Vigna unguiculata*) from
Nigeria and the USA. (Data taken from the FAO Agricultural database;
FAOSTAT, faostat.fao.org/site/291/default.aspx.)

management conditions, and a degree of resilience, but they also
consume resources and arguably do this more efficiently. Growing
the same intercrop on a piece of land will exhaust the soil just as a
monoculture will. What matters is what is practised over time, as well
as over space, and we will return to that later. It should also be noted
that agroforestry and intercropping systems are typically employed
in situations where farmers have little access or ability to purchase
other inputs that can provide increases in yield and resilience to environmental stress. This can make a major difference in yield terms. For
example, Figure 2.14 is a comparison of cowpea (dry seed) yields in the
USA, where it is grown entirely as a sole crop, and Nigeria, where it is
almost entirely grown as an intercrop (data provided by the United
Nations Food and Agriculture Organisation). Cowpea was domesticated
by human beings in Nigeria so that country can be thought of as its
home, and indeed the world germplasm collection of cowpea is held at
the International Institute of Tropical Agriculture based in Ibadan, Oyo
State, Nigeria. Cowpea was introduced to the USA by Africans during
the slave trade and is mostly grown in the south-east of the country
where it is known as black-eyed pea, on account of its distinctive seed-
coat colouration. While yields in both countries have shown an
increase with time, yields in the USA have been significantly higher
than those in Nigeria since 1961, and in the past eight years or so the
yield of cowpea has increased dramatically in the USA. It is remarkable
how yields of cowpea have shown relatively little increase since 1961,
but sole cropping as practised in the USA does allow for a surge in yield
with increased use of inputs allied with new varieties. In intercropping
systems this is far more difficult to achieve. Cowpea is a crop which is
plagued by pest attack and application of insecticide can make a major

difference to yield; spraying at the correct rate and time and is far easier when the crop is grown by itself.

2.5 TOTAL FACTOR PRODUCTIVITY: A MICROCOSM OF SUSTAINABILITY

So far the discussion has centred on agricultural sustainability envisioned as the maintenance of production at an 'acceptable' level over time, and we have explored how different cropping systems allow trade-offs between production, use of inputs and resilience to environment stress. From a farmer's, and indeed a consumer's, perspective this is obviously important. If production is not maintained then at best prices will increase, which is bad for the consumer, and at worst farmers and their families may starve. Thus, the maintenance of production over time is understandably seen as a key feature of agricultural sustainability, although it can be argued that in more agribusiness systems it is economic viability rather than production which is the critical aspect, and sustainability should equate to maintenance or improvement in economic viability (Lehman *et al.*, 1993). Given that the world's population is set to increase, then mere maintenance of production is not enough, production also has to increase and we will need to do something about distribution of the produce. However, as we have seen with the discussion of over-yielding in intercrops, production comes at a cost of resources, and the supply of these resources needs to be maintained for production to continue. Given this linkage, some have attempted to present production and sustainability in terms of efficiency of resource use, and an example is provided by one of the most influential concepts in economics, that of total factor productivity (TFP) (Lynam and Herdt, 1989; Spencer and Swift, 1992; Thirtle and Bottomly, 1992). TFP is one of the few economic concepts which has been the subject of a biography, in this case written by Charles Hulten (2000). While the idea may seem sound and uncontroversial, TFP has been the subject of a vigorous debate as to how it should best be measured or indeed how important it is. The heyday of TFP was the 1980s, but it is widely employed across the globe in a variety of geographical and sectoral contexts. Here I will concentrate on the application of TFP within agriculture.

In basic terms, we can describe yield as a function of inputs:

$$Y = \text{function}(L, K)$$

Where Y = yield (product/area), L = inputs of human capital (i.e. labour) and K = inputs of physical capital (fertiliser, pesticide, seeds, machinery etc.). Thus the more K and L we put in then the higher the yield, at least up to a point. There is a law of diminishing return which operates with such inputs, as we have already seen with light intensity and photosynthesis. Yield may increase to a point after which it levels off and can eventually decline as plants can become damaged. Fertiliser provides a good example. Application of nitrogen will boost the yield of many crops, but at a certain point no extra gain is realised, as the plants simply cannot make use of the additional nutrient. If application rates increase even further then the plants can become damaged. At even higher rates the plants will die. In reality, of course, farmers will want to ensure that they get the best return on inputs they use, so rarely will they get to the point of damaging their crops. But there is also an input from knowledge, farmer experience or the fruits of research, to consider. Thus we can restate this basic equation as:

$$Y = \text{function}(L, K, A)$$

Where A represents 'state of knowledge', which in effect adjusts L and K to allow for enhanced knowledge as to how best we can use L and K. We call A the total factor productivity (TFP), and the form of this function linking L, K and A is often expressed as a 'Cobb–Douglas' equation:

$$Y_t = A_t(K_t)^{\alpha}(L_t)^{1-\alpha}$$

Thus, the three components are multiplied together to give the yield (Y) and A is the conversion of inputs to output at that time. In effect, A is how much output we get for units of K and L. The value of A can be enhanced through research, for example, thereby getting more out of each unit of K and L we put in. Note that we have to specify a time (t) as, of course, the values of A, K and L will change over time. The term α is technically referred to as the 'marginal product of capital'. It is an adjustment for the relative contributions made by human and physical capital, and will of course vary depending upon the scale and the nature of the enterprise. For example, if α is 0.3 then $(1 - \alpha)$ is 0.7, and human capital (L) would be making a larger contribution to yield than physical capital (K).

While the measurement of K and L would seem straightforward, how can we find the TFP? How can we gauge the benefits of knowledge? One way of achieving this is by estimating K, L and α and seeing how these match an observed growth in yield. We can assume the difference

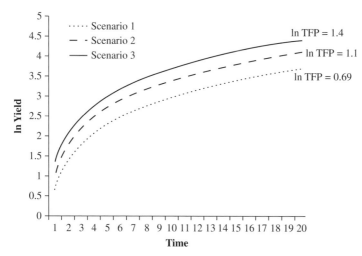

Figure 2.15 Effect of Total Factor Productivity on yield.
   The 3 scenarios represent different levels of TFP, with scenario 3 being the best and scenario 1 the worst. In all other respects the three scenarios are identical; same values of physical (K) and human (L) capital over the 20 time periods and same marginal product of capital (0.3). An increase in TFP increases the return (yield) on capital. The values used to construct the graph are logarithm (base e; Ln).

to be due to TFP. Employing a theoretical example, if crop yield over, say, 10 years increased by an average of 2% a year and physical and labour capital inputs increased by 3% and 1%, respectively, then we have the following (assuming the marginal product of capital is 0.3):

contribution to yield increase from physical capital
$$(K) : 3 \times 0.3 = 0.9$$
contribution to yield increase from human capital
$$(L) : 1 \times 0.7 = 0.7$$

These two together (0.9 + 0.7) account for 1.6 out of the total growth in yield of 2%. The balance of 0.4% each year is the contribution to the increase coming from TFP. Perhaps this was the result of new crop varieties coming on stream, better types of fertiliser or pesticide, or knowledge as to how to use all of these inputs in a more effective way via application rates, placement or timing. In effect, the efficiency of the production has increased as farmers are able to generate a 'value-added' component from their use of physical and human capital. Figure 2.15 is an illustration of the impact that TFP has on yield. The graph employs identical values of K, L and α for the three curves and the only difference is in TFP, which increases from 0.69 to 1.4. Note that these curves are based on the logarithmic form of the Cobb–Douglas equation:

$$\ln(Y_t) = \ln(A_t) + \alpha \ln(K_t) + (1 - \alpha)\ln(L_t)$$

Where ln is logarithm to the base e (e is Euler's number; one of those never-ending numbers which approximates to 2.71828182846). When numbers are converted to their logarithmic form, multiplication becomes addition (division becomes subtraction). The TFP values are the intercepts on the ln (Yield) axis when time is zero.

So what has all this to do with sustainability? Changes in TFP over time can be regarded as one measure of sustainability (i.e. change in productive capacity of the system). In its simplest form, an increase or stability in the TFP equates to sustainability, while a decrease indicates unsustainability. Rearranging the earlier Cobb–Douglas equation (non-logarithmic form) we have:

$$A_t = \frac{Y_t}{(K_t)^\alpha (L_t)^{1-\alpha}}$$

or, put another way:

$$TFP = \frac{\text{outputs from farming system}}{\text{inputs into farming system}}$$

For two time periods we can use the ratio:

$$\frac{TFP_2}{TFP_1} = \frac{\dfrac{\text{output}_2}{\text{input}_2}}{\dfrac{\text{output}_1}{\text{input}_1}}$$

or

$$\ln\left(\frac{TFP_2}{TFP_1}\right) = \ln\left(\frac{\text{output}_2}{\text{input}_2}\right) - \ln\left(\frac{\text{output}_1}{\text{input}_1}\right)$$

This is the same as:

$$\ln\left(\frac{TFP_2}{TFP_1}\right) = \ln(\text{output}_2) - \ln(\text{input}_2) - \ln(\text{output}_1) - \ln(\text{input}_1)$$

or, when re-ordered:

$$\ln\left(\frac{\text{TFP}_2}{\text{TFP}_1}\right) = \ln(\text{output}_2) - \ln(\text{output}_2) - \ln(\text{input}_1) - \ln(\text{input}_1)$$

$$= \text{rate of growth of outputs} - \text{rate of growth of inputs}$$

This ratio has to be one or more to equate to sustainability.

But while this assumption has logic, there are some problems. Firstly, the ratio can hide a decline in output which parallels a decline in input. Also, the terms 'output' and 'input' as expressed here are simple aggregates of what can be quite diverse entities. In practice, many inputs will be used (plant nutrients, pesticides, irrigation, energy etc.) and there could be a number of 'outputs', especially within intercrop and agroforestry systems, but also within mixed farms which combine elements of crop and animal production. How are these placed into the same units in order to allow the calculation of a ratio? The obvious answer is to convert to monetary value. For example:

$$\text{input}_1 = a_1b_1 + a_2b_2 + a_3b_3 \ldots a_nb_n$$

or

$$\text{input} = \sum_{i=1}^{i-n} a_ib_i$$

Where a is the cost and b the quantity of each of the n inputs which are used. The symbol Σ means to sum up over the range from i equals 1 to i equals n.

Between the two time periods there could be a number of changes. An obvious one is that prices for the same input may change. Therefore, an increase or decrease in TFP could be caused by a change in price rather than any change in quantity of output or input. In that sense the TFP becomes a measure of economic sustainability rather than reflecting any fundamental shift in biological performance. In order to focus on the latter, the ratio of TFPs can be based on a constant price. There are two possibilities, use the prices for time period 1 (start) or time period 2 (end). Laspeyres version of the TFP index uses prices based on period 1 and Paasche's version of TFP uses prices based on time period 2 (in both cases the assumption is that prices are lower in period 1 relative to period 2). It is possible to take the geometric mean (square root of the product) of these two as a further measure of TFP:

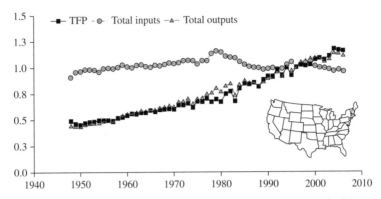

Figure 2.16 Values of the TFP in the USA (data available at United States Department of Agriculture, Economic Research Service; www.ers.usda.gov/Data/AgProductivity).

$$\text{Fisher TFP} = (\text{Laspeyres TFP} \times \text{Paasche TFP})^{0.5}$$

Figure 2.16 shows the trend in TFP for agriculture in the USA (see Mundlak, 2005 for a detailed analysis and discussion) from the late 1940s till 2008. TFP in this case is the ratio of an index for output (crop and livestock) divided by inputs (capital, land, labour and 'intermediates', i.e. inputs consumed within a year, such as petroleum, electricity, pesticides and fertiliser). Total inputs and outputs are also shown in Figure 2.16, and TFP is the ratio of these two. Clearly there has been an increase in TFP in the USA over the 60 years and the trend largely mirrors that of outputs and not inputs. A more detailed breakdown of the outputs is shown as Figure 2.17, where it can be seen that the one which mirrors total outputs most closely is crops. Other 'farm-related' outputs have shown a rapid increase since the early 1980s and livestock and livestock products have also shown a steady increase, but it is crops that show the closest correlation with the total. A breakdown of the inputs is shown in Figure 2.18. Labour has shown a dramatic decline over the 60 years, while material (includes pesticides and fertiliser) has increased and the capital input has remained steady. The result of all this is an input trend that is remarkably stable, with the decline in labour being compensated for by an increase in materials. What are the impacts on this trend in TFP for consumers in the USA? Basically it is a 'good news' story, as prices they have paid for primary farm products have declined as efficiency of production has improved (Gopinath and Roe, 1997). The story seems to be one of sustainability and 'winners all round', but there are complications.

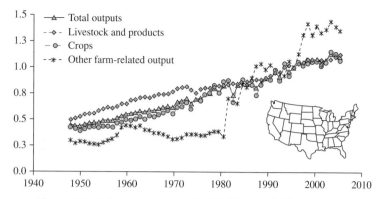

Figure 2.17 Output components for TFP (data available at United States Department of Agriculture, Economic Research Service; www.ers.usda. gov/Data/AgProductivity).

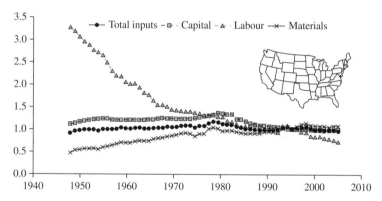

Figure 2.18 Input components for TFP (data available at United States Department of Agriculture, Economic Research Service; www.ers.usda. gov/Data/AgProductivity).

TFP can be applied to a wide range of agricultural systems, including those based on intercropping and agroforestry (Ehui and Spencer, 1993). It should also be noted that the TFP is fundamentally an economic approach, although the same idea could be applied to any common unit, such as energy input and output. The problem, of course, is that there are inputs into the system that we may not know anything about in precise terms. All we do know about are what the farmers are doing and the returns which they get. For example, soils contain plant nutrients to varying degrees and not all those used by the plant will come from applied fertiliser or organic inputs that we can measure. These are the so-called 'common pool resources'. In effect, we can derive a high TFP, even if only for a short period, by limiting the use of purchased inputs and using up the common pool resources already present in the soil. This would not be sustainable, of course, and over a period of time the TFP would inevitably decline, but much depends upon the time period over which it is being measured. Thus using TFP as a measure of sustainability over short timescales could be highly misleading. Unfortunately in many parts of the world we simply don't have the sort of quality datasets used to construct Figures 2.16 to 2.18 for the USA. Also, as we will discuss later, the reality is that many sustainable development projects have to make judgements on what to promote over relatively short timescales. Can TFP be employed in such cases?

To compensate for the common pool resources we could try and include them as 'inputs' within TFP. One obvious complication is that the common pool resource is not a static one, and while some resources will be utilised by crops, there will also be some replenishment from rainfall, weathering etc. Thus, it is important to know the dynamics of this change and not just the static picture of what is present at any one time. Figure 2.19 is a summary of some data provided by Ehui and Spencer (1993) for four cropping systems in Nigeria between the years 1986 and 1988. System A is an intercrop having three components, albeit slightly different ones in 1986 and 1988, while system B is an intercrop in 1986 and a sole crop in 1988. System C is an agroforestry one, in this case based on alley cropping, and system D is a sole crop of plantain. The two sets of bars in Figure 2.19 are values of the TFP between 1986 and 1988. In one case the calculation does not take into account changes in the common pool resources while in the other it does. Thus, increases in soil nutrients, for example, would be an output within TFP in much the same way as yield would be. TFPs below a value of one indicate unsustainability, while values of one or more indicate sustainability. By this measure, system A (an intercrop) is clearly unsustainable, while system B (combination of an intercrop and sole crop) is sustainable. In both cases it makes little difference to the TFP if changes to the common resource pool are included, and there was a slight increase in soil nutrients between 1986 and 1988, but this had little impact on TFP. However, for systems C and D it does make a substantial difference as to whether changes to the common pool resources are included or not. If included then system C (alley cropping) changes

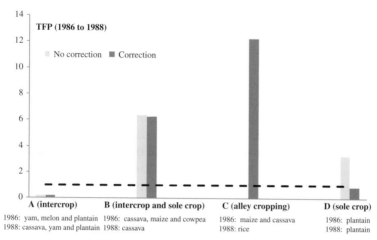

Figure 2.19 Total Factor Productivity for four cropping systems (A, B, C and D) in Nigeria spanning the years 1986 to 1988 (after Ehui and Spencer,1993).

No correction = no adjustment was made for using common pool resources.

Correction = adjustment was made for the use of common pool resources.

Values of TFP less than one (dashed line in the graph) indicate unsustainability.

from unsustainability to sustainability (TFP increases dramatically from 0.02 to 12.23). The difference is accounted for almost entirely by the nutrients which the leguminous alley plants are adding to the soil. Thus there is a substantial enhancement of soil nutrients. For system D the reverse is the case, as the sole crop plantain draws nutrients out of the soil. While plantain was also included as part of the intercrop in system A, the density was not as high.

While having the advantage of being able to use TFP over relatively short time periods and under subsistence conditions, the inclusion of flows into and out of the common pool resource is not as straightforward as implied here and would require a substantial and repeated regime of sampling and testing. As already mentioned, a crop requires a range of crop nutrients and we would need to measure all of them. The cost of doing all this is likely to be considerable. Another disadvantage of the TFP is that other environmental and social effects that many consider central to sustainability are not included. For example, farming can have effects on the wider environment, such as water pollution from pesticides and fertilisers. The rise in TFP shown for the USA in the above graph could have gone hand-in-hand with substantial pollution or perhaps with mass unemployment as human labour is displaced by machinery. Similarly a rise in TFP in itself does not guarantee that there will be no malnutrition. Much depends upon the price of food relative to what people earn, and there are also issues of distribution to consider. These effects are discounted (ignored) within TFP, but can be highly important in society. There have been efforts to create what is called a total social factor productivity (TSFP), which is meant to include at least some of these factors, but this approach has been criticised, largely because such social factors are not commodities being traded within the same markets as are the farm inputs and outputs (Byerlee and Murgai, 2001). Indeed, they may not be marketed at all. Thus TFSP attempts to integrate a set of quite different components.

2.6   ENHANCING TFP: GENETIC MODIFICATION

An example of one technology that has the potential to enhance TFP is genetic modification (GM; Herdt, 2006). Breeding of new crop varieties has provided a major contribution to TFP throughout the world, and indeed many of the crops we grow today are far removed in terms of their characteristics from their wild ancestors. The history of plant breeding is a long one and probably as old as agriculture itself, but once the laws of genetics had been formulated then the process became more methodical. Breeders can identify genes for desired characteristics and introduce them into existing varieties. However, they quite literally have to work with millions of genes, but may only be interested in a few: the ones that code for a desired characteristic. The consequence is a laborious and time-consuming process of crossing to transfer the desired genes, selection for the desired characteristic(s) and back-crossing with the original lines to retain desired 'background' characteristics. After all, the aim is to improve upon the existing lines and not necessarily to supplant them. This process is more complex and lengthy with characteristics that are multigenic (polygenic), i.e. controlled by a number of genes rather than only one, but the result can be a crop variety which makes better use of nutrients or water, can grow in saline environments or perhaps have has an enhanced resistance to pests and disease. As a result, TFP will increase, at least in the short term. However, this may not last. If no further improvements occur then yields will become static or, even worse, if the benefits of a technology go into reverse then TFP will decline. For example, there are examples where varietal resistance to an insect or pathogen may last for some years, but if applied over a large area it will place a selection pressure on the pest population and eventually the resistance will break down. It's not that the genes coding for that resistance have gone away, it is just that the pest population has developed 'resistance to the resistance'.

GM can be employed as an adjunct to traditional plant breeding. It is the transfer of a gene or genes from one species to another by circumventing biological boundaries that prevents different species from exchanging their genetic material. Genes are inserted directly into plant cells, which are nurtured into a full plant, thereby circumventing the plant's own reproductive process. There are various ways in which this can be achieved, including a 'shotgun' approach involving the literal shooting of genes on the surface of gold particles into recipient cells, or the use of biological carriers such as the bacterium *Agrobacterium tumefaciens*. Once the transformed cells have produced a full plant then it follows that every cell of the plant will have a copy of the inserted genes, and when the plant reproduces, the inserted genes will be passed to their offspring. Provided they can be made to express (to function) in their new environment, the inserted genes will confer a new characteristic. GM techniques can be used to transfer genes within the same plant species. The process is more precise as it allows the genetic background to be kept intact and negates the need for field-crossing, selection and back-crossing. All we need do is identify the cells that are expressing the gene(s) we are interested in and use them to produce a plant. However, the same technology can allow genes from any source (plant, animal or bacteria) to be used, and it is here that matters become contentious. However, it should first be noted that cross-species exchange of genes does happen in nature, and, indeed, this has been of great importance in the origins of agriculture. Bread wheat (*Triticum aestivum*), for example, is said to have originated in part from natural crosses between related grass species in the 'Fertile Crescent' of the Middle East (Figure 2.20). It is unlikely that humans crossed the wild grasses in a purposeful sense. Instead there was probably much selection by humans for plants with desirable characteristics once natural crossing had occurred.

GM is claimed to have advantages over traditional plant breeding techniques that should provide a significant enhancement to TFP. Plant breeders are no longer restricted to looking for genetic variation within the same species or a close relative and, in theory, this allows crops to have an almost limitless set of desired characteristics, including characters which help boost production, such as the enhancement of

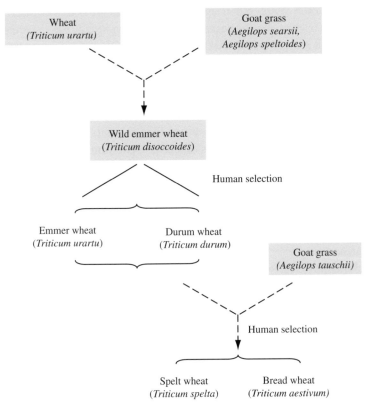

Figure 2.20 Hypothesised domestication of bread wheat (*Triticum aestivum*) from its wild ancestors in Western Asia. The diagram is a simplified version of wheat domestication. Shaded boxes represent wild grass species and the dashed lines represent the hypothesised natural crosses that may have occurred.

photosynthesis mentioned earlier, and/or an improvement in the quality of plant products (seeds, fibre, tubers etc.) or indeed generate entirely new products in a much more cost-effective way. An example of the latter is to engineer crops to produce biofuels, pharmaceuticals or even vaccines to human and animal disease. Second, it is argued that GM allows for a more targeted and quicker approach to generating new varieties.

Much of the commercial GM to date has focused on genes conferring resistance to pests and herbicides, although there are other examples where GM has been used to improve nutritional status, shelf life and tolerance to drought. An example of using GM to confer resistance to insects is provided by genes from a bacterium, *Bacillus thuringiensis* (abbreviated as Bt; Metz, 2003). Bt is a pathogen of many species of insect within the Lepidoptera (butterflies and moths) and Colleoptera (beetles), some of which are important crop pests. The Bt pathogen has genes that produce a variety of endotoxin proteins, which when ingested by susceptible insects cause death. While Bt is one of the first generations of GM insect resistance in crops there are further developments, including the stacking of separate resistance genes so as to limit the chances of a pest population overcoming that resistance (Christou *et al.*, 2006). Pests would need a number of beneficial mutations to happen more or less in tandem for them to overcome this 'stacked' plant resistance, and the chances of that happening are much lower than for a single mutation. Herbicide resistance has been engineered by introducing genes which confer the ability to degrade specific herbicides. There are two types: 'Roundup Ready' crops, which can degrade the broad-spectrum herbicide glyphosate, and 'Liberty Link' crops, which can degrade glufosinate. The former group carry the gene coding for a glyphosate-insensitive form of the enzyme 5-enolpyruvylshikimate 3-phosphate (EPSP) synthase, which derives from the bacterium *Agrobacterium* sp. strain CP4 (Funke *et al.*, 2006). Glyphosate normally works by blocking this important enzyme in plants and this eventually results in death. Crop plants engineered to be insensitive to the herbicide will be unaffected, while the weeds die (Cerdeira and Duke, 2006). Glyphosate is a very effective and relatively cheap herbicide, and hence farmers would be able to significantly reduce their costs rather than have to use more expensive and selective herbicides that kill some weeds, but not the crop. The tolerance of Liberty Link crops is due to introduced genetic material from another bacterial group, the *Streptomyces* (Block *et al.*, 1987; Thompson *et al.*, 1987).

When defined in terms of TFP then GM crops which reduce the need or cost of inputs or which enhance output should enhance sustainability, and GM crops have certainly grown in popularity over the past 10 years. In 2006, some 22 countries grew GM crops, comprising 11 developing countries and 11 developed countries, and the countries where the technology is especially prevalent are shown in Table 2.8. The USA had some 55 million hectares of GM crops in 2006 and the figure is likely to have grown since then. Indeed there are calls for GM to be allowed to make a major contribution to the lives of farmers and their families in developing countries, given the immediacy of the problems that they face (Ozor and Igbokwe, 2007), and targets to

Table 2.8 *Example of countries growing GM crops in 2006.*

Country	Area (million ha)	Biotech Crops
USA	54.6	Soybean, maize, cotton, canola, squash, papaya, alfalfa
Argentina	18	Soybean, maize, cotton
Brazil	11.5	Soybean, cotton
Canada	6.1	Canola, maize, soybean
India	3.8	Cotton
China	3.5	Cotton
Paraguay	2	Soybean
South Africa	1.4	Maize, soybean, cotton
Uruguay	0.4	Soybean, maize
Philippines	0.2	Maize
Australia	0.2	Cotton
Romania	0.1	Soybean
Mexico	0.1	Cotton, soybean
Spain	0.1	Maize

Source: James (2006)

increase food production such as those set by the UN. The countries most notable for their absence from Table 2.8 are those of Europ, where public opposition to GM is strong. The only EU member listed in Table 2.8 is Spain.

The rationale for opposition to GM crops is varied, and a review of some of the problems that GM crops have been proven and hypothesised to posses is provided by Craig *et al.* (2008). Perhaps the most immediate concern is that GM products may not be safe to consume (Key *et al.*, 2008). Whilst there may not be any consistent evidence of toxicity in the short term, the argument made here is that GM food products can cause health problems if consumed over long periods, and as yet they have not been around long enough for these effects to surface. This is a difficult issue for science to address given the long-term nature of studies which would be required (Dona and Arvanitoyannis, 2009). Some also argue that there is potential for gene escape from the crop to closely related species (Andow and Zwahlen, 2006), thereby creating 'super weeds' (Guarnieri *et al.*, 2008; Mallory-Smith and Zapiola, 2008). An example of this concern is provided by Roundup Ready alfalfa sold in the USA between

2005 and 2007. The acreage of the GM crop was low, only 300 000 acres (1200 km^2) out of the total alfalfa acreage of 21 000 000 acres (85 000 km^2), but in May 2007 the California Northern District Court issued an injunction order prohibiting farmers from planting the GM alfalfa until the US Department of Agriculture (USDA) completed a study on the variety's likely environmental impact, especially the possibility of the herbicide resistance gene escaping to other plants. Others are opposed to the technology on ethical grounds, as it breaks down the barriers between species and thus is 'unnatural'. No matter what research results say about GM varieties being environmentally safe or posing no threat to human health, those against the technology on ethical grounds will continue to regard them in derogative terms as 'Frankenstein Food' (Scott, 2000).

Going back to the beginning of this chapter and the various definitions provided for sustainable agriculture, one can argue that GM crops can help with the achievement of sustainability in most of those provided, and could potentially help with the UN's target of increasing food production by 70% by 2050. GM crops can be beneficial if they improve yield and if they result in less contamination from fertilisers or pesticides, and provided they are proven not to have any deleterious effects on human health or the environment. If GM varieties help with enhancing income and quality of life for farmers and their families then this has to be another plus for sustainability. These are all big 'ifs' of course, and proof of success is needed in each environment where the varieties are due to be released. Hence the testing and regulation regime has to be strong. Even if a GM crop successfully passes all of these tests there are other issues to consider. GM seed is usually far more expensive that non-GM seed, so there are issues of affordability and social differentiation to consider in poorer societies. Will the GM crop variety only make some farmers richer (the ones who can afford the seed)? In fairness it has to be said that this issue is also as old as agriculture and is not new to GM crops. There will always be some farmers better able to access and make use of any technology (fertiliser, irrigation, processing mills etc.) than others. However, having said all this, one of the definitions provided earlier for sustainable agriculture was:

> A sustainable agriculture must be economically viable, environmentally sound, and socially acceptable... it must also be politically achievable. (Zimdahl (2005))

At present, GM crops are socially acceptable and 'politically achievable' in some countries, as evidenced by Table 2.8, but not others, and even within a country where they are legally planted there will no doubt be groups wishing that they were not there. Thus, if we apply this definition then sustainability becomes highly differentiated both geographically and socially, and herein rests a central conundrum which we will continue to come across within this book, as sustainability can mean many things to many people.

2.7 CONCLUSION

This chapter has focused specifically on sustainability within an agricultural context, and, in particular, sustainability seen as the maintenance or increase in production over time. This focus on but one industry and indeed one face of sustainability would seem to facilitate a precise definition, but as we have seen there are many issues and perspectives involved that inevitably cloud matters. Agriculture does inevitably mean a change from a natural ecosystem to a managed one. The change might be large, as, for example, a shift from a tropical forest to a monoculture, or less so, as, for example, with agroforestry systems, but it is a change nonetheless. Take the management out of the equation and the ecosystem will revert to the natural state. Thus any agricultural system is sustainable only in so far as people are present. Beyond that fundamental point much depends upon what is meant by sustainability. A system such as organic farming which is excellent for maintaining soil quality and yield over long periods would be unsustainable if it means that the farmers cannot earn a living or if people cannot afford to buy what is produced. Indeed one could imagine such a system collapsing after only a few years as farmers simply abandon it. Similarly a highly intensive monoculture system which generates high yields and profits, but which exhausts the soil would also be unsustainable and eventually collapse.

The maintenance or enhancement of production as the basis for sustainability is important and can be captured with concepts such as TFP. Here the inputs are considered alongside outputs and it is possible to compare systems as well as explore changes in an area over time. It is even possible to extend the idea to cover changes in the common resource pool and explore the impacts of a technology such as GM crops to TFP. But production is not everything when it comes to sustainability, even if most of the definitions of sustainable agriculture include it. There are other concerns which are not captured by a device such as TFP. Production might be sustainable, but that might be at the expense of wider environmental damage, loss of biodiversity and negative impacts on social factors such as employment or even sub-jective factors such as enjoyment of the countryside. TFP does not include any of these and given the assumptions behind its construction it is hard to see how they could be included in any meaningful way. It has to be said that this is by no means a new insight. While there is science underpinning biological sustainability in agriculture and this can be investigated and addressed, the 'fuzzier' dimensions are much harder to consider, but no less important. We have seen here how GM crops have polarised opinion between those who think that they can make a positive contribution to TFP and farmer livelihood, especially in developing countries, while others take a critical stance which is not necessarily founded on science, but is no less important.

It is perhaps ironical given the call from the United Nations to increase global food production that in recent times we have also wit-nessed a movement in the developed world (the Global North of the planet) towards post-productivism. The argument here is a sort of 'production-plus'; it's not only production that matters, but also the impacts of that production. Thus there have been trends towards the promotion of organic farming, diversification of farmland and the inclu-sion of environmental groups in policy-making, all sharing the goal of moving away from what is perceived as a simplistic emphasis on pro-duction at any cost (Wilson and Rigg, 2003). Sustainability seems to be all about a messy world of trade-offs. None would argue against the need to increase our production of food to be able to address the obvious shortfalls that many will continue to face, but it is how we do it that matters most of all. It's not only the end, but the means to that end which counts. Some would accept GM as a welcome means by which we can increase production and quality of produce, but others feel the environmental and social price is too high.

The final point to highlight here is the importance of indigenous technical knowledge (ITK). As biologists we are used to perceiving the value of knowledge in terms of refereed journal publications and other outlets. The knowledge distributed in this way has been gleaned from a rigorous process of experimentation and the use of methodologies that can be replicated by others. ITK is knowledge passed typically by word of mouth amongst peers and between generations, and, while it may not be 'published', it is the life-blood of survival for many.

3

Sustainable management of fisheries

3.1 INTRODUCTION

Sustainable management of a resource was the theme of Chapter 2, with specific reference to agriculture, but there is obviously much more to this topic. We specifically explored production as well as some of the underlying biological principles of relevance. Thus we looked at the link between the biodiversity of agricultural systems and output, including the importance of system resilience and what farmers are trying to achieve. Farmers in many countries look to crop diversity as an insurance policy against crop failure, especially as they may lack access to inputs such as fertiliser, pesticide and irrigation. Underlying this is the concept of the niche and compatibility of crops.

But agriculture is only one source of food, albeit the most important one on a global scale. In this chapter we will continue the production theme, but look instead at the management of a wild animal resource, notably fish stocks. Fish farming aside, people manage fish stocks primarily through the means by which they harvest them. Wild fish stocks are not directly replenished by people in the same way that farmers plant crops or breed farm animals. Instead, the management is by controlling the rate of extraction of the stock or by the size (equates to age) of the animals which are removed. Thus, the management regime is more one dimensional than that of the systems we discussed in Chapter 2. Allied to this is the fact that many fisheries are not 'owned' by one person or even by one country. Instead they are regarded as common property resources, with access open to anyone with the means to harvest the population (Gordon, 1954). This results in what has been called 'The tragedy of the commons' which was mentioned in Chapter 1; a virtual decimation of many fish stocks as a result of over-fishing.

One of the central tenants in fishery management has been the concept of maximum sustainable yield (MSY; Ostrom, 2001), and the MSY will be the main focus of this chapter. The idea behind the MSY is straightforward in biological terms:

> Given a population of a species what is the number or biomass of individuals that can be removed without reducing the population?

The idea applies, of course, to any harvested population, be it animal or plant. However, perhaps the strongest association is with wild fish populations. MSY builds upon some of the central ideas in ecology, notably population growth and carrying capacity, and thus has held an almost mythical place in fishery management. Indeed, while it may be rare to come across biographies of economic concepts such as total factor productivity, it is even rarer for ecological concepts to be the subject of a prayer, but Peter Larkin (1924 to 1996), a Canadian fisheries biologist based at the University of British Columbia, Vancouver, published a now famous paper entitled 'An epitaph for the concept of maximum sustained yield'. Why he uses the term 'epitaph' we will see later in the chapter, but in his paper we have the prayer:

> *Any species each year produces a harvestable surplus,*
> *and if you take that much,*
> *and no more,*
> *you can go on getting it forever and ever.*
> *(Amen)*

Larkin (1977)

Amen indeed!

The chapter will begin by setting out the theoretical basis for the MSY and thus provide the rationale as to the popularity of the concept. From here we will explore some of the limitations of the MSY when applied in practice, along with examples of fishery collapse when managed with incomplete knowledge. Indeed, this chapter will highlight the importance of good knowledge (data and models) for the sustainable management of animal populations.

3.2 THE ENTICING CONCEPT OF MAXIMUM SUSTAINABLE YIELD

The MSY was developed in the 1930s as the rational (scientific) basis for fisheries management strategy and, if anything, increased in popularity during the 1950s (Ostrom, 2001). Its promise of being able to manage a resource so that the best yield could be obtained indefinitely has always been an alluring one, and it can be argued that this same ethos rests at the very heart of our current enthusiasm for sustainable development.

But what is the theory behind MSY? To set this out we need to go back in time to some of the original work on population dynamics. Population growth is a function of birth rate, death rate, immigration and emigration. Birth and immigration increase the population, while death and emigration reduce population size. In populations that are growing it is clear that the combination of birth rate and immigration is greater than the combination of mortality rate and emigration. In such populations we can regard the excess as an 'interest'; if we can harvest that excess and no more then we have a sustainable yield. It is akin to living off the interest on your bank account. As long as you don't eat into your capital then you are fine. Maximum simply refers to removing the excess at the time when the population growth rate is at its highest; thus we are living off the interest when the rate is at its highest. Sounds straightforward in theory, but, as anyone who has tried to live off interest on capital will acknowledge, much depends upon the size of the capital and the interest rate, and the latter can fluctuate wildly. So how can we set this out in biological terms?

The key to all this is knowledge of the population growth rate, but how can we determine this? Some of the earliest (and simplest) approaches were based on the fundamental idea that at each time (t) one individual in a population (represented by N) becomes two or more. Note that here we are assuming that the 'parents' at each generation do not live to the next. The population at time 1 ($N_1 = 4$) are the offspring of the two individuals living at time 0 and not the sum of both ($2 + 4$). Thus the population progresses from 2 to 4 to 8 to 16 to 32 and so on. We can present this change as a graph (Figure 3.1), and what we see is an example of organic (exponential) growth. The trend shown in Figure 3.1 is a curve with an increasing rate of ascent, as distinct from a linear growth with a constant rate of ascent. Population growth rate is the change in the number of individuals over a time period, and is represented by the slope of the line in the graph. Note how the population growth rate is greater for larger populations. In our example (where one 'parent' reproduces to give two offspring) the overall effect will be an acceleration of population increase with time. The increase over time 1 to 2 is 4 individuals, while the increase over time 4 to 5 is 32 individuals. In other words, population growth rate is a function of population size, which in this

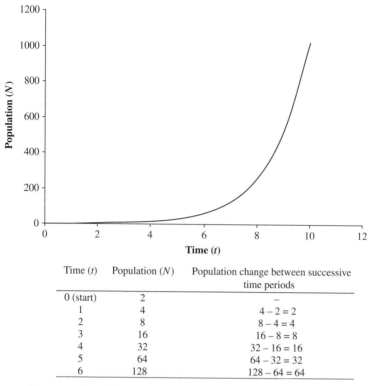

Time (t)	Population (N)	Population change between successive time periods
0 (start)	2	–
1	4	$4 - 2 = 2$
2	8	$8 - 4 = 4$
3	16	$16 - 8 = 8$
4	32	$32 - 16 = 16$
5	64	$64 - 32 = 32$
6	128	$128 - 64 = 64$

Figure 3.1 Population growth curve based on an assumption that in each generation one individual reproduces to give two.

model is a function of time. Note that an assumption here is the constancy of multiplication rate over all the generations. Thus at a 'generational' scale we can find the population at N_{t+1} provided we know N_t and the multiplication rate (often abbreviated as λ, which equals 2 in the above example). Higher values of λ will give population curves of increasing steepness, but it can be surprising how sensitive the curves are to λ. Figure 3.2 shows four populations with values of λ ranging from 2 to 5. The resulting curves are markedly different, even over just six generations.

The same curve can also be explored mathematically using differential calculus. We can start by making the reasonable assumption that change in population over a time period (growth rate) is a function of the population size at the start of that time and a multiplication constant which is related to the number of offspring that individuals produce. In the above we were looking at change over a generation

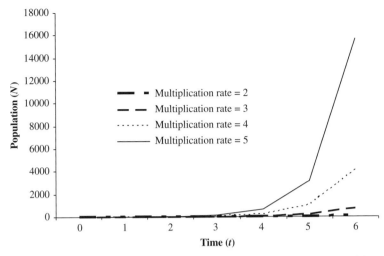

Figure 3.2 The influence of multiplication rate on the 'steepness' of the population growth curve. Note that higher multiplication rates increase the steepness of the population growth curve.

(t to $t + 1$), but this is somewhat 'lumpy'. We can smooth out the change by bringing the time intervals down to very short periods, so that population growth rate becomes:

$$\frac{dN}{dt} = \frac{\text{difference in } N \text{ over time d}t \text{ (will be very small)}}{\text{very small change in time (d}t)}$$

Where 'd' is a mathematical term meaning 'a very small change in' or perhaps more accurately 'an instantaneous change in'. Please note that dt is not d multiplied by t ($d \times t$), but instead is a mathematical short-hand. Thus given the assumption above, we can say:

$$\frac{dN}{dt} = \text{population size } (N) \times \text{constant}$$

This might seem rather simplistic, and indeed it is as we will discuss later, but it does succeed in allowing us to model the curves in Figures 3.1 and 3.2. By convention, the constant is given the symbol r and is referred to as the intrinsic (or innate) rate of population increase. Hence:

$$\frac{dN}{dt} = rN$$

The maximum value of r for a particular environment is called the maximum intrinsic or innate rate of increase, or sometimes the biotic potential (abbreviated as r_m). While r is operating over instantaneous time scales and λ operates over generations, there has to be a relationship between them. Indeed, the value of r can be found by taking the natural logarithm of the number of individuals produced by one individual at generational time scales.

$$r = \ln(\lambda)$$

In our example where one individual has two offspring in each generation:

$$r = \ln(2) = 0.6931$$

While this approach of exploring instantaneous population growth rate for each value of N might be mathematically elegant, it doesn't seem to be of much practical use. We need to modify this equation by bringing it up to more intuitive timescales; in other words changing dt to t and dN to N. Fortunately, the differential equation can be 'rearranged' and we can solve the differential equation using the method of separation of variables:

$$\frac{dN}{dt} = rN$$

and

$$\frac{dN}{N} = rdt$$

To get this equation away from dN and dt, we need to integrate both sides and there are rules for integration which simplify matters. The ones which apply here are:

Rule 1: Integration of dN/N is given by $\ln(N) + C_1$
Rule 2: Integration of rdt is given by is $rt + C_2$

The terms C_1 and C_2 are integration constants.
Thus:

$$\ln(N) + C_1 = rt + C_2$$
$$\ln(N) = rt + (C_2 - C_1)$$

Let's simplify this by renaming the difference of the two constants $(C_2 - C_1)$ as a single constant C.

$$\ln(N) = rt + C$$

To get ln(N) back to N we need to take its exponent and we also need to do that for both sides of the equation. The exponent of natural logarithms is e (2.71828 etc.), and therefore:

$$e^{\ln(N)} = e^{rt+C}$$

which is the same as:

$$N = e^{rt}e^{C}$$

The e^{C} component of the equation is a constant given that both e and C are constants, but what is it exactly? We can answer this question by making the e^{rt} component equal to one and we can achieve that by assuming that $t=0$. This makes the product rt equal to zero and e^{0} is equal to 1. Therefore e^{C} is the value of N at time zero and we can re label it as N_0. To avoid confusion we can also re label N as N_t (the population at time t). The result is:

$$N_t = N_0e^{rt}$$

This equation can give us the population at any time (N_t) by knowing the size of the starting population (N_0), the value of r and the time (t) which has elapsed. For example, if N_0 is set at one individual (as in the above example) and $\lambda=2$ ($r=0.6932$) then we can find the number of individuals at each generation, as shown in Table 3.1. The derivation of the population growth rate given here is intended to illustrate a number of key points that will emerge throughout this chapter. The population growth rate (dN/dt) is dependent on just one variable, the size of the population. Therefore the population growth is density dependent (i.e. population growth rate depends on the size (density) of the population). As r is a constant, it is density independent (i.e. its value does not depend on the size of the animal population). The validity of these assumptions will be discussed later, but there is a problem in all of this. In reality, populations do not increase to infinity as limitations of space and food usually become apparent. A population tends to increase up to a certain point, but then these limitations (space and food) start to operate and the growth rate slows down. Eventually the growth rate (dN/dt) becomes zero (i.e. the population is static). Fortunately this can be easily accommodated in the basic population growth curve already described

Table 3.1 *Calculation of population size at time* t *based upon a starting population (N$_0$) of one individual and an intrinsic population growth rate (r) of 0.6931.*

Time (t)	Calculation (integral form)	Estimated population at time t (N_t)
0	–	1
1	$1 \times e^{(0.6932 \times 1)}$	2
2	$1 \times e^{(0.6932 \times 2)}$	4
3	$1 \times e^{(0.6932 \times 3)}$	8
4	$1 \times e^{(0.6932 \times 4)}$	16
5	$1 \times e^{(0.6932 \times 5)}$	32

e = the exponential constant (2.71828 etc.)
Note how N_t is set as a function of t and not the population size in the proceeding generation.

by introducing a 'correction' depending upon how close the population is to this limit.

$$\frac{dN}{dt} = r \left(\frac{K - N}{K} \right) N$$

or

$$\frac{dN}{dt} = r \left(1 - \frac{N}{K} \right) N$$

This is called the logistic model of population growth, and K is yet another constant commonly referred to as 'carrying capacity'. Population growth rate (dN/dt) changes depending on how close the population is to K. As N approaches the value of K, the $(K - N)/K$ part of the equation becomes closer to zero and hence the growth rate also gets closer to zero. One way of regarding the $(K - N)/K$ element is to think of it as providing a density-dependent correction for the value of r so that as N gets closer to K the adjusted value of r declines. Eventually when $N = K$ the value of r becomes zero and the population stays at K:

$$\frac{dN}{dt} = r \left(\frac{K - K}{K} \right) K = 0$$

As before, the differential form of the equation can be altered to provide

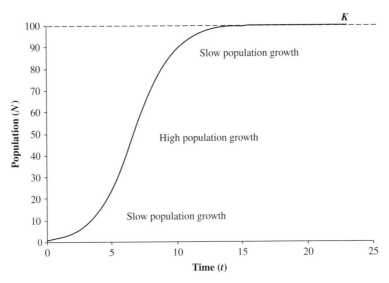

Figure 3.3 The logistic growth curve.

an integral form. I will not go into that detail here, but the result is:

$$N_t = \frac{K}{1 + e^{a-rt}}$$

The new term in the denominator, a, is another integration constant. For example, if we use values for $K = 100$ and $r = 0.6931$ (as before), and a arbitrarily set at 4.6 to give an intercept (N_0) of approximately 1, the result is the curve shown in Figure 3.3. The growth rate per individual of the population is shown plotted against population size in Figure 3.4. As the population increases in size towards K then the growth rate per individual declines.

It is possible to find the value of r in logistic curves, although this is more complex than with the simple exponential equation. We need to have a reasonable idea as to the value of K, and we also need to know the values of N for various times (t). We can plot the value of $\log ((K/N_t) - 1)$ against t, and a declining straight line indicates logistic growth, with the slope of the line providing an estimate of r (Figure 3.5).

What do these theoretical equations and graphs have to do with sustainable yield? Even simple equations such as these provide the basis for an understanding of the meaning and indeed complexities of sustainable yield. In logistic population growth, the MSY corresponds to the point on the graph where there is a maximum surplus of births over deaths; in other words where the population growth rate is the highest. Taking the logistic curve presented earlier and plotting population growth rate against population size, as shown in Figure 3.6,

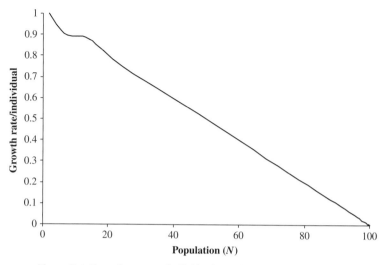

Figure 3.4 Growth rate per individual as a function of population size.

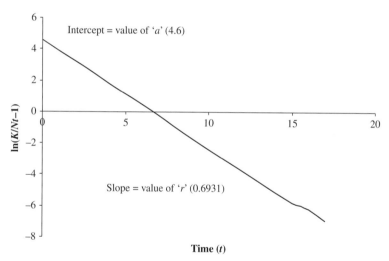

Figure 3.5 How we can test for logistic growth and find the value of r (the intrinsic rate of increase).

the maximum growth rate occurs once the population reaches 56 individuals. At this point of inflexion the population growth rate is 17 individuals per time period. Provided we only begin harvesting at this point and provided we only remove 17 individuals in each time period and don't become greedy then the population will remain static and the yield will be sustainable. This point corresponds to the MSY. What can

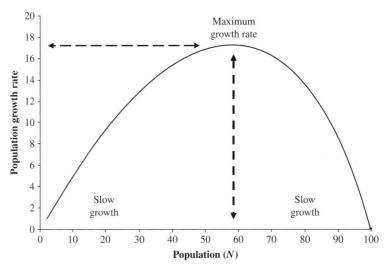

Figure 3.6 The rate of population growth as a function of population size.

be considered the intuitive answer – harvesting the population when it is at carrying capacity (K) – will reduce the size of the population as at K there is no excess of births over deaths. This is an example of a surplus yield model or more precisely as a biomass dynamics model, and in theory provides the scientific basis for a sustainable management regime (Gause, 1934).

However, in practice the logistic equation would be difficult to use for sustainable management of a renewable resource in the form given here. To begin with we would need to know the values of r and K, and this requires a very detailed biological knowledge of the population. However, there are deeper concerns to do with the relative simplicity of these equations and the assumptions upon which they are built. First, there is the focus on change over very short periods of time (dN/dt), which implies an instantaneous change in N that does not seem to be logical. In 'real' populations there is a time lag for this density-dependent influence. Second, Secondly we can question whether the assumed constants really are constants. There are two main constants included in the above equations (not including the integration constant a): r and K. Is it realistic to assume that carrying capacity is a constant? After all, real environments fluctuate greatly from year to year, or even day by day, and hence the value of K may also fluctuate. Also, what about r? Real populations are made up of two groups:

(1)   Individuals which can contribute to population growth
       (i.e. reproductively active)
(2)   Individuals (too young or too old) which cannot add to
       population increase.

It is the first group that contributes to population growth and hence would have an influence on r; the second group would have no influence. Figure 3.7a is an example of an age distribution, with 10 categories based on age and the proportion of that category in the total population. Perhaps only categories 3 to 7 are reproductively active, and they make up 46% of the population. The remaining 44% are not reproductively active. In this example there is a steady mortality operating through all of the age groups, but there can, of course, be a higher rate of mortality operating on younger age groups, as shown in Figure 3.7b. In this case there is greater mortality operating between age groups 1 and 2 than others, perhaps because they are more vulnerable to predation or disease. This may be more realistic for wild populations of animals, where the young are not protected and hence are more vulnerable. Categories 3 to 7 make up 40% of this population. The species relies on high multiplication rates to ensure its survival (so called 'r-selected' species). The other extreme would be a high survival through early age groups (Figure 3.7c), which can happen if the young are protected in some way by older age groups. Mortality rates get higher for older age groups perhaps because of increased vulnerability to disease or loss through predation. This species relies less on high multiplication rates, but on better survival (so-called 'K-selected species'), and humans are an example. For our model, the shape of the curves is immaterial. What does matter is the consistency of the shape over time. The assumption that r is a constant will only be true if the proportion of reproductively active individuals in the population remains stable. However, in practice, age distributions may not be stable over time as a result of natural or indeed human-induced pressures.

3.3   MANAGING WITH THE LOGISTIC CURVE: THE SCHAEFER MODEL

While the logistic curve highlights the theory behind MSY, it is of little practical use. However, it can be modified to produce an equation that is of more use. If we take the logistic equation as our starting point:

$$Y_{\text{equil}} = FK \left(1 - \frac{F}{r} \right)$$

This can be rearranged as:

$$Y_{\text{equil}} = FK - \frac{F^2 K}{r}$$

Assuming K and r are constants (as before) then this equation has the general form of a quadratic curve:

$$Y_{\text{equil}} = aF - bF^2$$

Where $a = K$ and $b = (K/r)$. A plot of yield (when population is assumed to be in equilibrium) against fishing mortality rate generates a curve with a maximum. If the fishing mortality rate exceeds this point then yield will decline. Time-series yield data are available for many fisheries, even sub-divided into different species, but how can we find values for F? The fishing mortality rate will depend upon a number of factors, but at a basic level we could deconstruct F into two components:

(1)   Fishing effort (number and size of trawlers, how many days they spend at sea etc., U)
(2)   Catchability (quality of the fishing gear, skill of the fishers, how easy the fish are to catch etc., q).This can be be thought of as efficienty.

such that $F = Uq$ (effort × efficienty). Then the equation becomes:

$$Y_{\text{equil}} = UqK \left(1 - \frac{U\,q}{r} \right)$$

This also has the generic form of a quadratic equation if we assume that q, K and r are constants:

$$Y_{\text{equil}} = aU - bU^2$$

Where a in this case is shorthand for (qK) and b is shorthand for $(q^2 K/r)$. Thus, when using this equation to manage fish stocks we don't need q, K and r but just a and b. We can now plot yield against fishing effort (U), as shown in Figure 3.8a, and the latter can in turn be proxied by available data, such as the size of the fleet and how many days they spend at sea. This equation is referred to as the Schaefer model and the graph in Figure 3.8a as the Schaefer curve after its creator (Schaefer, 1954, 1957). Yield per unit of fishing effort (Y_{equil}/U), at equilibrium can be found by:

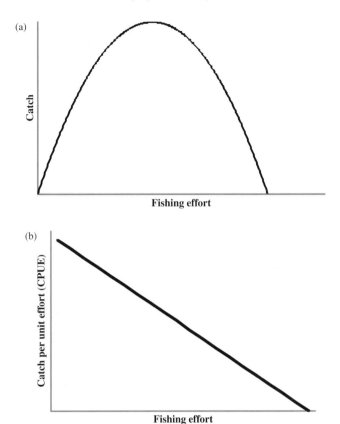

Figure 3.8 Theoretical relationship between yield (catch) from a fishery and the fishing effort: (a) catch as a function of fishing effort; this is referred to as the Schaefer curve; (b) catch per unit effort (CPUE) as a function of fishing effort.

$$\frac{Y_{\text{equil}}}{U} = qK \left(1 - \frac{Uq}{r} \right)$$

Multiplying out the right-hand side gives:

$$\frac{Y_{\text{equil}}}{U} = qK - \left(\frac{Kq^2}{r} \right) U$$

which is a linear equation of the form:

$$\text{CPUE} = a - bU$$

where CPUE is 'catch per unit of fishing effort', a is shorthand for (qK) and b is shorthand for (Kq^2/r). The equation tells us that CPUE will

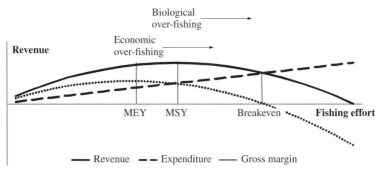

Figure 3.9 Maximum economic yield (MEY) for a fishery. Revenue is determined by yield (catch) × price (assumed to be a constant). Expenditure is given by fishing effort × cost of each unit of that effort (assumed to be a constant). Gross margin = revenue – expenditure.

decline with increasing fishing effort as shown in Figure 3.8b. CPUE has similarities with Total Factor Productivity (output/input), discussed in Chapter 2.

It is also possible to combine the catch-based Schaefer curve with economic considerations such as the cost of fishing (i.e. the cost of F) and the revenue obtained for the yield. An example is the maximum economic yield (MEY) shown in Figure 3.9. The graph shows the same curve as that of Figure 3.8a only with yield changed to revenue (yield × price). In Figure 3.9 there is yet another simplifying assumption that price remains constant, whereas in reality of course it is likely that price will change according to the law of supply and demand. Also shown is a plot of expenditure, in this case given by fishing effort multiplied by the unit cost of that effort (again assumed to be a constant), and gross margin which is revenue – expenditure. The MEY occurs at a different place along the horizontal axis than does MSY. MEY represents the fishing effort where there is the largest gross margin (economic yield) and not necessarily at the effort corresponding to the MSY (which is a biological yield). While fishing beyond the MEY might give more yield and still be profitable, the profit would be less than it is at the MEY. At a certain point, of course, the cost of fishing breaks even and beyond that point fishing becomes uneconomic.

Thus an economically rational management of the fishing effort would suggest that it be kept at MEY. Where the resource is subject to a less controlled fishing effort then it is quite possible for MEY to be exceeded. It is, after all, an economic threshold and not a biological one and its placement on the fishing effort axis will depend upon the relative balance of price for the fish and cost of fishing, and these will vary over time. While the model suggests that exceeding MEY will not be detrimental to the fish population, the gross margins of those fishing the resource will be lowered. However, once the uncontrolled fishing effort exceeds MSY then the model predicts that the fish stock will go into decline.

The above derivation of the Schaefer model from the logistic may have been somewhat protracted, but was not meant to be mathematically exhaustive. My aim has been to highlight the many assumptions that have been made in its creation. The model uses the logistic equation as a starting point and builds from there. A surplus-production model such as the one given here does have the significant advantage of being easy to fit to data that are often readily available (Prager, 1994). The calculation of the model parameters can be readily achieved with a spreadsheet or even a calculator. However, the edifice is built upon a number of key assumptions and unfortunately these are all too readily ignored. To begin with it assumes that the population remains in equilibrium when we are taking our catch; hence, we purposely employed the terms N_{equil} and Y_{equil} to remind us of this. Thus, we are attempting to take the excess of births over deaths without driving the population down. It also assumes that values of r (growth rate) and K (carrying capacity) are constant, but as we have already seen in reality it is unlikely that they will be. Similarly is it reasonable to assume that q is also a constant? Indeed what does 'catchability' really mean in practice? Here, it can be regarded as a measure of the efficiency of the fishing effort so that fishing mortality is a simple product of fishing effort (hours spent fishing by a number of boats) multiplied by how effective each of those boats is at catching fish. Effectiveness could be a complex measure of a number of influences such as how good the equipment, captain and crew are, the weather conditions, decisions over where they fish (the distribution of fish in three dimensions will not be even) and so on. As with the TFP discussion in Chapter 2, it does not seem reasonable to assume that all of these will remain constant over time. Thus, we are trying to manage a complex resource with a rather simplistic tool.

3.4 APPLYING THE SCHAEFER MODEL

As already mentioned, one of the major advantages of the Schaefer model is that it can readily be estimated from data on fishing effort and catch, and such data are available for a number of important fisheries, although quality of the data may be variable (Watson and Pauly, 2001). As a result of this relative ease of use, the Schaefer model has proved to be highly popular in fisheries management. Four examples have been chosen here and I in no way wish to imply that these are the only such examples that could have been selected. Instead, the examples have been chosen to illustrate different aspects of the use of scientific knowledge to sustainably manage fisheries.

The first is for cod in the North Sea and is employed here merely to illustrate how easy it is to fit a Schaefer model to a set of data. Catches of cod from 1906 to 1959, spanning two World Wars, are shown in Figure 3.10a. There is a data gap for the First World War, while data are available for the Second World War, although note how the catches declined. Fishing in the North Sea has its dangers at the best of times, but is far riskier during a war. A Schaefer model can be readily fitted to these catches and corresponding effort data which are also available, and the results are shown in Figure 3.10b. The curve which can be seen in the graph is a quadratic 'least squares' fit to the data using the model:

$$Y_{\text{equil}} = aU - bU^2$$

There is no need for any specialised software to achieve this. The estimated MSY is around 500 units and only a few data points are above that. The relationship between catch per unit effort (CPUE) and fishing effort is shown in Figure 3.10c.

The second example is the South Atlantic Albacore (*Thunnus alalunga*) fishery. The Albacore is a type of tuna found in many oceans. North Atlantic stocks of the species are now regarded as critically endangered by the IUCN as a result of over-fishing and are listed in their 'Red Book' of populations and species at risk. Indeed both the South and North Atlantic Albacore fisheries are regarded as being 'data deficient' by IUCN. A graph of catch and fishing effort for the North Atlantic Albacore is provided in Figure 3.11 (covers 1967 to 1989; the source of data is Polacheck *et al.*, 1993). There are three separate curves in the graph giving three different estimations of the MSY. MSY (1) is akin to a simple 'least squares' quadratic curve fitted for cod in Figure 3.10a. It provides an estimation of the MSY as approximately 50 000 tonnes per annum, although it should be noted that this is well above any of the data points. The other two curves to the left-hand side of the graph are based upon estimated values for q, K and r rather than a simple 'least squares' fit to the data. These two curves are constructed in a 'bottom up' fashion using the equation we derived earlier:

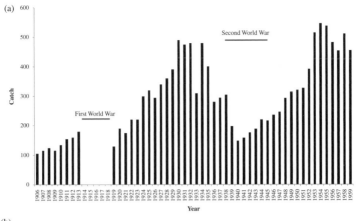

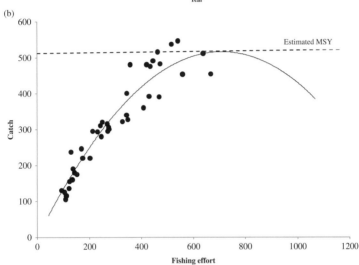

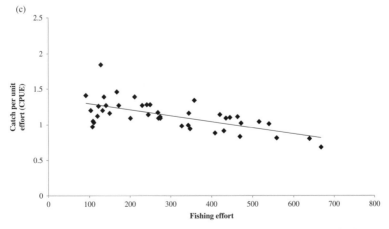

Figure 3.10 Estimation of the MSY using a Schaefer model, cod in the North Sea (1906 to 1959): (a) catches of cod; (b) fitting of a Schaefer model to catch and fishing effort data; (c) catch per unit fishing effort (CPUE) as a function of fishing effort.

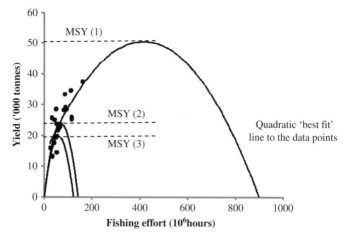

Figure 3.11 Differing estimation of the MSY using a Schaefer model for data from the South Atlantic Albacore fishery (1967 to 1989). (After data provided in Polacheck *et al.* (1993).) MSY (1) is the simple fitting of a quadratic model akin to the model in Figure 3.10a for North Sea cod. MSY (2) and MSY (3) are based upon Schaefer model parameters estimated from different assumptions.

$$Y_{\text{equil}} = U\,q\,K\left(1 - \frac{Uq}{r}\right)$$

But the curves differ in their assumptions and values for q, K and r also end up being different. The details need not be discussed here, but it should be noted that MSY(2) and MSY(3) are much lower than MSY(1); figures are approximately 20 000 and 24 000 tonnes per annum, respectively. MSY(1) and MSY(2) have been generated from a more sophisticated process than has MSY(1) and the outcomes are quite different. If MSY(1) is taken as the target, then clearly none of the data points are even close to exceeding it. A manager might therefore assume based upon this evidence that fishing effort can be increased rather than reduced, although it should be noted that Figure 3.11 does not have values of the MEY. On the other hand, both MSY(2) and MSY(3) are much lower than MSY(1) and there are some data points which have exceeded the MSY. Based upon these estimates, it might be reasonably assumed that fishing effort needs to be controlled rather than increased. The result is a set of mixed messages leading to quite different recommendations for management, depending upon the basis employed to find the MSY.

A third example of a Schaefer model is provided by the Peruvian Anchovy fishery, and, indeed, this is perhaps one of the most spectacular examples of the collapse of a fishery we have witnessed to date (Boerema and Gulland, 1973; Idyll, 1973; Laws, 1997; Ibarra *et al.*, 2000). The fishery was established in the 1950s and at one time accounted for almost a quarter (22%) of all fish caught throughout the world. The Anchovy were converted to fishmeal for animal consumption as this increased the commercial value by some 300%. Indeed, sale of this product accounted for 25 to 30% of Peru's foreign exchange in the 1970s. The fishery exists largely because of the combination of various currents along the coast resulting in deep water bringing nutrients to the surface. These nutrients encourage the growth of phytoplankton which in turn provides a source of energy for the whole ecosystem (Espinoza and Bertrand, 2008). Such upwellings occur throughout the world, but the Peruvian upwelling has been shown to be three to ten times more productive than others and the reasons why this is so are still under some debate (the so-called 'Peruvian Puzzle'; Cury *et al.*, 1998). Anchovy (*Engraulis ringens*) lives in shallow-water ecosystems off the Western coast of South America, but the Peruvian fishery is especially productive. The fish can live up to four years and reach reproductive age after only six months. Catch and effort data for the Peruvian fishery were readily available in the 1960s and a Schaefer model can be used to estimate the MSY, as in the case of the previous two examples. The result is shown in Figure 3.12, where it can be observed that the MSY is just over 10 million tonnes, and occurs at a fishing effort of about 30 million gross registered tonnage (GRT, referring to the size of the fishing fleet). In this case the curve is a simple 'least squares' fit to the data akin to the MSY(1) of Figure 3.11 and the MSY for cod in Figure 3.10b. While some of the data points are near to the MSY there is no evidence from the graph that the MSY was being exceeded and fishing effort was consistently below 30 million GRT.

However, the Anchovy fishery collapsed in dramatic fashion in 1972 and the niche left behind was occupied by the less profitable Sardine (*Sardinaps sagax*). Both species feed on the same organisms, but Anchovy and Sardine larvae are normally separated in space and hence there is little competition between them. The two species appear to follow an inverse cyclic behaviour in many fisheries (Al-Jufaili, 2007), such that as one increases the other declines. The collapse of the Anchovy population occurred for two main reasons. Firstly, despite the reassuring picture provided by Figure 3.12, the extraction was especially heavy between 1967 and 1970, and this hit recruitment

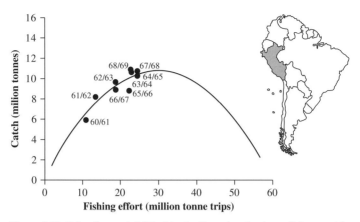

Figure 3.12 Schaefer model fitted to the Peruvian Anchovy fishery catch for the 1960s. Point labels are the season over which the fishing took place. Model parameters: predicted catch = $0.722U - 0.0121U^2$ (where U is fishing effort).

hard. In effect, the value of r had been reduced. Secondly, the fishery was subject to a natural oscillation in the Pacific every two to ten years; the El Niño event. In the early 1970s, an El Niño occurred which brought warmer water into the fishery, and with it came increased numbers of predators of Anchovy which placed further pressure onto the Anchovy population. The warm water also reduced the upwelling and the flow of nutrients to surface waters. El Niño does seem to have a significant impact on the ecosystem off the Peruvian coast (Niquen and Bouchon, 2004). The combination of increased predation, fewer nutrients, continued fishing effort and a fall in recruitment resulted in the collapse. This was a biological disaster, but one which had a number of important social and economic consequences (Glantz, 1990). The industry was nationalised by the military government of Peru and effectively reduced to half its size. The number of boats was cut from 1 500 to 800, the number of fishmeal plants was reduced from 100 to 50 and the number of people employed was reduced from 25 000 to 12 000. The Anchovy has recovered since then, and Figure 3.13 shows landings of the Anchovy and Sardine from the 1950s to 2006, as well as the timing of some strong El Niño events. The El Niño of 1997–98 clearly had an impact on the fishery, but recovery was good.

Sadly, the Peruvian Anchovy is far from being the only example of over-fishing as a result of our poor knowledge of ecosystems or unwillingness to act. The fourth example to be discussed here, albeit

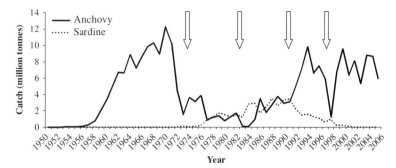

Figure 3.13 Catches of the Peruvian Anchovy and Sardine (data sourced from FAO). Arrows indicate some major El Niño events since 1970.

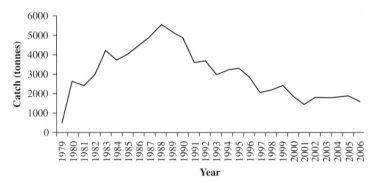

Figure 3.14 Catches from the New Zealand Orange Roughy fishery (data sourced from FAO).

one that contrasts with the Peruvian Anchovy in a number of regards, is provided by the New Zealand Orange Roughy Fishery. Unlike Anchovy, the Orange Roughy (*Hoplostethus atlanticus*) is a deep-water species and for understandable reasons it is difficult to study the biology of such fish and their ecosystems, and this does not aid management (Pankhurst, 1999). What is known is that such deep-water species tend to be long-living. The Orange Roughy, for example, can live to 100 years of age and reach sexual maturity between 23 and 31 years of age. The fish has firm flesh that produces a white boneless fillet which has proved to be highly palatable to consumers. Indeed the original name of 'slimeheads' was changed to 'roughy' to make the species more marketable. New Zealand is the main supplier in the world today and the USA is the main consumer. The New Zealand roughy fishery has only recently been exploited and catches are shown in Figure 3.14. The

1980s were a main period of activity, with a peak catch of 55 000 tonnes in 1988. It was initially thought that the Orange Roughy had a relatively short lifespan and bred relatively quickly, hence the stock could recover quickly from exploitation, but this was not the case and catches declined dramatically in the early 1990s. By 1994 the catch levels had already declined to around 25% of the original level. Clearly the exploitation had a major impact on the population of the species and also on the genetic diversity of the surviving population, which had significantly narrowed (Smith *et al.*, 1991). We now know that such deep-sea species are slow to recover from exploitation (Clark and Tracey, 1994). Controls on catches were quickly changed and at present the total catch of the species is set at roughly 30% of what is assumed to be the pre-exploitation biomass levels. For example, in the 2008/09 fishing season, the total allowable commercial catch was set at 12 532 metric tonnes. But even so, the sustainability of this resource has been questioned, given how little we know about it, the low reproduction rate and ease of capture (Francis and Clark, 2005). Others have argued that, given the gaps in our knowledge, it should be assumed that current exploitation of this resource is already optimal and we are taking the MSY (Hilborn *et al.*, 2006).

3.5   SUSTAINABILITY, CHAOS AND STRANGE ATTRACTORS

The examples given in the previous section reinforce what we know; nature is complex and can be unpredictable. Founding a management regime on wrong assumptions and far from complete knowledge of what is in an ecosystem and how the components interact over time and space is a recipe for disaster. The smooth logistic and Schaefer curves in the previous sections are aesthetically attractive and, while useful in a theoretical sense for illustrating the biological logic which rests behind management of a dynamic resource, they are misleading in their simplicity when it comes to practical management. Indeed, it doesn't take much to change the equations to reflect what we often see in practice and thereby illustrate the problems of achieving MSY. Instead of relating population size (N) to time (t), what happens if it is related to the size of the population in the previous generation? After all, this seems a more logical stance to take. Population growth will obviously be directly related to the population size of the previous generation more than to some absolute notion of time.

$$\text{population this} = \text{population last} \times \text{number of offspring}$$
$$\text{year } (t+1) \qquad \text{year } (t) \qquad \text{per individual}$$

or

$$N_{t+1} = N_t \, \lambda$$

where

N_{t+1} = population in generation t+1
N_t = population in generation t
λ = multiplication rate (number of offspring/individual between
    time t to t+1)

Allowing for 'carrying capacity' (K) limitations, as in the logistic equation:

$$N_{t+1} = N_t \left(\frac{K - N_t}{K} \right) \lambda$$

This seems to be straightforward, but unfortunately such a logical starting point can generate very complex population curves as they incorporate the notion of feedback. Indeed it can produce chaotic behaviour, especially with higher values of the multiplication rate. The graphs in Figure 3.15 illustrate what happens when λ increases from 2 to 4 (starting population is 1 and K = 100). With a λ of 2, the picture is reminiscent of the logistic curve with a steady increase in population towards a plateau, but note that the population does not reach carrying capacity. With a value of λ equal to 3 there is some evidence of instability. The population reaches 75 and then begins to oscillate, although as time progresses the degree of oscillation dampens. With a λ of 4 there is apparent chaos with no clear pattern in the population curve over time. Don't forget that these three quite different patterns have come from the same equation, and one that on the surface does not look all that different from the logistic. The difference has been brought about by linking population at one generation to the population of the previous generation and not simply to time. There is a feedback process at play.

What about predictions of MSY in such populations? As might be expected, this becomes problematic when values of λ are high. When λ equals 2 the curve is 'well behaved' and a MSY of approximately 12 seems appropriate, and even with a λ of 3 there is a discernible point of inflection (this time suggesting an MSY of approximately 30). However, once λ becomes 4 the possibility of finding an MSY disappears. The result is a wild circularity with no clear single point of inflection;

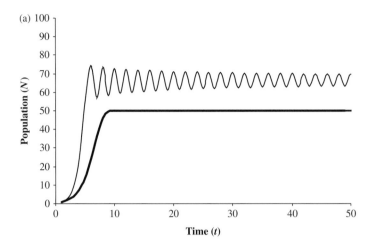

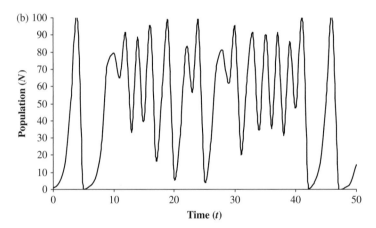

Figure 3.15 Growth curves based on the assumption that population in one generation is solely a function of population in the previous generation and multiplication rate: (a) multiplication rates of 2 (solid line) and 3 (dashed line); (b) multiplication rate of 4.

instead there are many! Don't forget that with all these graphs the value of λ, as well as K, are held constant over the generations. There is no fluctuation in environmental conditions built into these graphs.

A simple rearrangement of the basic population growth equation allows us to estimate the population increase per individual:

$$N_{t+1} = N_t \left(\frac{K - N_t}{K}\right) \lambda$$

$$\frac{N_{t+1}}{N_t} = \left(\frac{K - N_t}{K}\right) \lambda$$

$$\frac{N_{t+1}}{N_t} = \lambda - \left(\frac{\lambda}{K}\right) N_t$$

Given that (λ/K) is itself a constant, this equation is equivalent to $y = a - bx$, the equation for a straight line, and that is indeed what we see when λ equals 2 (Figure 3.16a). However, note how this 'straight line'

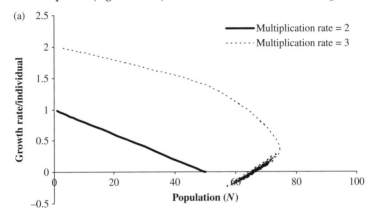

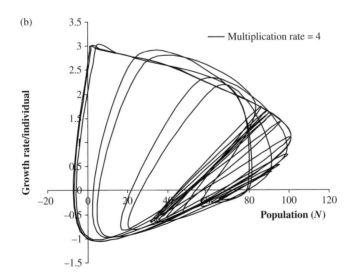

Figure 3.16 Population growth rate per individual: (a) multiplication rate of 2 (solid line) and 3 (dashed line); (b) multiplication rate of 4.

(a)

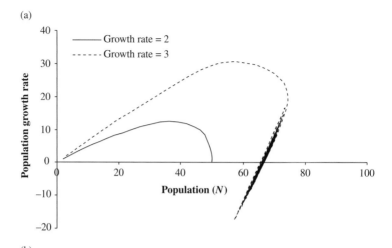

(b)

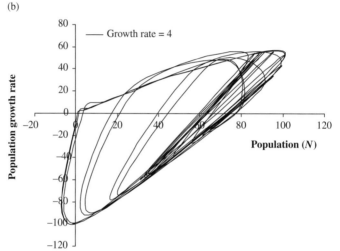

Figure 3.17 Population growth rate as a function of population:
(a) growth rates of 2 (solid line) and 3 (dashed line); (b) growth rate of 4.

prediction breaks down once λ is increased to 3 and disappears alto-
gether once λ reaches 4, as shown in Figure 3.16a and 3.16b. The same
chaos occurs when we plot population growth rate against population
size (Figure 3.17), the relationship we used to derive the MSY earlier in
the chapter. The smooth curve we observed with the differential
equations breaks down once λ is greater than 2. Unfortunately for
sustainable management, chaotic patterns such as those of
Figure 3.15b are often what we see with animal populations in

practice (Fielding, 1991). Wild populations do fluctuate widely (an effect caused by an array of environmental and biotic factors) and don't just increase smoothly to a maximum before levelling. Finding an MSY for such populations based on the equations given here seems impossible.

However, isn't there another way to proceed rather than try and make fixed predictions based on simple models as we have done here? Given the complexity we expect to see in nature, surely it makes more sense to constantly monitor the population and set our fishing effort relative to the density of the population that we find. This sounds like an intuitively obvious thing to do, and in fact is practiced in fisheries such as the Orange Roughy where populations are monitored. In effect, we make the removal from fishing a density-dependent relationship to the size of the fish population rather than have a single figure for an MSY applied each year. This approach is referred to as a 'state-dependent strategy' (SDS; Hunter and Runge, 2004). We can model removal from fishing easily enough by allowing for a loss from the basic population growth equation used earlier:

$$N_{t+1} = \left(N_t \left(\frac{K - N_t}{K} \right) \lambda \right) - F$$

where F is the number removed by fishing between t and $t+1$. As we discussed earlier, F is a function of fishing effort (U) and 'catchability' (q). The value of F can be made density dependent so that the rate will vary as the fish-population varies. As fish-population increases, so will the fishing effort, and vice versa. But much depends on the time delay of the density dependence. For example, using the same starting conditions as before ($N_0 = 1$ and $K = 100$) and a multiplication rate of 2 we can easily build-in a fish catch per fishing vessel (and make it a constant), but assume that the number of fishing vessels will be positively density dependent. For the sake of simplicity, if we set our fish catch at 2.2 individuals/vessel (please forgive the decimal point) and our density dependence at 7 (for every seven fish in a generation there is one fishing vessel) the result is shown in Figure 3.18a. Note that I have also built in a delay at the start to give the fish population a chance to get going. As we would perhaps expect, as the fish population increases, so doed the number of vessels, and both populations level off at exactly the same time (the response is instantaneous). For the 150 generations of this graph the two populations are in complete harmony; we have reached sustainability.

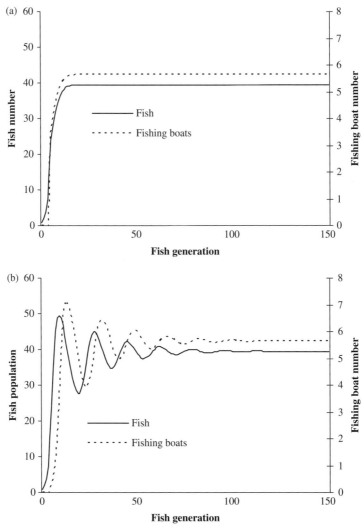

Figure 3.18 Number of fishing vessels as a function of fish density: (a) no time delay in the response; (b) with a delay in the response.

We can also include a delay factor in the density dependence. After all, monitoring will need to take place some time prior to the fishing fleet setting sail and with current technology it may be unrealistic to expect that fishing effort can be set at the same time as monitoring. But between monitoring and decisions made over the number of vessels to send out, the fish population may well change. In that case, the fishers are

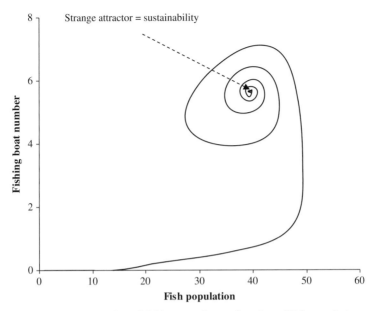

Figure 3.19 Number of fishing vessels as a function of fish population.

responding to what is perceived to be the fish population some time ago, and not what it may be at the time of fishing. The outcome is still sustainability, but the means by which the fish and fisher populations get there is different. Figure 2.18b is based on exactly the same parameters as before, but this time there is time delay in the density-dependency relationship of four fish generations (vessel numbers reflect the size of the fish population four generations ago). Note that the two populations have offset responses. At times the fish population will be declining while the fishing boat population is increasing and vice versa. But the end result is still a dampening down of the fluctuations and eventually a pair of parallel lines emerges as before. Plotting the two populations against each other yields the graph in Figure 3.19. The line winds into itself until eventually a single point – sustainability – is reached, where fisher and fish numbers remain at the point. This sort of behaviour has long been observed with systems having feedback relationships, and the central point in the graph has been given the enticing name of 'strange attractor'. In this case it represents the Holy Grail that we have strived for throughout this chapter – sustainability.

So what are lessons here for the fishing industry? The obvious utopian answer is to make fishing effort and efficiency density dependent so that at any one time the number of fishing vessels and the catch of each vessel are kept set in such a way as to create a balance.

But the problem, yet again, is that we are dealing with something far more complex than our simple models allow. To begin with, the regular and detailed monitoring which is being advocated here would be very expensive and who is going to pay for it, even if it was technically feasible? The obvious answer might be to tax the fishers and let them pass that cost on to the consumer, but prices may rise as a result and that may not be popular. Secondly, what about the fishers told to stay in port while others fish? While these are not insurmountable problems given enough will and, more important of all, resources, they do seem to be well beyond our reach at the time of writing. In the previous section we heard about the 'data deficiency' surrounding the North and South Atlantic populations of Albacore and also the difficulty of monitoring deep-sea fish such as the Orange Roughy.

We still continue to hear of problems of over-fishing, even with relatively well-monitored stocks such as those in the North Sea. Time and time again the issue appears to come down to economics and politics and the trade-offs which take place rather than biology. Economics has not featured all that much in this chapter, but will be the focus of Chapter 5.

3.6   CONCLUSION

The concept of a fixed MSY for fish stocks assumed to be at equilibrium has proved to be popular and resilient (Larkin, 1977; Jennings *et al.*, 2001). However, as a result of the issues raised above, the use of MSY, at least as defined and set out in this chapter, in order to manage fisheries has been heavily criticised. Instead, a more flexible approach is adopted to managing such a dynamic resource and fisheries scientists and managers aim for a maximum average yield (MAY; Mace, 2001). Thus the MSY applied to fish stocks provides a further affirmation, if one were needed, that sustainability is complex and in order to best be able to achieve it in practice we need much good quality data, as well as good theories. But obtaining such data on a routine basis does not come cheaply and what we are often left with is a compromise: a rough rule of thumb that we hope allows us to utilise a resource without driving it to extinction. In the case of the Orange Roughy the allowable commercial catch is set at 30% of what is thought to be the natural equilibrium population, but this is based on current knowledge and perhaps can be seen as no more than a best guess! In other cases, such as the Peruvian Anchovy, the influence of El Niño on the fishery was not known and neither was the event anticipated. Thus, we have a conundrum; we know that we are dealing with complex systems, yet we all too often try to manage those systems with highly simplified tools, even when we know that the assumptions behind those tools may not apply.

It is true, of course, that our knowledge is improving and the previous paragraph and indeed the chapter should certainly not be read as a message of hopelessness; that we should give up any attempt to unravel this complexity. We are somewhere in between a mechanistic view of populations, where knowledge of parameters such as growth rates, recruitment, age structure and so on can be used to model change, and a chaotic view of nature (Gaichas, 2008). There is a need to re-think fishery management and MSY and MEY in less absolute terms and take on board this fusion of the mechanistic with chaos (Mous *et al.*, 2005; Gaichas, 2008). Some have suggested that a new emphasis should be upon on a more ecosystems-based approach (Garcia *et al.*, 2003) and the ecologically sustainable yield (ESY), the yield an ecosystem can sustain without shifting to an undesirable state (Katz *et al.*, 2001). More on this later in the book, but all too often we do ignore the extent of our ignorance and that can have devastating effects. Even recent reports on the state of the world's fisheries produced by the FAO have contradictions as to whether we are more or less fishing at the MSY for most of them, whether many are seriously depleted and in danger or whether there is scope for enhancing the fishing effort as we are not yet at the MSY (Holt, 2009). So how does biological knowledge and indeed the uncertainty which is present in most cases regarding fish-stock dynamics translate to management and policy? The policies employed to manage fish stocks are varied and are typically the setting of a constant catch, fishing mortality rate and/or escapement (fish not caught), all based on various degrees of knowledge and uncertainty. Indeed there has been surprisingly little research on the comparative effectiveness of these tools (Deroba and Bence, 2008) or indeed on the institutional landscapes which are charged with governance (Young, 1998). This is a point that will be returned to later. The danger is that while many may espouse the need for sustainable management of fisheries, the implementation may not be so apparent (Corten, 1996; Shelton and Sinclair, 2008), and even when clear plans are put in place for recovery there can be problems in reducing exploitation (Rosenberg *et al.*, 2006). 'The tragedy of the commons' does unfortunately mean that unregulated exploitation is more the norm than the exception (Hilborn *et al.*, 1995) and regulation in itself is not enough unless there is rigorous enforcement and closing of loopholes.

4

Applying sustainability to industry

4.1 INTRODUCTION

In Chapters 2 and 3 we have explored sustainability in two industries: agriculture and fisheries. Both, of course, involved the harvesting of organisms and thus are essentially 'biological' industries. In this chapter we will cast the net wider and look at how biology has had an impact upon visions and practice of sustainability in industry.

The first point that needs to be made is that the central notion of 'carrying capacity' in biology, which was discussed in Chapter 3 with relation to MSY, can equally be applied to humans, and human population growth, and has long been seen as of critical importance to the utilisation of the planet's resources. These resources are not only used to produce food, but to enhance our quality of life. The relationship between population and sustainability is perhaps most associated with Paul Ehrlich, a Stanford University zoologist. Ehrlich was one of the pioneers of planned biological control as an alternative to the use of pesticides. However, it is his writing on human populations that have received the most attention. His 1968 best-selling book *The Population Bomb* (1968) and the sequel in 1990 *The Population Explosion* (1990) along with various articles in scientific journals and the popular press raised awareness of the dangers of population growth with their graphic predictions of poverty and starvation as a result of limited resources having to be redistributed amongst more and more people. As an undergraduate in the UK during the 1970s I remember these messages of a doom-laden future only too well, and Ehrlich wasn't the only source and food and famine weren't the only foci. A magazine *The Ecologist* (1972) carried a special edition in 1972 called *Blueprint for survival* written by a number of eminent scientists and later published in book form. *Blueprint for survival* appeared ahead of the world's first Environmental Summit and set out future predictions of reserves of natural resources such as oil and gas as extraction rates continued to increase. Some quotations from *Blueprint for survival* highlight the enormity of the challenges we were thought to face in 1972:

> *At present rates of consumption, known reserves of natural gas will be exhausted within 35 years, and of petroleum within 70 years. If these rates continue to grow exponentially, as they have done since 1960, then natural gas will be exhausted within 14 years, and petroleum within 20. Coal is likely to last much longer (about 300 years), but the fossil fuels in general are required for so many purposes other than fuel – pesticides, fertilisers, plastics, and so on – that it would be foolish to come to depend on it for energy . . .*

> *. . . at present rates of consumption all known reserves of these metals [list includes tin, iron, zinc, nickel and lead] will be exhausted within 100 years, with the exception of six (aluminium, cobalt, chromium, iron, magnesium and nickel). However, if these rates of consumption continue to increase exponentially at the rate they have done since 1960, then all known reserves will be exhausted within 50 years with the exception of only two (chromium and iron) – and they will last for only another 40 years! (Blueprint for Survival*, Appendix D: Non-renewable resources)

At the time of writing this book some 34 to 36 years have passed and gas and oil supplies have not yet been exhausted and neither do we seem close to exhausting our supplies of iron and chromium. Indeed predictions of almost immediate catastrophe, as some would say, have sometimes provided an easy focus for attack by critics of sustainability and as such have helped to discredit the underlying messages; ironically the very opposite of what was intended. In 1980, Ehrlich took on Julian Simon, an economist, with a bet that commodity prices were bound to rise in the relative short term (10 years) as inexorable human population growth increased demand. Simon predicted the opposite trend: that commodity prices would fall as humans can respond to shortages rather than being inflexible. So what happened? The trends of some commodity prices (metals and oil) are shown in Figure 4.1. There has been volatility in prices since 1980, but no sign of a surge in price reflecting a shortage of supply relative to demand until recent years, with increased demand from the rapidly growing economies of China and India. But over the 10 years specified in the Ehrlich–Simon bet (1980 to 1990) the trend for the commodities in Figure 4.1 is either level or downward. Needless to say that Simon won the bet! It's a pity for Ehrlich that the bet didn't extend into the first decade of the twenty-first century; he may well have won. The surge in commodity prices between 2005 and 2008 have indeed been followed by a crash and it is

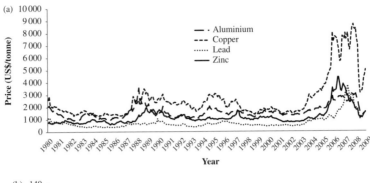

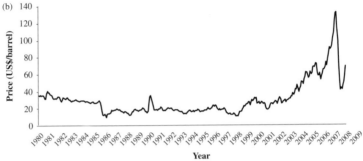

Figure 4.1 Trend in some commodity prices (1980 to June 2009):
(a) metals; (b) oil.
(Data obtained from the International Monetary Fund, www.imf.com.)

anyone's guess where they go from here. It just goes to highlight one of the central conundrums of sustainability. On the one hand it is necessary to make 'predictions' based on the best science we can muster to make politicians, and indeed society, listen to what can go wrong if we manage matters badly, but no one knows the future, and humans are a very adaptable species! While sustainability is founded on a notion of futurity – what we do now must not damage future generations – the only reliable knowledge upon which sustainability can be founded is that derived from history.

There are, of course, many industries, each with their own set of characteristics and constraints. Rather than attempt to cover all of them, we will instead begin with a theme which emerged at various points in Chapters 2 and 3, namely energy. We will explore how researchers have analysed the use of energy in industrial production and make analogies to energy flows in ecosystems. From here we will explore some generic approaches that people have taken to analysing the

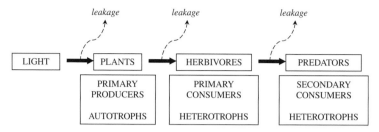

Figure 4.2 Energy flow and trophic structure.

interaction that industries have with their environment and, indeed, the social systems within which they are embedded.

4.2 ENERGY, EMERGY AND EXERGY

One of the central concepts in ecology is the 'food chain': the transfer of energy between organisms (Figure 4.2). Light energy enters the system and is passed through the various trophic levels from herbivores to predators. The transfers are not perfect and, as we have seen with photosynthesis in Chapter 2, there are inefficiencies and losses do occur. With this simple chain we can often use terms such as:

Standing crop: amount of living matter present in the ecosystem at a particular time

Productivity: the flow of energy/area/time

Primary productivity (or gross primary productivity): the amount of organic matter fixed by the primary producers in an area over time

Net primary productivity: the amount of energy fixed minus that lost through respiration.

Estimating productivity in terms of energy flows has been fashionable in ecology for 60 years or so, and there are many estimates for different ecosystems. For some classical examples, see Odum (1959, 1975). The example in Figure 4.3 has been adapted from a diagram in Odum (1975) and provides an example of energy flow through a generalised ecosystem, from incident solar radiation through to predators. The figure at the far right-hand side of Figure 4.3 (the top of the food chain) is a very small proportion indeed of the energy entering. There are losses (represented by the 'earth' symbol) which are incurred at various steps in the transfer of energy from autotrophs to heterotrophs. Note also that

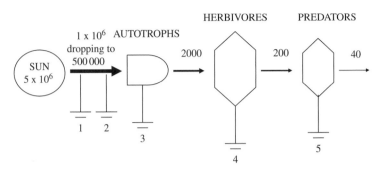

Figure 4.3 Energy flow (kcal/m²) through an ecosystem (after Odum, 1975, page 62). 1 = atmospheric heating, driving hydrological cycles, weather systems; 2 = warming the ecosystem, driving internal cycles; 3 = losses incurred in the conversion of energy to plant matter; 4 = losses incurred in the conversion of plant to herbivore; 5 = losses incurred in the conversion of herbivore to predator.

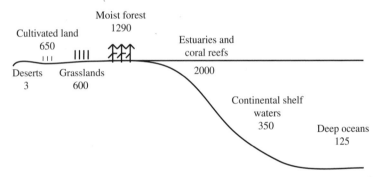

Figure 4.4 Example estimates of average net primary productivity (g/m²/ year; data from Odum, 1959).

the energy being referred to here is not 'free' as such, but is 'held' within complex organic materials in much the same way that oil, gas and coal can be said to 'hold' energy. Also, energy dissipates as it passes through the chain. Much of the chemical energy is eventually 'released' (mostly as heat) or becomes 'locked' within carbon-rich deposits (coal, oil, gas).

Different ecosystems have quite different net primary productivities, and an example is presented as Figure 4.4, based upon data in Odum (1959). It is perhaps no surprise that deserts have so little primary productivity, given the paucity of water, but the reader may be surprised to see the comparatively low figure for the continental shelf

(350 g/m^2/year) and especially the oceans (125 g/m^2/year). Nutrients are often limiting in these environments, hence the importance of upwellings in coastal fisheries such as the Peruvian Anchovy, which bring nutrients to the surface, thereby facilitating primary productivity. The very low productivity in deep oceans has led some to suggest that we 'seed' them with limiting nutrients so as to encourage phytoplankton growth and hence sequester CO_2 from the atmosphere. A number of attempts have been made to do this by adding iron (Boyd et al., 2007), although there is much debate as to the effectiveness of the technique (Buesseler et al., 2008).

The burning of carbohydrate generates carbon dioxide; whether this takes place via respiration or, indeed, by fire. Some of the CO_2 release can be re-fixed, of course, via photosynthesis, but if the rate of release is greater than the rate of absorption then the gas will accumulate in the atmosphere. Values of the CO_2 concentration in the atmosphere are published by the National Oceanic and Atmospheric Administration (NOAA) in the USA and are available on their website. Prior to the industrial revolution it has been estimated that concentrations of CO_2 in the atmosphere were stable at around 280 parts per million (ppm; equivalent to 280 mg/litre). The concentration of CO_2 in the atmosphere today is around 370 ppm and increasing. The CO_2 has largely come from the combustion of fossil fuel as an energy source. Indeed, the current consensus amongst scientists is that this accumulation of CO_2 in the atmosphere is a causal factor, along with the release of other pollutants such as methane, in global warming (Keller, 2007). A graph of the trend of CO_2 and global temperature is shown as Figure 4.5 (based upon data available at the NOAA website). In effect, CO_2 and the other greenhouse gases (water vapor, methane and ozone) trap heat at the planet's surface. It has to be stressed that Figure 4.5 is by no means the only evidence of a human-mediated global warming. There are historical data gleaned from tree-ring and ice-core data that also point to a causal relationship between greenhouse gas concentration in the atmosphere and temperature. However, even a cursory glance at Figure 4.4 would suggest that global temperature fluctuates a great deal due to a host of factors, such as the El Niño events we looked at in Chapter 3 and even volcanic eruptions. Unfortunately the scatter apparent in Figure 4.4 makes it all too easy for some commentators to come to a conclusion that the evidence for a CO_2-mediated global warming is weak, to say the least (Bellamy and Barrett, 2007). We have even seen such sentiments at a high

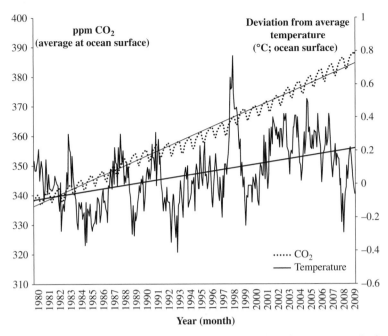

Figure 4.5 Recent trends in global carbon dioxide and temperature. Both variables have been measured at sea level.
(Source of data: NOAA ESRL.)

level in politics. The following is an extract from an interview Sarah Palin, Governor of Alaska until 2009 and a US Vice-Presidential candidate in the 2008 election, gave to 'Newsmax'.

> *A changing environment will affect Alaska more than any other state,*
> *because of our location. I'm not one though who would attribute it to being*
> *man-made.* (Sarah Palin, (29 August, 2008))
> www.newsmax.com/headlines/sarah_palin_vp/2008/08/29/126139.html

While accepting global warming as a reality, this senior politician was clearly not convinced by the scientific evidence that points towards a major contribution from human beings to global warming, and she is far from being alone. The following quote is from an article in the *Daily Mail* newspaper by Professor David Bellamy, a famous botanist in the UK:

> *For a start, carbon dioxide is not the dreaded killer greenhouse gas that the 1992*
> *Earth Summit in Rio de Janeiro and the subsequent Kyoto Protocol five years later*
> *cracked it up to be. It is, in fact, the most important airborne fertiliser in the world,*
> *and without it there would be no green plants at all ... Increase the amount of*
> *carbon dioxide in the atmosphere, double it even, and this would produce a rise in*
> *plant productivity. Call me a biased old plant lover but that doesn't sound like*

much of a killer gas to me. Hooray for global warming is what I say, and so do a lot of my fellow scientists.' (David Bellamy (*Daily Mail*, 9 July 2004))

In line with much of what we have discussed so far in this book, the complexity of the global climate and the dynamics involved only allow us to make best estimates as to causality and what might happen in the future. The following is a quote from an Intergovernmental Panel on Climate Change publication of 2007 (summary version for policy-makers; page 5).

> *Most of the observed increase in global average temperatures since the mid-20th century is very likely due to the observed increase in anthropogenic [man-made] GHG [greenhouse gas] concentrations. It is likely that there has been significant anthropogenic warming over the past 50 years averaged over each continent (except Antarctica).*

In this report 'very likely' is defined as 'the assessed likelihood, using expert judgment', being 90%, and 'likely' as being 66%. But 90% and 66% are not the same as 100%, and the gap is, by definition, uncertainty. While scientists can point to this uncertainty and make a reasonable call for more research on the causes of global warming (Florides and Christodoulides, 2009) it does provide the 'wiggle room' which some can exploit for whatever motive. After all, while the science might be convincing, even if at 90% and 66% likelihood, the ramifications for our economy and society are immense (Keller, 2009). The response, unfortunately, has all too often been to call upon others to stop polluting, while carrying on oneself (McLean, 2008).

However, while providing many original insights, diagrams such as Figure 4.3 can be rather simplistic. It suggests that energy is the most important commodity passing through the system and can ignore requirements such as plant nutrients, which can be limiting, as we have seen with the iron seeding example given above. It also emphasises the relationships between trophic levels rather than within them. Even so, the analogy of these ecological models of energy flow and efficiency of conversion have not been lost to those interested in the analysis of industrial productivity where there are also producers and consumers. Indeed, the analysis of energy flow through industrial systems has also become a focal point within analyses of sustainability. However, there is one complication in that most industries do not operate directly with solar energy as do plants. Not only are the energy sources fossil fuels, but most industries also 'buy in' the products of other industries for their own process. Therefore, as shown in Figure 4.6, the finished product from company D (automobiles for

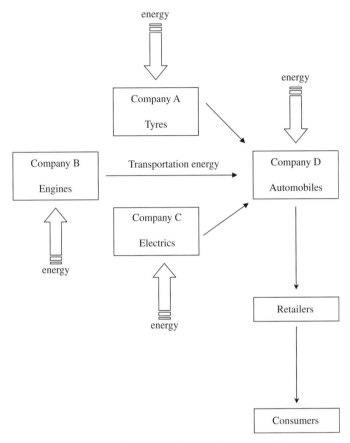

Figure 4.6 Summary of energy used to produce automobiles.

example) is not just a function of energy used directly by that company, but also the energy consumed by other industries (A to C) in the manufacture of components of automobiles or provision of services. To fully account for the energy used by company D in the production of automobiles, we also need to take into account the energy used throughout the chain, including transportation of the raw materials and components. Indeed, beyond that point we can also consider the energy used in getting the automobiles to the consumers. Hence the concept of 'embodied energy' or emergy; a sort of 'energy memory' (Herendeen, 2004), which can take account of this varied sources of energy coming together into a production process. Emergy is the available energy of one kind previously required, directly and indirectly, to make a product or service. The units may be emjoules, emkilocalories etc. to distinguish from energy units (Odum, 1988, 1996). Also following the concept of productivity, 'empower' is the emergy flow per unit time (units: emjoules per unit time). Emergy is typically expressed in terms of solar energy equivalents (e.g. solar emjoules). While emergy can be used to calculate the solar equivalent energy needed to generate a product or service, its use does have problems in practice, largely because of practical issues of determining solar energy equivalents within a chain of production, along with misunderstandings as to what emergy is (Hau and Bakshi, 2004a).

According to the First Law of Thermodynamics, energy cannot be lost from a closed system; it can only change from one form to another, with mass being a form of energy. Thus the passage of energy through Figure 4.2 results in much loss from start to end point, but the incident solar radiation becomes converted to other forms or is transferred away as radiation or heat. But change of energy can do work; fossil fuels can be burnt, releasing CO_2 and heat energy. Thus, one stable state, for example fossil fuels in the form of a liquid or solid, is changed via combustion to another stable state (gas and energy dissipated into the environment thereby raising its temperature). In between is the potential for some of the energy held in the fossil fuel to do work: move an automobile or run a power station. The total energy in the system does not change during this process; all that happens is that it is transformed from one form (fossil fuel) to another (mostly gas and heat). But once this change has occurred, it is difficult to harness the energy in its new forms to do more work. Thus, the quantity of energy in the system remains the same (i.e. it is conserved), but the quality of that energy seen in terms of its ability to do useful work for us declines. The heat becomes dissipated, as do the gases. Indeed, in terms of the Laws of Thermodynamics we can't strictly speaking have an 'energy crisis' as energy can't disappear. Instead what we do have is an exergy crisis; we lose 'good quality' (usable) energy resources, which are replaced by 'poor quality' (unusable) ones.

Why is exergy an important concept in biological terms? Well, life on Earth is far from being in a state of thermodynamic equilibrium; its organisation depends upon a constant input of energy from the sun or elsewhere (Wall, 2008). Without that energy then life would eventually cease to exist. The quantity of energy flowing through biological systems can be measured in line with the Laws of Thermodynamics, as shown in Figure 4.2. All the numbers moving along the trophic levels and leaked out through heat or radiation have to add up to what comes into the system in the first place. But an analysis based on exergy will show that exergy can increase (energy is converted to biomass and structure) and also decline as energy becomes lost to the system as heat or is reflected away (Hau and Bakshi, 2004b). Thus exergy can be viewed, albeit simplistically, as a function of biomass (standing crop) in the ecosystem (Christensen, 1995); the more biomass we have then the greater the exergy. This is another way of looking at the production issues we have covered in Chapters 2 and 3, and an example for agricultural, forest and phytoplankton primary production in China is provided by Chen *et al.* (2009). The basic model employed by Chen *et al.* (2009) is shown as Figure 4.7. This is at heart an input–output diagram, but with inputs classified in terms of renewable (which add exergy) and non-renewable (which destroy exergy), and those which are 'free' and those which have to be purchased. Examples of each are also provided in Figure 4.7. There is a further input which the authors refer to as 'virtual environmental input' and define as 'the cost of the environment supporting the system' (page 398). Examples of the latter are pollution from animal waste, fertiliser and pesticide. In terms of 'free' resource inputs to the system (the common pool resources discussed in Chapter 2), the largest component is sunlight. Without wishing to go into the details of all of the exergy calculations, the sunlight input is basically the solar radiant energy for the land area of China corrected for PAR, photosynthetic efficiency and consumption of carbohydrate through respiration. Their estimation is founded upon three assumptions or steps:

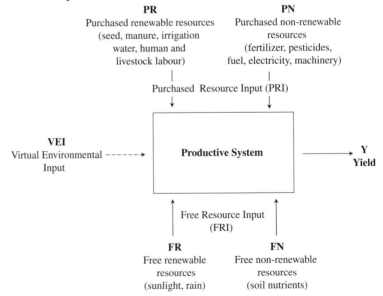

Figure 4.7 Simple systems diagram for a primary production-based system such as agriculture.

First assumption: estimate the surface area receiving insolation

Land area of China: 7.06×10^{12} m^2 (cultivated land, orchards, forest)

Water area of China: 2.87×10^{12} m^2 (inland water, fishing grounds of the continental shelf and cultivated seashore)

Total area: 9.93×10^{12} m^2

Second assumption: adjust this surface area for photosynthetic efficiency

Total energy input via sunlight: 5.2×10^9 joules/m^2/year

Virtual P/S efficiency (as a percentage of this total energy input) is assumed to be:

0.2% for land plants: 1.04×10^7 joules/m^2/year

0.05% for algae: 0.26×10^7 joules/m^2/year

Note: these figures take into account not only the efficiency of the conversion of light energy into carbohydrate (gain in exergy), but also the consumption of some carbohydrate via respiration (a loss of exergy).

Third assumption: multiplying surface areas derived by the first assumption by the efficiencies found under the second assumption gives the photosynthetically derived exergy such that:

Exergy = energy input adjusted for P/S efficiency × surface area

and therefore

Land plants = $1.04 \times 10^7 \times 7.06 \times 10^{12} = 7.342 \times 10^{19}$ joules

Algae: $0.26 \times 10^7 \times 2.87 \times 10^{12} = 0.746 \times 10^{19}$ joules

Total P/S exergy: 9.09×10^{19} joules

As we have seen before, it is clear that a number of simplifying assumptions have been made in the calculation. Chen *et al.* (2009) go on to derive exergy values for all of the inputs and outputs of Figure 4.7 on a national scale, along with various ratios of inputs and outputs, and the results are shown in Figure 4.8. This analysis has a familiar feel to the TFP approach outlined in Chapter 1, only with exergy replacing a common unit of monetary value, and, indeed, we can adopt the same TFP ratio of output/ input with exergy. The results are shown in graphical form as Figure 4.9. Note how input exergy is so much higher than output and the resultant TFPs are much less than one as a result. The trend between 1980 and 2000 is an increase in input TFP, largely reflecting an increased use of non-renewable inputs, and a moderate increase in yield. The result is an exergy TFP which is more or less flat over those 20 years.

Sustainability can thereby be defined in part as the need to conserve and enhance exergy, for example by the encouragement of renewable energy resources (Suganthi and Samuel, 2000; Dincer, 2007; Hepbasli, 2008; Rosen *et al.*, 2008). A part of this, of course, is the need

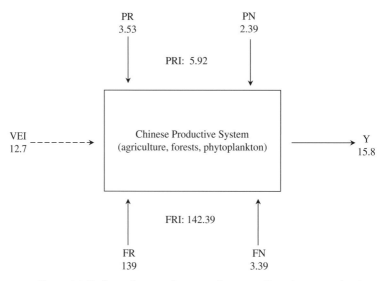

Figure 4.8 Estimated exergy inputs and outputs for primary production in China (after Chen *et al.*, 2009).

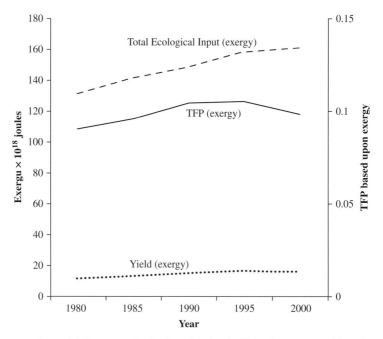

Figure 4.9 Exergy analysis of production in China (1985 to 2000) based upon total factor productivity (yield/total ecological input). (Based upon data in Chen *et al.*, 2009.)

to enhance efficiency of benefits gained from a loss of exergy (Apaiah
et al., 2006). More sustainable systems are arguably those that have
the most return on loss of exergy. However, it has to be said that the
usefulness of exergy analysis within ecosystems has been questioned,
and in particular where it is linked to economics (Dewulf *et al.*, 2008).

4.3   BALANCING INPUTS AND OUTPUTS: MATERIAL INTENSITY

As described with energy, emergy and exergy, one obvious way of
thinking about sustainability in an industrial sense is to consider the
efficiency of production – inputs used to deliver outputs such as a
product or service. Thus TFP can equally be applied to any industry as
it can be to agriculture. But this is not just a matter of analysing energy –
a similar criticism applies to the danger of over-emphasising the importance of energy flows in ecosystems and ignoring other important
flows such as water and inorganic nutrients. Table 4.1 illustrates the
wide range of inputs and impacts to consider, including those on the
quality of life of people living near or distant to an industry and not
employed there.

Table 4.1 *Some environmental impacts of industrial activity (after Tyteca, 1996)*

Category		Items to consider	Impacts
Resources	Raw materials		Negative impacts on biodiversity, the landscape, human health and quality of life.
	Energy	Fossil fuels	
Waste products	Released into water	Suspended solids	
		Nitrates, phosphates	
		Heavy metals	
		Acidity and alkalinity	
	Released into air	Carbon dioxide	Contributions to global warming, acid rain and depletion of the ozone layer.
		Nitrogen oxides	
		Sulfur dioxide	
		Methane	
	Solid wastes	Spoil tips	Negative impacts on other industries.
	Noise		

The analogy between biological organisms and industrial activities is strong, given that both are materials-processing systems driven by a flow of energy. The obvious difference is in the means of regulation within the system. Industrial activity is regulated by humans in the sense that it is we who provide the labour which guides the process and also because people are the consumers. Supply and demand is balanced via price and competition. In much the same way as we saw in Chapter 2 for agricultural systems, there is competition between companies producing similar products, and we can talk of 'market niche' and 'aggressivity'.

The idea of balancing inputs and outputs in industrial processes so as to minimise environmental impact is an old one (Ayres, 1978), and there are various approaches that can be taken in practice (Daniels and Moore, 2002). An example is material intensity analysis (material intensity per unit service or function; MIPS) developed by Prof. 'Bio' Schmidt-Bleek and the Wuppertal Institute, Germany, between 1989 and 1993. The aim of the approach is to analyse the entire production or service process in terms of both energy and material consumed (Spangenberg et al., 1999; Giljum, 2006). Each product or service has what can be called an 'ecological rucksack'. An example often quoted in the literature is in order to extract one tonne of copper from the Earth we may have to move some 500 tonnes of non-renewable resource. This gives us an 'ecological rucksack' ratio of 500:1 (MacDonald and Peters, 2007). This can be changed, of course, perhaps by increasing the efficiency of the extraction process; a strategy which is referred to as 'dematerialisation' (Hinterberger et al., 1997). Thus, the aim would be to reduce the 500:1 ratio, perhaps by a factor of 10, to say 50:1. Hence the phrase 'factor 10' which often crops up in MIPS studies (Schmidt-Bleek, 2000). But, of course, there are other elements to increasing efficiency than reducing consumption of materials during production. In Figure 4.10 there is a chain from raw materials through production to the consumer, as there was in Figure 4.6, but now we have included 'use' of that product/service as well. Materials are consumed both during production and eventual use, and the ratio of A:B (raw material/product), while important, is but a part of all this. MIPS aims to take this complete chain into account, and a MIPS-based analysis of Figure 4.10 would in fact be:

$$\text{MIPS} = \frac{A + C}{D}$$

The efficiency ratio is a reversal of the TFP ratio of output/input, but the idea is fundamentally the same. The higher the value of the MIPS ratio

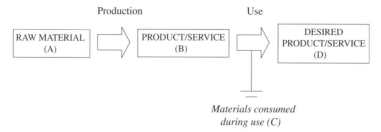

Figure 4.10 Chain of production from raw materials to desired product/service.

then the more material which is being consumed for each unit of desired output of a good or service, and thus the greater the potential for a negative impact on the environment. Thus MIPS can be thought of as a measure of eco-efficiency where higher values can indicate potential unsustainability.

While MIPS does have an advantage in providing a clear focus on potential environmental impact during the life of a product, at least in terms of materials which are consumed in the process, there are also important disadvantages, some of which are listed as follows:

(1)   MIPS does not take account of other resources consumed, but not necessarily included in the calculation, such as surface area. Agriculture and forestry do take up a large surface area and this in itself has an impact, even if only aesthetically.

(2)   MIPS is focused on quantities of material consumed and does not take into account differing toxicities of wastes which are generated. Thus a lower MIPS ratio could in theory be achieved by using less material, but with emissions of waste that have a much greater negative impact on the environment.

(3)   MIPS can lack a geographic dimension. The inputs for production may come from many different countries, or indeed spatial units within a country, and impacts associated with gaining those resources may thus be quite different in some places compared to others. Indeed the inputs may come from a very different place than where use takes place. A reduction in the MIPS ratio, while good news on a large scale, may be associated with an enhanced impact in some places and upon some people.

It should also be mentioned at this point that the concept of 'life-cycle' analysis (LCA) for industrial products has become fashionable (Lee *et al.*, 1995; Hertwich, 2005; Tukker and Jansen, 2006). While the two are related in the sense of being process or 'flow based' (Krotscheck, 1997), LCA is a broader concept than MIPS in that it includes everything associated with a product or service so as to aid in the selection of processes which are least damaging to the environment (Lee *et al.*, 1995; Rebitzer *et al.*, 2004).

> *Life-cycle assessment is a recognized analytical method for evaluating the environmental burdens associated with a product, process or activity by identifying and quantifying the energy and materials used and wastes released to the environment.* (Strange *et al.* (2008, page 238))

LCA is often referred to as a holistic assessment in that it includes many dimensions. The units employed are typically energy, and indeed some have criticised LCA for its general avoidance of economic units as this can limit its appeal to business executives charged with maximising profits. Also, as with the other 'flow-based' approaches such as MIPS, the focus on processes involved in manufacture and use can also be criticised for failing to include social costs and benefits as well as not allowing for geographical differentiation of impact (Raugei and Ulgiati, 2009). Indeed just where can system boundaries be drawn in geographical as well as conceptual terms? Drawing such boundaries is a crucial step in both MIPS and LCA and much depends in practice upon the decisions that have been made. Different boundaries will generate different conclusions, even for the same industry (Villanueva and Wenzel, 2007). Much the same is true, of course, when it comes to identifying ecosystem boundaries. What might make sense in LCA terms as a means of limiting the energy cost of production might result in large-scale unemployment and thus have social as well as political ramifications. Thus, it is claimed by some that while LCA has value, it should only be employed in conjunction with other social and economic assessments of the production and indeed consumption process when priorities are being set (Field *et al.*, 1994). A discussion of the latter with regard to LCA in fisheries is provided by Pelletier *et al.* (2007).

An example of an LCA applied to a genetically modified (GM) crop, in this case canola, is provided by Strange *et al.* (2008). Canola (CANadian Oil, Low Acid) is a name used to describe a number of varieties of *Brassica napus* and *Brassica rapa* bred to have low concentrations of glucosinolates and erucic acid. The latter chemicals, while providing plants with an element of protection from herbivores, do make them unappealing for use in animal feed and foodstuffs. Much of the original breeding work took place in Canada during the late 1960s; hence the 'CAN' in Canola. *Brassica* plants do normally require significant applications of nitrogen fertiliser, and the GM characteristic analysed in the Strange *et al.* (2008) paper is nitrogen-use efficiency (GMNUE). The GMNUE canola can maintain its yield relative to non-GMNUE varieties, but with less nitrogen, and this should be beneficial to both the environment (less pollution, less energy consumption and reduced loss of exergy) and farmer (less expenditure on fertiliser and its application). The LCA methodology applied by Strange *et al.* (2008) was based on guidelines set out by the International Organisation for Standardisation (ISO) in 1998. The methodology and assumptions made by the authors are summarised as follows:

4.3.1   Goal and scope definition

Examine and compare two farming systems, one based on GMNUE canola and one based on conventional (non-GMNUE) canola, each producing 1 tonne of product. The 'farm-gate' (i.e. the spatial unit of the farm) was used as the system boundary (Figure 4.11). Note that the LCA in this case does not include processes involved once the product has left the farm (transport, packaging, retail etc.). The authors assumed that these processes would be the same for both the GMNUE and non-GMNUE products.

4.3.2   Inventory analysis

This comprises a list of all resources requirement in the production process and emissions which occur. In this study the processes included:

(a)   Manufacture, packaging and transport of nitrogen fertiliser (in this case urea)
(b)   Field operations (sowing, cultivation and application of inputs)
(c)   Manufacturing, repair and maintenance of farm machinery
(d)   Production and use of fuel for tractors
(e)   Transport costs
(f)   Construction, maintenance and ultimate demolition of buildings for machinery storage.

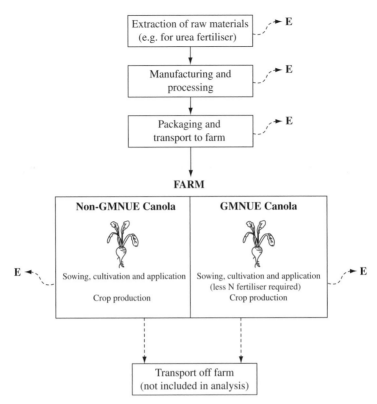

Figure 4.11 System boundary for canola cropping systems in the USA employed by Strange *et al.* (2008) in their Life-cycle Analysis; GMNUE (genetically modified, nitrogen use efficient) compared with non-GMNUE varieties.

E = emissions into the environment.

In line with the choice of the system boundary being the 'farm' then these are the processes involved in growing the crops, as well as the production of the materials which are consumed during production, notably the urea fertiliser which GMNUE canola should make better use of compared with non-GMNUE.

4.3.3 Impact assessment

Emissions were characterised so as to measure potential effects on the environment. At the heart of this stage is the calculation of what is called an impact category indicator (ICI). This is found for a range of emission categories (emissions which have similar impacts are grouped together). The technical formula for each ICI is:

$$ICI_i = \sum_{j=1}^{j=n} E_i \text{ or } R_i.CF_{ij}$$

where i is used as a label for each of the emission categories and j is a label to differentiate each of the emissions within the category. In this equation the symbol E stands for 'emission' while R is consumption of resource per functional unit. Thus, impact is either via the pollutants released into the environment upon use or via consumption of resource. The multiplier CF stands for 'characterisation factor' and is used to provide the relative impact weighting of the emissions or consumption within each category. Thus category 1 ($i = 1$) might have 5 emissions ($j = 1$ to 5) within it, all having quite different environmental impacts, and thus the CF would be different for each of them. The categories are set out within ISO, and include global warming, human toxicity, acidification, eutrophication and ecotoxicity. One emission can be in a number of these categories. There is inevitably a degree of simplification which occurs when environmental impacts are being gauged like this. As we have already seen with MIPS, it is possible for impacts to be concentrated in certain geographic areas and less pronounced elsewhere. Thus 'human toxicity' is treated as a single category, but the impacts upon this may be far worse during the mining and manufacture of the urea fertiliser than for the farmers applying the material.

4.3.4   Interpretation

This comprises an evaluation of the results of the LCA. In this study the results suggest that yields for GMNUE canola were at least equal to and often higher than non-GMNUE canola, and with an overall energy saving of some 22%. Therefore, although exergy was not included in the analysis, it seems reasonable to conclude that GMNUE canola would also destroy less exergy than non-GMNUE.

The results of the project suggested that emissions of methane and CO_2, two gases which contribute to global warming, were less for the GMNUE canola than for the non-GMNUE canola. The latter emitted some 16% more of these gases than the former. This difference was largely due to the energy required to produce, transport and apply the extra nitrogen needed by the non-GMNUE canola.

Emissions of CO_2 have been identified by others as a key factor in how we should assess agricultural sustainability (Glendining *et al.*, 2009). GMNUE canola also resulted in less acidification and eutrophication than non-GMNUE.

4.4   THE NATURAL STEPS: SETTING OUT RULES FOR SUSTAINABILITY

The canola LCA example given in the previous section does highlight the need to consider impacts of production and emissions within an industrial context. It is not just energy and exergy which need to be measured, but cognisance needs to be made of the overall picture, including impacts of pollutants and indeed social and economic concerns. When considering industrial production, the following broad principles, or variations of them, are commonly espoused for a sustainable society:

(1)   Waste emissions must not be greater than the assimilation capacities of the Earth's environment

(2)   Waste emissions must not be allowed to accumulate in the Earth's environment

(3)   The basis for the productivity and diversity of the Earth's environment must not be diminished

(4)   Resource use must be fair and efficient, so as to allow us to meet our needs.

The first three of the principles tell us what we must not do (i.e. despoil), while the last brings out the importance of equity, within human societies of today as well as tomorrow. Notice how they are set out as scientific statements, akin to the Laws of Thermodynamics mentioned earlier, and indeed these Laws are employed in part to provide the theoretical underpinning of the four principles. They are referred to as the Natural Steps (TNS; Bradbury and Clair, 1993; Hardi *et al.*, 1997; Robèrt *et al.*, 1997; Curwell and Cooper, 1998; Broman *et al.*, 2000; Robèrt, 2002; Johnston *et al.*, 2007), and have become the basis for a movement founded in Sweden in 1989 by Karl-Henrick Robert. The principles arose out of a consensus among that country's top scientists as to what conditions are required for a sustainable society, but they were certainly not new in the 1980s. Blutstein (2003) points out that they were articulated in a similar form by Sir Frank Macfarlane Burnet, an Australian virologist who made many commentaries on what we now call sustainability during the

1960s, and we have already come across the notion of sustainable yield. The need to reduce pollution is also obvious and Chapter 2 began with a brief set of references regarding the impacts of agriculture on the environment from the early days of Islamic Science. TNS implies that society should move away from a linear process of production, consumption and waste into a more cyclical process which Curwell and Cooper (1998) refer to as the 4 Rs: reuse, repair, recycling and reconditioning. Thus TNS encourages activities such as better management of renewable resources so as to make them sustainable over the longer term, less reliance on non-renewable resources, a reduction in waste and pollution, more efficient use of energy and materials and an investment in repairing the damage that has already been done to the planet.

At first glance the principles set out in TNS seem obvious, so what has it contributed to sustainability that is new? TNS re-envisions sustainability so as to give it a more scientific basis. Quoting from Robèrt *et al.* (1997; 78–79) we have the following as a starting point:

a. The model must be based on a scientifically acceptable conception of the world.

b. The model must contain a scientifically supportable definition of sustainability.

c. The overall perspective must be applicable at different scales, and must see the economy as a subsystem of the ecosystem at each scale. Individuals must see how their actions aggregate from micro scales up to the macro scale, and thus understand their role in the overall move toward sustainability.

d. The micro-economical perspective should not require individuals to act against self interest. We may need some altruistic behaviour in the political task of setting up the rules of the game, but in the actual playing of the game we should not expect individuals to behave altruistically.

e. The model must be pedagogical and simple to disseminate so that it can support a public consensus necessary to be put into practice democratically.

f. The model must not engender unnecessary resistance or be adversarial.

g. The model must be able to get started without first requiring large scale societal changes. It should be implementable within today's economic reality. Business corporations, political parties and the public should be able to use the model directly.

h. It would be an advantage if the model could also be used as a starting point for developing 'new economics' – as a way to recognize a new and larger pattern of scarcity to which old and basic economizing principles must be applied.

Note the emphasis on science (items a and b) as the foundation and the requirement for a new economics (item h) which should fit into existing economic reality (item g) and not act against individual self-interest (item d). Thus the starting point of the four principles is almost a statement of what is needed for a new approach to ensure its acceptance. Indeed the creators of TNS purposely avoided the more economic dimension of sustainability, which they regard as doing nothing more than encouraging appealing rhetoric and 'business as usual' (Johnston et al., 2007). They suggest that the world should embrace a 'new economics', although they are not so clear what that is. Some have criticised TNS precisely because it side-steps socio-economic concerns which are important in sustainability (Varga and Kuehr, 2007) and for implying an ideal of 'zero growth', at least in the physical parameters of the economy (Upham, 2000a, 2000b). There are also contradictions within the principles and the underlying requirements that helped generate them. The notion of equity within sustainability can span anything from complete equality in terms of access to resources (which can be measured) in a way which even communist societies failed to achieve or it could mean equity in terms of opportunity or perhaps access to the basics for a good quality of life (health care, income, education). Equity is a highly subjective term. Similarly with the list of requirements there are somewhat vague statements about the need to avoid conflict and have public consensus. This is a difficult wish list to achieve in practice, as we shall see later.

Ironically, given what has been said already about TNS and its emphasis on the 'physical' rather than socio-economic dimension of sustainability, the ideas at the heart of TNS do provide guidance for the key activities of production and consumption and thus can be 'sold' to companies in terms of both their corporate responsibilities, but also in terms of the 'bottom line' (an enhanced profitability). TNS does have an appeal and has been influential, albeit in various incarnations within communities and indeed business and industry (Burns, 1999; Jonsson, 2000; Anon, 2002; Nattrass and Altomare, 1999, 2002; Craig, 2004; Ny et al., 2006; Garcia-Serna et al., 2007; Zimmerman and Kibert, 2007).

4.5 GAIA: OUR SAVIOUR?

A commonly expressed opinion is that while industry releases CO_2 and other pollutants, the Earth has an innate capacity to deal with them and thus minimise or even avoid negative impacts such as global warming. In effect, life on the planet is said to act as a cleanser which helps protect us against our worst excesses. This idea of a 'Mother Earth' which cushions us has an old pedigree and has been associated with a number of theories as to how life on Earth interacts with its environment, and one of these is the Gaia hypothesis. During the 1960s and 1970s James Lovelock and other planetary scientists noticed that the environment of the Earth seemed to be regulated in such a way as to make life possible. Lovelock began his career in medicine and biophysics before joining NASA as part of their team working on instruments for spacecraft designed to travel to the moon and the innermost 'rocky' planets. He quickly turned his skill to an understanding of the Earth's environment and was one of the first to discover, in 1972, high levels of chlorofluorocarbons (CFCs) accumulating in the atmosphere. CFCs, often employed as refrigerants, were later shown to cause damage to the ozone layer over the north and south poles and are in the process of being phased out and replaced by other chemicals that are less environmentally damaging. The apparent regulation of the Earth's environment to make it just 'right' for life appeared to Lovelock to be in complete contrast to the environments of our near planetary neighbours (Venus and Mars) with their extremes of heat and cold, and the atmospheres of these planets are quite distinct from that of Earth. So why should this be so? Lovelock and his colleagues proposed the notion that life on Earth is self-regulating in the sense that it alters the environmental conditions to suit itself (Lovelock and Margulis, 1974), and they used the name 'Gaia' to describe this system (Lovelock, 1987). In this theory, the Earth is more than just a collection of separate ecosystems, but is almost an organism in its own right. Some even began to talk of Gaia as a sort of deity, a stance later decried by Lovelock and his supporters, but frankly not helped by the title or content of the last chapter ('God and Gaia') in one of Lovelock's books (*The Ages of Gaia*, 1988) and text such as the following from that chapter:

> *That is why, for me, Gaia is a religious as well as a scientific concept, and in both spheres it is manageable.* (page 206)

> *How can we use the concept of Gaia as a way of understanding God? Belief in God is an act of faith, and will remain so. In the same way, it is otiose to try to prove that Gaia is alive. Instead, Gaia should be a way to view the Earth, ourselves, and our relationships with living things.* (page 207)

> *God and Gaia, theology and science, even physics and biology are not separate but a single way of thought.* (page 212)

The idea that such apparent atmospheric disequilibrium seen on Earth is a stamp of life has since been questioned by a number of people (Nielsen and Ditlevsen, 2009), but here we will concentrate on the notion of life on Earth acting as a self-regulating entity. At first, and indeed to this day, biologists attacked the idea of life acting almost as a single entity to support itself, as it seemed to go against the nature of 'tooth and claw' resting at the heart of natural selection (Dagg, 2002). Why would one species act 'altruistically' to help modify the environment for the benefit of others? What would it gain in this struggle for survival? All species interact, of course, with each other and with the environment, as we discussed in the context of intercropping in Chapter 2, but a distinction needs to be made as to whether species act to change the environment so as to aid other species or whether the interactions are via by-products (Volk, 2003)? This is a fine line to draw, given that species co-evolve and natural selection by 'tooth and claw' could well produce an apparent picture of co-operation (Kirchner, 2002; Staley, 2002). Perhaps unsurprisingly, the debate continues to this day (Free and Barton, 2007). To help illustrate the Gaia hypothesis Lovelock et al. proposed a simple model of two species of plant, white and dark daisies, existing on a planet (they called 'Daisyworld') experiencing the same sort of solar evolution as our own sun (Wood et al., 2008). As the sun aged from its beginnings it released more energy and the Earth's surface temperature increased. The equation for this increasing luminosity with time is given by:

$$\text{Solar luminosity} = 0.6 + (0.006 \times \text{time})$$

Without life, the surface temperature of the planet would keep on increasing as a function of solar energy intensity, as shown in Figure 4.12. This acts as a pressure on the system, as life can only exist within certain temperature limits. In the original model, the optimal temperature for daisy growth (the only life assumed to exist on the planet) is 22.5°C within an acceptable range of 17.5°C either side of this, as represented by the shaded zone in Figure 4.12. So what happens when life in the form of the two types of daisy are introduced into the model? Firstly, Lovelock and his colleagues made a number of assumptions that govern daisy growth on this world. First they assumed that two species do not directly interact with each other either by competition or by 'partnership'. They also assumed that growth of each type of daisy is entirely a function of temperature not time, although with the

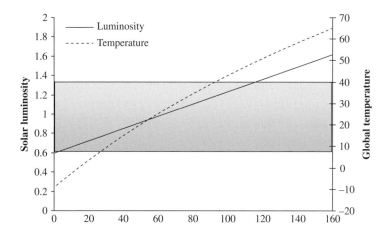

Figure 4.12 Global temperature of a Daisyworld without daisies as a function of solar luminosity.

passage of time the global temperature increases. Within a certain range amenable for growth of both daisies, as temperature increases so does the population of the daisies. There are echoes here of the sort of population growth models described in Chapter 3, only in this case population growth is expressed as areas rather than numbers and is only a function of temperature.

The key facet of the model is that daisy area provides feedback into the temperature of the local environment, and it is this process that rests at the heart of regulation in the model. Planetary temperature is a function of the albedo of the surface, which itself is a combination of the albedo of the bare surface (no daisies) as well as the respective albedos of black and white daisies. Black daisies absorb heat better than white daisies (i.e. black daisies are better at converting incident energy into heat – they have a lower albedo). White daisies, on the other hand, reflect light and are not so effective at converting incident energy into heat. As a result, when planetary temperatures are low the black daisies can flourish, while the white daisies cannot. As time progresses and the planet receives more energy from the sun, the white daisies can begin to flourish. Therefore daisy growth is a function of local temperature, which in itself is a function of planetary temperature, which in turn is a function of planetary albedo and daisy growth. There is a feedback process in place.

Table 4.2 *Stability of global temperature in various versions of Daisyworld*

Type of Daisyworld	Number of time periods with a temperature between 20 and 25°C (out of a total of 170)
No daisies (abiotic)	11
Only white daisies	20
Only black daisies	1
Both white and black daisies	82
White and black daisies and seven types having shades of grey	35

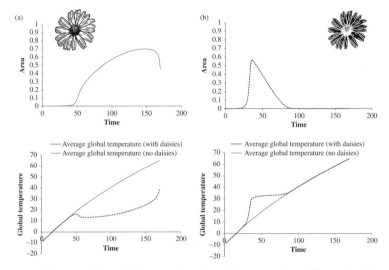

Figure 4.13 Population growth and resulting area of a world populated by either white or black daisies as a function of time: (a) white Daisyworld; (b) black Daisyworld.

The outcome of this model for a world populated by either white or black daisies is shown in Figure 4.13. For either type of daisy the graph at the top is the proportion of the globe covered in the plant and the graph at the bottom is the resulting global temperature compared to a world where there is no life. It is not easy to get an assessment for how much stability there is in global temperature just by looking at these graphs, so Table 4.2 presents the number of time periods (out of 170 in total) where global temperature is between 20 and 25°C (2.5°C either side of the optimal temperature for daisy growth of 22.5°C). As one would expect, black daisies tend to do well at low levels of solar luminosity (low global temperatures) and at their maximum extent (around time period 40) they cover some 60% of the global surface area. Black daisies absorb heat, so the planet warms faster than it would without any daisies. At a point the temperature warms beyond the optimum for daisy growth and the population goes into decline (area decreases) and eventually becomes extinct. Only one of the time periods has a temperature between 20 and 25°C; less than for a planet without any daisies. With a world populated entirely by white daisies, population growth is delayed relative to black daisies until solar luminosity reaches the point where global temperature becomes amenable for the plant. As the area of the white daisy increases more light is reflected back into space and results in a cooling of the planet. However, global temperature continues a steady increase with solar luminosity until eventually the daisy population declines and becomes extinct. In this case there are 20 time periods with a global temperature between 20 and 25°C.

The results of mixing these white and black daisies are shown in Figure 4.14. Black daisies again do well at the start, while it takes white daisies some time to increase. Over a relatively long period there is co-existence, with both species being present, and the existence of the black daisy population is prolonged relative to the planet where only black daisies existed. On a global scale, with the two species of daisy present, we begin to see a regulation of the temperature so as to keep it within a tolerable (for life) band. In Figure 4.14b we can see this difference between the temperature of an abiotic and biotic planet. We now have 82 time periods where global temperature is between 20 and 25°C, and the overall effect is a regulation of planetary temperature, even though the two daisies do not co-operate in any sense of the word. What we see is life overcoming an external pressure.

The Daisyworld model is imperfect in a number of regards, and there have been various attempts to improve upon it by, for example, including a hydrological cycle with clouds (Salazar and Poveda, 2009) and a local spatial interaction (Lenten and van Oijen, 2002). Some have criticised the assumption of only two species, arguing that the buffering would disappear with many species. It's hard to see why this should be so, and indeed is counter-intuitive, given the diversity we see in the world, but it can be tested easily enough. The results from such a model, identical to the one outlined

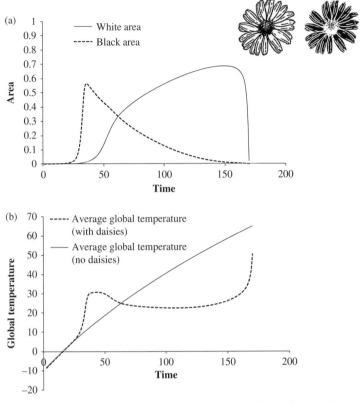

Figure 4.14 Characteristics for a world populated by both the white and black daisies:

(a) Area of white and black daisies as a function of time;

(b) global temperature (with and without daisies) as a function of time.

above in all of its characteristics, but with nine types of daisy (white, black and seven shades of grey in between) are shown in Figure 4.15. In this more diverse world, albeit one still driven by a steady increase in solar luminosity, the initial surge in temperature due to the black daisies becomes dampened and global temperature is maintained. However, the number of periods where global temperature is between 20 and 25°C is only 35. The latter is more than for a planet populated entirely by white or black daisies, but is less than for the Daisyworld where there are only white and black forms. A second criticism rests with the use of growth equations which while having some similarities to those of Chapter 3 are also quite different. However, despite these specific criticisms of

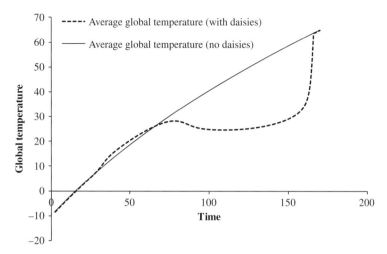

Figure 4.15 Global temperatures of a Daisyworld with a total of nine types of daisy spanning white and black at the extremes and seven 'shades of grey' in between.

Daisyworld as an example mechanism of how homoeostasis could happen in Gaia and the highlighting of other mechanisms that could equally play a role (Waltham, 2007), it is generally accepted today that the fundamental idea of the biosphere interacting with its environment so as to maximise survival is well established (Karnani and Annila, 2009).

One of the criticisms of the Gaia hypothesis is the notion that life can serve as the ultimate buffer for the excesses of humankind. Thus, it can be hypothesised that, while Gaia cannot replace resources at a rate which is proportional to the speed at which we extract them, it can at least buffer any potentially negative 'side-effects' of our development, such as pollution. The central pressure in the Daisyworld model is solar luminosity, which drives global temperature, but cannot the same apply to many human-mediated pressures, such as the release of greenhouse gases? Thus, we can have the comforting thought that if global temperature increases as a result of human-mediated release of greenhouse gases (methane, CO_2 etc.) then Gaia will adapt and regulate.

> Gaia has cause for concern about the long-term decline of carbon dioxide, but the rise of carbon dioxide is, for her, just a minor perturbation that lasts but an instant of time. She is, in any case, tending to offset the decline. (Lovelock (1988, page 157))

Indeed on a broader front we have the following comment:

> It is now generally accepted that man's industrial activities are fouling the nest and pose a threat to the total life of the planet which grows more ominous every year. Here, however, I part company with conventional thought. It may be that the white-hot rash of our technology will in the end prove destructive and painful for our own species, but the evidence for accepting that industrial activities either at the present level or in the immediate future may endanger the life of Gaia as a whole, is very weak indeed.' (Lovelock (1987, page 108))

In fairness, it has to be stressed that these words were written over 20 years ago and knowledge moves on, but the sentiment expressed in these passages is still articulated today by those unwilling to accept 'human-made' global warming. Such apparent complacency about the self-regulating ability of Gaia can imply a 'carry on as you are' approach to the environment, even if this is far from what Lovelock and others had intended. To be fair, the authors do go on to warn against the short-term repercussions of adding CO_2 as, while life may adapt to long-term environmental stress, this could take thousands of years. Indeed, the increases in CO_2 we have seen in our atmosphere have apparently yet to be regulated by Gaia, and if anything the evidence suggests that far from dampening any swings in CO_2 and other greenhouse gases, the biosphere can exacerbate them (Kirchner, 2003). Reality, as yet, does not seem to match theory. It does not look as if Gaia will be our saviour; we have to save ourselves.

Nonetheless, Gaia remains a powerful symbol for environmental groups. The contrast these groups make could not be starker; Gaia is being wounded by our actions, ignorance and greed, while GM (for example) is pictured as a Frankenstein technology (Scott, 2000). That is perhaps Gaia's legacy: a powerful symbol of deep ecology rather than a comforting mechanism that will save us from ourselves.

4.6 CORPORATE SUSTAINABILITY

The sections covered so far in this chapter have viewed sustainability in an industrial context through the eyes of production, inputs and pollution. Processes have been described in terms of energy and exergy, and TNS sets out basic principles that need to be followed. However, the reader may have noted the absence of people in much of this discussion, with the notable exception in the fourth Natural Step that resource use must be equitable. The 1990s saw an increasing awareness amongst companies that being 'sustainable' was a good thing and that shareholder value could be enhanced by embracing sustainability rather than ignoring it. The theory is a simple one; companies that plan their present and future performance so as to take account of environmental and social factors, not only economic ones, are likely to continue to perform well, and hence maintain and increase the value of dividends paid to their shareholders. To paraphrase – sustainability makes good business sense! But sustainability is not just a matter of improving the efficiency of resource use, minimising exergy and/or reducing pollution, as we have seen earlier. It is also about the broad context of a social responsibility; making a positive contribution to society as a whole.

Corporate sustainability is a substantial topic in itself and, as with much else in this book, it is only possible to provide an outline of the philosophy and an example of putting it into practice. Corporate sustainability (CS) overlaps with perhaps the better known approach of corporate social responsibility (CSR; Moon, 2007; Lee, 2008; Bazin, 2009; Weyzig, 2009), indeed some see them as much the same thing, albeit with different historical origins (Montiel, 2008). It has been argued that the origins of CSR rest with the Cold War of the 1950s and a sense of what is a good society rather than environmental concerns per se (Spector, 2008). CS and CSR certainly have much in common, but corporate sustainability has perhaps a stronger signal that shareholders matter; so-called firm-level sustainability, which goes hand in hand with a concern for the sustainability of the environment of which the company is a part (Stubbs and Cocklin, 2008). Thus CS includes a need for the company to survive and do well in a competitive sense.

One specific programme designed to facilitate CS is that of the Dow Jones Sustainability Index (DJSI; www.sustainability-index. com.); the first global kitemark of CS. DJSI was first published on 8 September 1999 and utilises the name of the prestigious 'Dow Jones' financial index in the USA. In 2003 there were 50 DJSI licenses held by asset managers in 14 countries, having a total value of 2.8 billion Euro. Companies wishing to be listed on the DJSI (i.e. to obtain the DJSI kite-mark) apply by completing a questionnaire. In 2003 the questionnaire comprised 60 specific questions requiring highly structured answers. In addition, the company has to submit a set of reports (environment, health and safety, financial etc.) as evidence of its achievements in CS. An outline of the questionnaire employed in 2003 is shown in Table 4.3. The questionnaire is divided into the three dimensions of sustainability, economic, environmental

Table 4.3 *Structure of the questionnaire used for validation of Dow Jones Sustainability Index (DJSI) kitemark of Corporate Sustainability.*

Dimension	Section	Number of specific questions	Weighting (%)
Economic	Corporate Governance	10	4.2
	Investor Relations	3	3.6
	Strategic Planning	2	4.2
	Scorecards/Measurement Systems	2	4.2
	Risk and Crisis Management	3	4.2
	Codes of Conduct/ Compliance/Corruption and Bribery	5	4.2
	Customer Relationship Management	2	3.0
	Industry-specific Criteria (Analyst)	–	Depends on industry
	Total	**27**	**27.6**
Environmental	Environmental Policy/ Management	5	4.8
	Environmental Performance (Eco-efficiency)	1	3.6
	Environmental Reporting	Based on publicly available information	1.8
	Industry-specific Criteria (Analyst)	–	Depends on industry
	Total	**6**	**10.2**
Social	Labour Practice Indicators	3	3.0
	Human Capital Development	5	3.0
	Talent Attraction and Retention	9	3.0
	Knowledge Management/ Organisational Learning	3	3.0
	Standards for Suppliers	1	2.4
	Stakeholder Engagement	2	3.6
	Corporate Citizenship/ Philanthropy	4	2.4

Table 4.3 (*cont.*)

Dimension	Section	Number of specific questions	Weighting (%)
	Social Reporting	Based on publicly available information	1.8
	Industry-specific Criteria (Analyst)	–	Depends on industry
	Total	**27**	**22.2**
	Overall total	**60**	**60**

and social, and within each of the dimensions there are sections. Each section has a number of associated questions, ranging from 10 (corporate governance) to 1 (environmental performance), and each section has a different weighting to the final score. The number of questions per dimension ranges from 27 from economic to only six for environmental, although, in fairness, some of the questions can be quite wide ranging. Under environmental performance (what the authors term as 'eco-efficiency') there is only one question in that respondents are asked to measure their performance with regard to the following indicators:

● Total direct greenhouse gas emissions (tonnes CO_2 equivalent)
● Total water use (m^3)
● Total energy consumption (GJ)
● Total waste generation (tonnes).

The company is expected to provide targets for reducing these indicators and explain its progress towards achieving those targets. The four indicators are not surprising, given the issues we have discussed so far in this chapter.

Only 60% of the total score in the DJSI is accounted for by the 60 structured questions. The remainder is allocated based on the research of industry-specific analysts familiar with the sector within which the company functions. The analysts peruse media stories and other publically available information about the company, as well as clear up any ambiguities in the information provided by the company in its returns. Companies are liable for inspection and if found to have provided misleading information the 'kitemark' can be revoked.

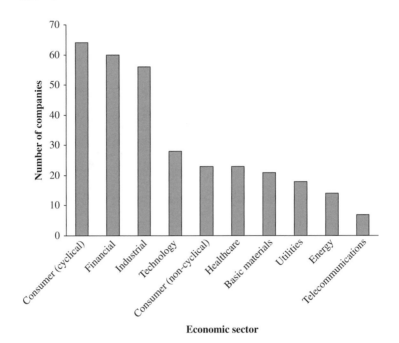

Figure 4.16 Number of companies having the Dow Jones Sustainability Index (DJSI) kitemark by sector.

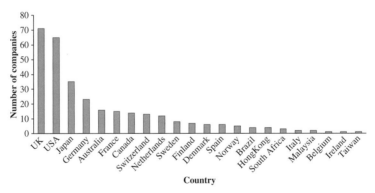

Figure 4.17 Number of companies having the Dow Jones Sustainability Index (DJSI) kitemark by country of registration.

Of the 314 companies with the kitemark in 2003 some 57% were in the consumer, financial and industrial sectors (Figure 4.16), and the majority of these companies were registered in the developed world (Figure 4.17). Indeed the UK and USA together account for over 40% of

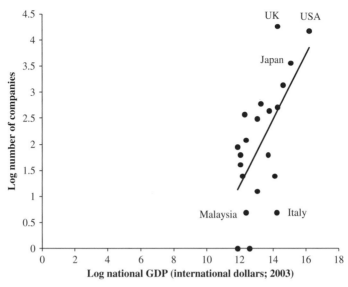

Figure 4.18 Relationship between the number of companies having the DJSI kitemark in a country and that country's wealth (as measured by GDP).

the 314 companies. A plot of number of companies having the DJSI kitemark per country against wealth of that country (measured as gross domestic product) does yield a linear relationship, as shown in Figure 4.18. This would be expected if wealth brings 'awareness', and hence the place where the companies are registered (and typically where the head offices are located) would be expected to influence the level of adoption of the DJSI kite-mark. The linkage between sustainability and wealth is another one of those recurring themes and will be explored in the next chapter.

While undoubtedly a positive step, the DJSI as a practical mechanism for facilitating CS does have problems. Firstly, it fails to incorporate variation in perspective as it represents the situation as seen, presumably, by senior managers in the company. They complete the questionnaire, but how would other employees answer the questions, let alone those not working for the company, but affected by it? Those living near to an industry may well be affected by pollution (air, water, noise) and have strong views as to environmental performance that may well be at odds with those of senior managers, even if the levels are within 'legally' defined limits and on target, as defined by the company. Some of these feelings may be found in publicly available material such as media stories, but not necessarily. How far would the external analysts go in looking for such divergent opinions? Secondly, the questionnaire provides a very rigid framework for assessment and, while it does cover many important issues in CS, it is likely that others would create a very different-looking questionnaire: different sections, phrasing of questions and weighting. Thus while the questionnaire has an objective 'feel', this can hide a large degree of subjectivity as to key decisions over what to include, how questions are asked and weighted. This is a point at the very heart of sustainability (whose sustainability counts?) and we will return to it later, but suffice it to say the claim of 'objectivity' is not as straightforward as it would appear.

In fairness, it has to be stressed that the DJSI has evolved and in 2009 there are a number of related indices rather than only one. But what are the incentives for a company to join the DJSI or indeed to engage in the closely related CSR? Indeed, some have questioned the notion of CSR as an oxymoron; how can a company which by definition has to look for its own survival and performance take on wider social responsibilities (Kallio, 2007; Caterina and Lorenzo-Molo, 2009; Devinney, 2009)? Is it nothing more than an exercise in public relations; the presentation of a good image? There is evidence that the adoption of CSR does make a difference (Smith and Langford, 2009; Vanhamme and Grobben, 2009). There is also evidence that companies adopting the DJSI kitemark are at an economic disadvantage, at least in the short term, compared with companies that do not adopt (Lopez *et al.*, 2007). This might at first glance sound reasonable, as schemes such as DJSI or, indeed, an involvement in CSR would be expected to increase costs. However, there are increasing reports in the literature that companies adopting a CSR strategy also perform well in business terms (Lo and Sheu, 2007; van Beurden and Gossling, 2008; Chang and Kuo, 2008; Shen and Chang, 2009). There are a number of reasons why this may be so, at least over the longer term, beyond arguments of enhanced efficiency in production or service delivery (Ambec and Lanoie, 2008). Adopting kitemarks such as the DJSI may generate a good image and thus help attract investment as well as sales, but it may also be indicative of a company that is imaginative, well managed, forward thinking and willing to innovate. Thus, having the DJSI kitemark or engaging in CSR could be an indicator of a company likely to have a good share price rather than the other way around. There may well be some feedback here in the sense that having DJSI or engaging in CSR could in itself promote market innovation and better employee motivation (Becchetti *et al.*, 2008) and thus an enhancement of competitiveness (Vilanova *et al.*, 2009). Having said all this there are powerful voices that decry these efforts by companies to take on more socially responsible faces (Pava, 2008), including how CS and CSR can mislead investors (Aras and Crowther, 2009). Some have highlighted the limitations of CSR and how it is not a substitute for good regulation by the state. An example of the latter can be seen with the illegal release of genetically modified organisms into the environment (Clapp, 2008).

But what are the contributions, if any, of CS and CSR to sustainability in broad terms? While we have discussed the benefits to companies, does it really make a difference to wider society if companies adopt kitemarks such as the DJSI? Are they really nothing more than window-dressing? This is a relatively unexplored area and much less is known about such potential impacts (Blowfield, 2007). However, one must take care to balance what companies say about such impacts in their own publications (Jones *et al.*, 2007). Clearly there is much scope for further research.

4.7 CONCLUSION

This chapter has shown how some basic principles employed in biological systems, namely energy flows and resource use, can also be applied to explore sustainability within industry. Sustainability equates to efficiency of production – making best use of resources and minimising waste – and this can be assessed in various ways. We can analyse energy flows through industry, while remembering that components of the process manufactured in other places would also have used energy. Hence, the important concept of emergy within such an analysis, to make sure we include as much as possible. We can also view energy balances in terms of a loss of exergy or 'quality energy'. Hence the burning of fossil fuels to release CO_2 and heat is strictly speaking a loss of exergy rather than a loss of energy. The heat generated will do work for us, which will be changed into motion, sound, friction etc., but the amount of energy in a closed system remains the same – what we have changed it to makes it less easy to harness. We have, to all intents and purposes, lost that energy once the work has been done, as we can no longer use it.

But energy flows are only a part of the story and we also need to consider other dimensions. Material-flow-based analyses can allow us to consider many aspects of a production or service-provision industry from raw materials through to final use. Included here, as we have seen with life-cycle analysis, is the environmental impact of a process.

Problems remain with such analyses, given that we have to define a system boundary. In other words, we have to make a decision as to what to include or not. Allied to this is the issue of geographical or indeed social spatiality of differing impacts. Sourcing of raw materials and eventual use of the product/service can take place in very different spaces, both in terms of geography and in terms of socio-economic groups. Thus, we can improve material intensity, for example, but this can go hand in hand with an increased negative impact on some groups. Is the trade-off worthwhile? Well, it depends who you talk to. Those who are more negatively affected by a change may not think it is worthwhile, even if a MIPS analysis suggests an overall improvement.

The Natural Step principles set out a set of rules that society needs to follow to move us towards sustainability, and one of these is somewhat nebulously put forward as a need for 'fair' resource use. While TNS attempts to ground sustainability within science, the inclusion of the word 'fair' only highlights the degree of value judgement that remains. Fair is a highly subjective term, but is nonetheless a word that one often hears in any discussion regarding sustainability. Is it fair that a local community should have a road bypass next to their village in order to help ease traffic congestion in a neighbouring town? Much depends upon where you happen to live, of course. Science can contribute to an enhancement of sustainability, but sustainability is not science.

It is sometimes claimed that the Earth has an absorptive capacity to help mitigate the detrimental impacts of our activity. Hence, an increase in CO_2 will not be detrimental, as plants will absorb it via photosynthesis. After all, it is argued, increased concentrations of CO_2 results in increased rates of photosynthesis and hence plant growth. In this chapter I have used the concept of Gaia to illustrate this argument, but also to provide a counter view. A simple model such as Daisyworld does indeed show how life can succeed under an environmental pressure, in that case increased solar luminosity, but it has to be remembered that the model is a very simple one. We cannot draw conclusions from this simple example for the whole of the planet. Indeed, so far all the data we have suggests that we could be witnessing a negative feedback loop where increased CO_2 in the atmosphere is exacerbated rather than mitigated by the biosphere.

The final point made in the chapter is that industrial sustainability is not only a matter of material, energy and pollution, but is also about people. Science can only take us so far. We can analyse energy flows using the concept of emergy to understand how efficient the production is, but this says nothing about the conditions of the people that work there or have to live near to where the production is taking place. Corporate sustainability (CS) and its close relative corporate social responsibility (CSR) have becomes fashionable in recent times and do seek to take on board the wider social impacts of a company beyond its workforce and shareholders. In this chapter we explored the Dow Jones Sustainability Index (DJSI) as one practical mechanism for promoting CS. But while CS and especially CSR can be all too easily dismissed as an oxymoron and perhaps a somewhat cynical attempt to help marketing more than to make a worthwhile difference to society, they are at least a step in the right direction.

5
Social and economic dimensions to sustainability

So far in this book we have focused on production and throughout the discussion we have touched upon social and economic aspects. Total factor productivity in Chapter 2 was expressed in monetary terms and, while MSY was derived from biological principles in Chapter 3, it was stressed how economics also matter (as with the extension of MSY to MEY). In Chapter 4 we explored energy (and related concepts), life-cycle analysis, Natural Steps and so on, but socio-economic dimensions continued to emerge. Towards the end of the chapter, social and economic issues were brought to the fore with a discussion of corporate sustainability and corporate social responsibility. This intertwining of biology with economic and social dimensions is inescapable in sustainability, and this theme will form the basis for this chapter.

The language of sustainability has often been expressed in economic as well as scientific terms. Science may provide the soul of sustainability, but the practice is often tied to economics, and hence to politics. Some use the term 'weak sustainability' to bring out a compromise between a desire to achieve the environmental changes necessary for sustainability and to express this in financial terms. This allows us to estimate the costs and benefits from a programme and thereby gauge the best value for money and make any trade-offs transparent. This contrasts with strong sustainability, where there is no such compromise. The argument here is that the environment is the primary consideration and there is no trade-off between that and economic benefits. Indeed, the relationship between national income and attempts to assess sustainability at the level of the nation state has received a great deal of attention in the literature. There is a strong logic here, given that all of us live under the jurisdiction of a government, and it is governments that primarily decide policy and raise the money to make that policy a reality. Thus, governments have power and can choose to make sustainability a reality, either through funding research or facilitating the changes that research suggests we need to bring about. Governments raise the necessary funds to pay for all this through taxation, and thus we have accountability to the population and electorates to please. Indeed national income has played a central role in these considerations of sustainability at the scale of the nation state.

This chapter will begin with an outline of the ways in which economic performance is measured and how some have sought to 'green' these measures and thereby illustrate how economic growth can impact upon the environment. From here we will look at how economic growth has been hypothesised to link to environmental degradation and whether these two can be de-linked. In other words, is it possible to have economic growth without any degradation of the environment? The chapter will end with a discussion of the sustainable livelihood concept in development, especially the advantages and disadvantages of this approach in practice.

5.2 LINKING ECONOMICS AND ENVIRONMENT

The main measure of economic performance is the gross domestic product (GDP). GDP is designed to measure the level of economic activity in a country, region or even smaller spatial units such as a city. The higher the value for GDP then the greater the level of economic activity. GDP is a headline indicator in the sense that it is often referred to by politicians in government, their opponents and others to stress how well (or badly) the economy is doing. The term crops up regularly in the media, often in the context of comparing the economic performance of nations.

GDP is a snapshot of economic activity at one specific time. A comparison of GDP over time provides us with a trend in economic activity. If economic activity declines over a period of time then it is called a recession. But how is economic activity measured? Let us assume that an economy takes the simplified form shown in Figure 5.1. There are a number of components in this model, as well as a number of flows, both of money, and goods and services. People earn income from wages and spend it on goods (food, washing machines, TVs etc.) and services (water supply, internet connections etc.). Figure 5.1 has a number of similarities to the energy diagram of Chapter 4, only with monetary flows taking the place of energy flow. In

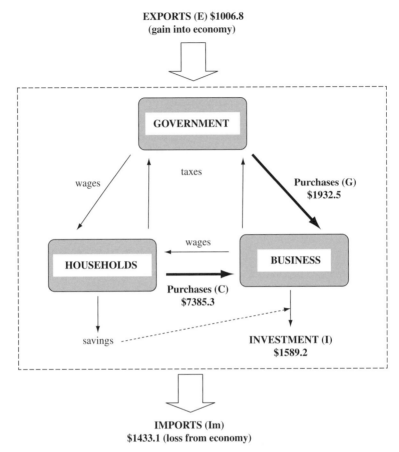

EXPORTS (E) $1006.8
(gain into economy)

GOVERNMENT

wages

taxes

Purchases (G)
$1932.5

wages

HOUSEHOLDS

BUSINESS

Purchases (C)
$7385.3

savings

INVESTMENT (I)
$1589.2

IMPORTS (Im)
$1433.1 (loss from economy)

Figure 5.1 The flow of money within an economy.

    This is a highly simplified model of a closed economy, where the money circulates between households, business and government as payment for labour as well as goods and services. GDP can be found by the sums of C, G and I and then adjusting for the trade balance (exports – imports). Figures are the values for the US economy in 2002 (billion dollars). The US GDP for 2002 was $10 480.7 billion.

order to judge the level of economic activity, we need to measure the flows in Figure 5.1 (assuming that money, like energy, is not destroyed within a closed system), but where are the best points in the diagram to do that? We could measure purchases of goods and services, or wages. As long as significant quantities of cash are not being hoarded under floorboards then these points of measurement should give the same result. Therefore, if we take expenditures on goods and services then we can find GDP as follows:

$$\text{GDP (expenditure)} = C + G + I + (\text{EX} - \text{IM})$$

where:

GDP = gross domestic product
C = consumers' expenditure on goods and services
G = government expenditure on goods and services
I = investment
EX = exports
IM = imports.

Hence, expenditure in the economy is the summation of expenditures by consumers (C) and government (G) on goods and services, with an allowance made for money spent on investment (I) and 'lost' or 'gained' via the trade balance (exports – imports). In this model 'investment' refers to private domestic investment and is a somewhat complex component. Only private investment by industry is included (new facilities, machinery etc.), since government investment to build infrastructure (roads, dams etc.) is included as a part of G. Much of the savings lodged by households is invested by banks into the private sector, and is therefore a 'sink' which locks up capital. Liquidating that investment will put cash back into the system. There are other complications to this simple model. For example, non-productive government expenditures such as social security benefits, unemployment compensation, welfare benefits, interest payments on the national debt and so on are not included in G, even though they are flows of money. Figures for these components of GDP for the US economy in 2002 are also shown in Figure 5.1. The expenditure components (C and G) together account for more than 80% of the US GDP and this has been consistently so since 1959 (Figure 5.2).

While the model in Figure 5.1 works in terms of measuring the size of an economy, there are various complications with its use in practice. It is not necessary to go into all of them and, indeed, we have already looked at one of the issues (purchasing power parity) in Chapter 1. However, it is worth pointing out two further complications as they will feature in other sections of the book. Firstly, looking at trends of GDP over time can be misleading, as inflation will also come into play. Prices tend to creep up within an economy as demand increases, and this leads to an increase in prices which in turn leads to an increase in wages. The opposite is deflation, where prices spiral down as a result of a drop in demand. Thus consumers will put off making purchases as they expect prices to drop further. In theory, even

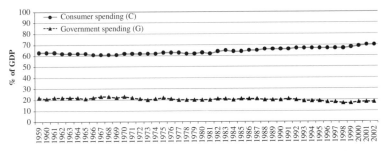

Figure 5.2 Consumer and government spending as a percentage of US GDP (1959 to 2002). Together these two components comprise approximately 82 to 88% of the total GDP in the USA.
(Source: US Department of Commerce, Bureau of Economic Analysis, www.bea.gov.)

if the size of an economy remains the same over, say, 10 years, but the currency diminishes in value through inflation, then we would get an illusionary increase in GDP. The apparent increase in GDP has been caused not by an increase in the number of items being purchased, but by an increase in their unit price. Economists get around this problem by calculating what is called 'real GDP'. In effect, they recalculate all the transactions relative to a single year and thereby remove any inflationary effects. For example, we could recalculate GDP from the 1950s to the present day in terms of what a dollar buys in the year 2000. Any change we see now reflects a genuine change in the size of the economy and will not be an inflationary artefact generated by inflation. The difference this makes can be seen in Figure 5.3, where we have the values of GDP shown in current dollars (i.e. for each of the years) and in dollars pegged to their value in the year 2000. There has been an increase in real GDP since 1959, but this is not as steep an increase as for GDP based on current dollars, which will also include inflation.

Secondly, the quantity of money flowing in an economy will also be partly a reflection of the number of people in that economy, as well as inflation. The more people there are then the greater the flow of cash in purchases and wages. Economists normally adjust for this by dividing national GDP by the number of residents. Thus you will often see terms such as 'GDP/capita' as a measure of national wealth, rather than just GDP.

From the point of view of sustainability, our main concern in this book, it should be noted that there is nothing in the GDP calculation as outlined here to allow for consumption or damage of natural resources.

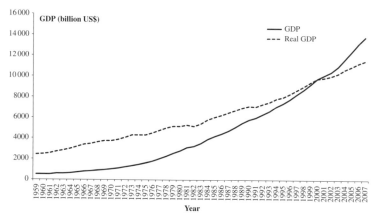

Figure 5.3 GDP and real GDP for the US economy (1959 to 2007). Real GDP is GDP where the US dollars have been 'chained' to their value in the year 2000. This removes the effect of inflation.
(Source of data: US Department of Commerce, Bureau of Economic Analysis, www.bea.gov.)

Within the broader system of accounting there are other measures that do take into account the use of natural assets (forests, minerals and fossil fuels, for example), but damage caused by pollution can be hard to assess. This implies that a country can generate, and indeed maintain, a substantial growth in GDP by completely destroying its natural habitats and resource base. This is obviously not sustainable in a 'weak sustainability' sense of the term unless the capital that is generated is invested in ways that can maintain economic growth. If not, then economic growth will eventually halt and go into reverse. Similarly, a high GDP can be created and maintained with most of the inhabitants either in poverty and/or with a very low quality of life, such as high levels of crime, bad working conditions and job security. As long as there are some who are very rich to maintain the flows of cash then GDP can be increased. So how can we allow for at least some of these in GDP? Recently there has been growing support for a new system of integrated environmental and economic accounting (SEEA) which does try to bridge the divide. In effect it is a promotion of 'green accounting' (Auty, 2007; Bartelmus, 2007; Dietz and Neumayer, 2007; Lange, 2007; Lawn 2007); the incorporation of 'environmental assets and their source and sink functions into national and corporate accounts' (Bartelmus *et al.*, 2008). One example of SEEA in practice is the environmentally adjusted net domestic product (EDP), and will be the only one covered here. The theory behind EDP is straightforward and can be expressed as follows:

$$EDP = GDP - \text{capital consumption (CC)} - \text{environmental costs (EC)}$$

where capital consumption is the replacement value of 'man-made' capital used up in the process of production and 'environmental costs' include depletion of natural resources (minerals, forests, water and so on), as well as environmental degradation through pollution, for example. It is possible to express EDP in two forms, depending upon what is included under the EC component:

EDP I: only includes natural resource depletion
EDP II: includes both natural resource depletion and environmental degradation.

Example calculations of EDP I and EDP II are shown in Table 5.1 for the USA and Africa. In both cases the EDP is obviously lower than GDP and EDP II is lower than EDP I. Indeed, the ratio of EDP and GDP provides one measure of sustainability; the lower this ratio then the greater the extent to which GDP is being 'bought' at the expense of capital consumption and/or damage to the environment. Figure 5.4 provides examples of this ratio for the USA and Africa. The ratio is reasonably constant in the USA between 0.8 and 0.9, but is showing signs of a slow decline. By way of complete contrast, in Africa the ratio has shown a rapid decline especially since 1995 and the reason for this can be seen in Table 5.1. In Africa there has been a surge in natural resource depletion and a much smaller increase in environmental degradation. The question then becomes whether Africa is re-investing the capital being generated from natural resource depletion in such a way as to allow for sustainability in economic growth.

However, one of the problems of the EDP is that it does include an element of 'trade-off' between man-made capital and the environment. It is possible to mask some environmental costs (depletion and/or degradation) by reducing consumption of man-made capital. The value of the EDP will deceptively remain the same in such a circumstance, but the negative impacts on the environment have been increased. This is a typical concern in green accounting; the masking of depletion and degradation by man-made capital. Another problem is the availability of good-quality data which can be employed to make these estimates. The flows in Figure 5.1 can readily be assessed from surveys and records, but even here there may be problems if

Table 5.1 *Calculation of the EDP for the USA and Africa (after Bartelmus, 2009). Figures are billion US dollars (current).*

	USA						Africa					
	1990	1992	1995	2000	2004	2006	1990	1992	1995	2000	2004	2006
GDP	5757	6287	7342	9765	11 657	13 192	514	525	536	605	828	1091
Man-made capital consumption (CC)	637	701	823	1,136	1,426	1,604	45	45	46	54	82	111
Environmental cost (EC)	82	63	72	146	188	310	63	53	50	101	168	307
thereof:												
Natural resource (NR) depletion	68	51	51	90	126	245	63	53	50	92	151	288
Environmental degradation	14	12	21	57	62	65	0	0	0	9	17	18
EDP I (GDP – CC – NR depletion)	5052	5535	6468	8539	10 105	11 343	406	427	440	459	595	692
EDP II (GDP – CC – EC)	5038	5523	6447	8483	10 043	11 278	406	427	440	450	578	673

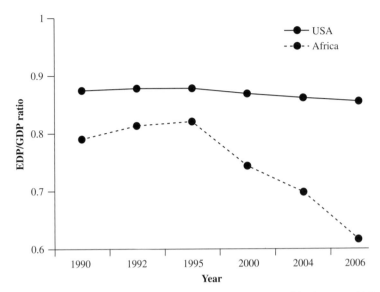

Figure 5.4 EDP as a proportion of GDP for the USA and Africa (1990 to 2006). (Source of data: Bartelmus, 2009.)

transactions are not recorded, as with Black Market activity for example. Values for consumption of produced capital are readily available from sources such as the United Nations Statistics Division (UNSD) and World Bank (note that GDP – CC is referred to by economists as the 'net domestic product' or NDP). The difficulty rests with estimating the value of environmental costs (Holub *et al.*, 1999). Just how do we assess natural resource depletion and environmental degradation in monetary terms? After all, they do not come in convenient packages sold in shops, are not traded, even on a wholesale basis and thus have no agreed price (Boyd, 2007). Financial estimates of natural resource depletion can be found in UNSD and World Bank datasets for energy, metals, minerals and forests, although it should be noted that not all resources are included. Fish stocks, for example, are notable for their absence in these datasets, although there have been some efforts to include them within an SEEA (Willmann, 2000), albeit with limited success (Danielsson, 2005). Environmental degradation is the most difficult component. There are two approaches that could be adopted:

1.   Estimate the financial impact(s) of degradation. For example, once we know what the level of pollution is we could estimate how this reduces forest and crop growth or how it reduces productivity amongst workers

2. Estimate the cost of reducing degradation below an 'acceptable' level (i.e. the maintenance cost).

The first of these options is not easy. We have to know what the impacts are, including any interactions that might occur between them, in order to be able to estimate the level of degradation. Bartelmus (2009) adopts the second of these two approaches and that is the basis for the data in Table 5.1 and Figure 5.4.

The EDP does not seek to change GDP. Instead it adjusts GDP by including costs of degradation and depletion of produced and natural capital. The way in which GDP is calculated is left intact and this is a significant advantage, given the established institutions and procedures in place to do the work and the widespread understanding and acceptability of GDP. People know what it means when GDP declines; they know it is bad news. Thus keeping GDP intact at the core of the sustainability assessment does have a strong logic, but another approach advocated by some is to re-design GDP from the bottom up rather than to adjust it. An example of this approach is the Genuine Progress Indicator (GPI), created by the organisation 'Redefining Progress' (Lawn, 2003). While GDP is a measure of the flow of money in Figure 5.1 the GPI attempts to include components which are deemed important in terms of quality of life and the environment, but which don't appear in Figure 5.1. The starting point of the GPI calculation is personal consumption (C) exactly as it appears in Figure 5.1 for GDP, but rather than add government spending, investment and foreign-trade balance there are various additions and subtractions based upon what is deemed by the creators of the GPI to be positive or negative contributions to society and the environment. Each of these positives and negatives are given an economic value. Indeed, the first adjustment is made to C in terms of income distribution in the society. If it is deemed that a more uneven distribution of income is a 'bad' thing for a society, and, after all, sustainability does have intra- and inter-generational equity at its heart, then C has to be altered to reflect that value. In the GPI, the adjustment can be made by dividing C by the Income Distribution Index (IDI) in each year and multiplying by 100. The result is a weighted personal consumption (C_w);

$$C_w = \left(\frac{C}{\text{IDI}}\right) \times 100$$

Therefore, the greater the unevenness of income distribution in society (i.e. the higher the value of IDI) then the greater the degree to which C is reduced. A flavour of the other adjustments (positive and negative) made to C_w is provided in Table 5.2 (details behind these assumptions can be found in Talberth *et al.*, 2007). These are the components in the 2006 version of the GPI released by 'Redefining Progress'. There are three categories; social benefits, social costs and environmental costs. The latter two categories exert a downward pressure on the GPI. Included under environmental costs are some familiar variables such as the cost of pollution (including noise pollution) and degradation of resources. Under social costs are variables such as the cost of crime. The GPI is then calculated as follows:

$$\text{GPI} = C_w + \text{social benefits} - \text{social costs} - \text{environmental costs} \pm \text{NCI} \pm \text{NFB}$$

NCI and NFB are net capital investment and net foreign borrowing, respectively. For example, in 2004 these components have been estimated as follows (note that all values have been pegged to the value of the US$ in the year 2000):

$$C_w = \left(\frac{7588.6}{120.1}\right) \times 100$$
$$C_w = 6318.57$$

and

$$\text{GPT} = 6318.57 + 4356.71 - 2400.8 - 3990.01 + 388.8 - 254.02$$
$$\text{GPT} = \$4,419.25$$

The 'environmental cost' adjustment of nearly $4000 was clearly a significant one in 2004. A plot of real GDP and GPI (on a per capita basis) from 1959 to 2004 is shown as Figure 5.5. GDP/capita has shown a steady increase from 1950 to 2004 (remember that these are 'real' GDP figures and thus the effect of inflation has been removed), but GPI/capita has been more or less level since the mid-1970s. The latter suggests that while the economy may have expanded, the net benefits to society have not kept up with that expansion. The values (again on a per capita basis) of the social and environmental costs included in the 2006 version of the GPI are shown in Figure 5.6. Both show a rather worrying increase over time, and the rate of increase of environmental cost is higher than that of social cost. Other examples of the GPI, based upon different sets of assumptions for the calculation over spatial and time scales can be found in Hamilton (1999) and Costanza *et al.* (2004).

Table 5.2 *Components of the GPI for 2006 (based upon Telberth et al., 2007).*

Item	How measured?
Group 1: Social benefits	
Household work and parenting	Value of hours of household work performed each year
Volunteer work	Value of volunteer work performed each year
Higher education	Annual social benefits that arise from higher education
Service of consumer durables	Value of the services provided by durables.
Service of highways	Value of the use of streets and highways
Group 2(a): *Social costs*	
Cost of crime	Measured by property losses and household spending on crime prevention
Cost of commuting	Time spent commuting valued at opportunity cost
Cost of consumer durables	Expenditures on consumer durables
Loss of leisure time	Value of leisure time lost or gained
Cost of under-employment	Value of psychological costs of underemployment of part-time employees who want to work full-time
Cost of car accidents	Costs of repairs and pain and suffering
Group 2(b): *environmental costs*	
Cost of household pollution abatement	Expenditure on equipment such as air and water filters
Cost of water pollution	Damage to the environment measured by the control costs of improving water quality
Cost of air pollution	Damage to humans and environment from noxious emissions measured mainly by health costs
Cost of noise pollution	Excess noise levels valued by cost of reducing noise to acceptable level
Loss of farmland	Costs to current and future generations from soil erosion etc., measured by forgone output
Loss of wetlands	Cost of wetlands which are lost
Loss of primary forest	Environmental values denied to future generations measured by willingness to pay
Resource depletion	Costs of shifting from oil and gas to renewables
Cost of ozone depletion	Annual emissions valued by future impacts on humans and environment
CO_2 emissions damage	Annual emissions valued by future impacts on humans and environment

Plus adjustments for income distribution in the economy, net capital investment (NCI) and net foreign borrowing (NFB).

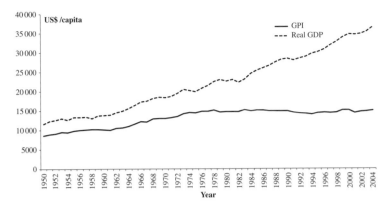

Figure 5.5 Comparing trends of GDP and GPI in the USA.
(Source of data: Talberth *et al.*, 2007.)

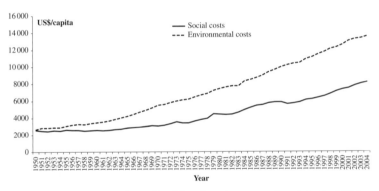

Figure 5.6 Comparison of social and environmental costs in the GPI for the USA.
(Source of data: Talberth *et al.*, 2007.)

While GPI and GDP are related, they are also quite different. Indeed, this difference is analogous in a broad sense to that between energy and exergy we encountered in Chapter 4. GPI attempts to provide an improved quality to the assessment of economic activity in much the same way that exergy is (to put it somewhat basically) 'quality' energy. However, while GPI does have an appeal, the approach has its critics, given the numerous value judgements it makes over what should be included and the valuations that are made (Neumayer, 2000; Lawn, 2003). Thus, GPI includes a great deal of subjectivity which can be hidden in graphs like Figure 5.5. Changing those value judgements over what to include in GPI, as well as how those components are assessed would make a major difference.

One final point needs to be briefly made here and will also be returned to later in the book. While 'green accounting' does have the advantage of bringing the environment into economics and thus providing a basis for managing progress towards sustainability, like all approaches it will mean little if it is not used to influence policy (Alfsen and Greaker, 2007). In a sense, we are reinforcing the same point we discussed in the earlier chapters of this book; the need for good-quality data and tools, but there must also be willingness for them to be employed in order to bring about positive change. While GDP is a politically powerful measure of economic performance and one that certainly resonates with those having power, is the same true of EDP and GPI? To be frank, the answer is probably no.

5.3   ENVIRONMENTAL KUZNETS CURVE: DE-LINKING ECONOMIC GROWTH AND ENVIRONMENT IMPACT?

In the previous section we saw how economists have tried to include the environment and, indeed, other social concerns into workhorse economic concepts and statistics such as the GDP. The EDP is an example, and in Table 5.1 and Figure 5.4 there is an implication that by this measure Africa is not doing as well as the USA in terms of sustainability. The ratio of EDP/GDP for Africa is showing an alarming rate of decline that suggests its capital (produced and natural) is being consumed and that the environment is being degraded. But is this not an expected state of affairs, given the relative poverty of the people of Africa compared with those of the USA? Surely many people in Africa have little choice than to consume and degrade in order to survive, even when they know of the consequences for future generations? The relationship between poverty and environmental degradation has long been explored. For example, there are the following quotations from the World Summit on Sustainable Development held in Johannesburg (2001; www.johannesburgsummit.org):

> The Summit reaffirmed sustainable development as a central element of the international agenda and gave new impetus to global action to fight poverty and protect the environment.
>
> The understanding of sustainable development was broadened and strengthened as a result of the Summit, particularly the important linkages between poverty, the environment and the use of natural resources.

What is surprising is not so much the statement of a relationship between poverty and sustainability, but the fact that it needs to be reiterated so often. Indeed, can we not assume that poverty is linked to environmental degradation and that as countries industrialise this will get worse? At a certain point it seems logical to assume that people will move out of poverty and begin to call for an improvement to the environment. They will put pressure on their government, who will in turn create and enforce regulations which reduce degradation, and this will encourage the development of new technologies to help with this reduction. The effect will be the sort of relationship between national wealth (income per head of the population) and environmental degradation (assessed as loss of biodiversity, for example) we see in Figure 5.7a. This is called the environmental Kuznets curve (EKC). The 'quadratic' shape of this curve is a familiar one from the sort of diminishing return curves of Chapters 2 and 3, where we looked at photosynthesis and maximum sustainable yield, even if the axes are different variables, but Figure 5.7a is fundamentally different. In Figure 5.7a beyond a certain level of income we have a de-coupling of degradation from economic growth; one no longer drives an increase in the other.

Although he didn't describe it during his lifetime, the EKC is named after Simon Kuznets (1901–85), a Russian-born economist and Nobel Prize winner famous for his work on estimating national income. One of Kuznets interests was the nature of an assumed link between national wealth and inequality of the distribution of that wealth (Kuznets and Simon, 1955). He hypothesised that wealth inequality increases with wealth, but at some point the curve turns and inequality declines as social support systems such as a minimum wage, better education etc. take effect. This is referred to as the inequality Kuznets curve (IKC). Kuznets did not make the same assumption for environmental degradation, but in 1991 other researchers suggested that the same relationship may hold sway (Ekins, 1997; Stern, 2004; Dinda, 2005). This was six years after Kuznets death, but both the EKC and the IKC have the 'good news' message that economic growth will eventually right wrongs. While there may be pain along the way, a worsening environment or greater inequality, they can be addressed. It is quite literally the pot of gold at the end of the sustainability rainbow; the promise that we will get there provided we can increase wealth. As can perhaps be imagined, the EKC theory expressed in Figure 5.7a has been the subject of a vigorous debate.

As with most of the other concepts discussed in this book, there is a substantial literature on the EKC which can only be touched

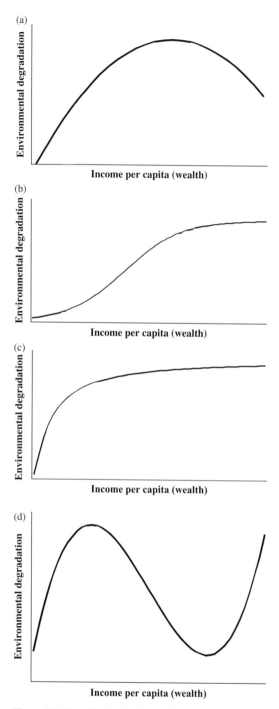

Figure 5.7 Hypothesised relationships between national wealth and environmental degradation:

(a) quadratic: the classic form of the relationship as set out in the EKC;

(b) logistic;

(c) logarithmic;

(d) cubic.

upon here. We have already looked at the problem of assessing 'degradation' in financial terms and how dependent this is on good-quality data. Perhaps understandably, this same issue has hindered the gathering of conclusive evidence for a quadratic form of the EKC and as a result, contradictory messages often emerge from the literature (Stern *et al.*, 1996; Ekins, 1997; Torras and Boyce, 1998; Cole, 2003; Perman and Stern, 2003; Stern, 2004; Galeotti and Lanza, 2005; Nahman and Antrobus, 2005; Aslanidis and Iranzo, 2009; Mills and Waite, 2009). Any attempt to generate a relationship between complex sets of empirical data on environmental degradation, with all the problems of time delay and trans-boundary effects as pollutants can easily cross national borders, will inevitably involve a simplification (Harbaugh *et al.*, 2002). After all, a number of lines of differing shape can be fitted using standard statistical techniques to any dataset and each fit may well be statistically significant (Harbaugh *et al.*, 2002). A quadratic-type EKC, as shown in Figure 5.7a, could be just one of these and thus we could easily deceive ourselves into believing that if such a line can be fitted then the economic theory behind it must be right (Galeotti and Lanza, 2005). Sobhee (2004), for example, suggests that the quadratic assumption may be wrong and a logistic-type model akin to those we looked at in Chapter 3 for population growth may be more appropriate (Figure 5.7b). In that case there is a flattening of degradation at some level of income and not an eventual decline. A slight variant on the logistic is the logarithmic model, where the line does level out, but keeps increasing, albeit at a slower rate (Figure 5.7c). Some have even suggested a 'two-hump' (cubic) polynomial curve which implies that, while degradation improves in the short term, with wealth it eventually worsens (Figure 5.7d; Rupasingha *et al.*, 2004; Bousquet and Favard, 2005). None of these options have anything like the 'good news' message of the quadratic form of the EKC.

So what evidence is there for a quadratic 'good news' EKC? Well, it has to be said that this is limited at best, even after a substantial effort to look for it (Ayres, 2008) let alone deriving an optimistic message for policy from what has been found (Ciegis *et al.*, 2008). Even when a convincing picture does emerge, it can disappear when the analysis is repeated with a different technique (Wagner, 2008). At times, the search for a 'good news' quadratic form of the EKC seems like trying to hold water in your hands. For example, Figure 5.8 presents the results of some analyses that were generated using national income data and components of what is called the 'environmental sustainability index' (ESI). ESI

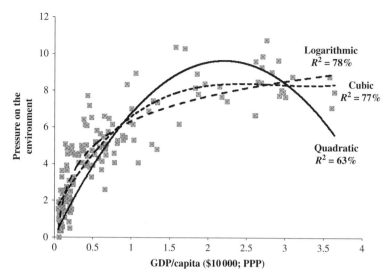

Figure 5.8 Attempts to fit various curves to a real dataset. Data points are values of GDP/capita and pressure on the environment for 145 nations. GDP/capita is for 2002 (adjusted for Purchasing Power Parity), while pressure on the environment is a composite indicator extracted from the environmental sustainability index (ESI; sedac.ciesin.columbia.edu/es/esi). The R^2 values indicate 'goodness of fit' of the lines to the data.

datasets include estimates of pollution for nation states and these can be plotted against income. While the ESI also has its critics, the authors do take great pains to present and explain their data. The vertical axis in Figure 5.8 is a complex indicator of pressure placed on the environment, and here it is assumed that this pressure is related to degradation. At first glance, the data would seem to match a quadratic trend, as hypothesised by the EKC. The R^2, a statistic which measures how well the line fits the data, is reasonably high at 63%. So is the case proven? Well, unfortunately not, as we can also fit logarithmic and, indeed, cubic lines to the same data, and if anything the R^2 is higher for these (77 and 78%) than it is for the quadratic. The problem is that we don't have enough points to the right of the graph to give us a better idea as to what happens with regard to degradation when countries get to that income. Instead, many of the points are bunched at the left side of the graph. But, while Figure 5.8 may not provide a decisive form of the relationship between wealth and degradation, it does reinforce the notion that a relationship of some form does exist. However, if we assume that the nature of the

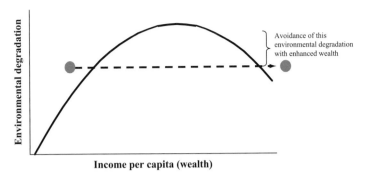

Figure 5.9 Tunnelling through a hypothesised quadratic relationship between national wealth and environmental degradation.

relationship between environmental degradation and wealth is quadratic then the trick is to try and 'tunnel' from the left-hand side of the graph to the right-hand side, while avoiding the supposed peak of environmental degradation, as shown in Figure 5.9.

It should also be borne in mind that the ability of people to survive – their resilience to adversity – could also be quite different as we move from the left- to the right-hand side of Figure 5.8. At the left-hand side, where pressure on the environment is relatively low, we may seem to have a contradiction of the quotation from the Johannesburg Summit given above. After all, in this part of the graph wealth is also relatively low, so surely this implies that development is a bad deal for the environment. So isn't the answer for all to move to the left of Figure 5.8 rather than the inexorable move to the right-hand side? It must be remembered that the components of the ESI are mostly those related to industrialisation, such as release of pollutants into the atmosphere and water. Thus, environmental degradation is being portrayed in but one way, and it is a vision chosen by the creators of the ESI and could miss or under-estimate other types of environmental degradation. For example, the ESI does not include a component for soil erosion, and that could be an important issue for subsistence farmers trying to survive in fragile environments or countries located to the left-hand side of Figure 5.8. The ESI shares the same underlying issue of subjectivity that we can find with GPI.

5.4   SUSTAINABLE LIVELIHOODS

So far in this chapter we have explored the relationships between economics and the environment at a relatively large scale: that of the nation state. But these same concerns of integrating the socio-economic with the environmental also play out at the level of house-holds and, indeed, individuals, and these smaller-scale impacts could well be hidden when we look only at larger scales. The devices we have discussed in Sections 5.2 and 5.3 will not be of much help here; they are designed for the macro scale and not the micro scale. Efforts have been made to try and apply approaches such as the GPI to smaller spatial scales such as cities, but the inherent problems of subjectivity do not go away and some even argue that they are intensi-fied (Clarke and Lawn, 2008).

The need to analyse sustainability at smaller social scales has led to the development of what is called the sustainable livelihood approach (SLA). SLA was designed to help with an appreciation of sustainability at the level of the household and is founded upon an analysis of availability and use of 'capital'. We have already come across the term 'capital' in Section 5.2 when we discussed the differ-ence between man-made (produced) capital, such as infrastructure and machinery, and natural capital (minerals, energy sources, forests and so on). The reader may have noticed that what is missing from this list is people, i.e. human capital (labour and skills). The reason is straightforward in the sense that EDP includes the economic cost of physical degradation of capital (roads crumbling, forests destroyed etc.) and this is not so easy with human capital. By way of contrast to 'green accounting', SLA includes a consideration of all types of capital and thus provides a much broader vision of the interaction between people and their environment.

SLA has been in vogue since the late 1990s, especially in the context of less-developed countries; populations existing to the left-hand side of the distribution in Figure 5.8. It has been a central plank of the strategy adopted by a number of aid agencies, including the UK Department for International Development (DFID). A White Paper produced by the New Labour government led by Tony Blair in 1997 stated their intention to:

> ... refocus our international development efforts on the elimination of poverty and encouragement of economic growth which benefits the poor. We will do this through support for international sustainable development targets and policies that create sustainable livelihoods for poor people, promote human development and conserve the environment. (DFID (1997, Summary, page 6))

This statement is perhaps not all that surprising, given the established linkage between poverty and environmental degradation already alluded to in this chapter, but what exactly are these 'sustainable livelihoods' that DFID intends to help create? One definition is provided by Chambers and Conway (1992) some five years before the White Paper was published:

> A livelihood comprises the capabilities, assets (stores, resources, claims and access) and activities required for a means of living; a livelihood is sustainable which can cope with and recover from stress and shocks, maintain or enhance its capabilities and assets, and provide sustainable livelihood opportunities for the next generation; and which contributes net benefits to other livelihoods at the local and global levels and in the short and long-term. (Chambers and Conway (1992, page 7))

In this definition we have a number of strands operating together. On the one hand there is a requirement for livelihood to be able to recover from 'stress and shocks', but also to be able to 'maintain and enhance' capabilities and assets into the future. A central element in this 'resilience' to stress and shocks is the diversification of capitals that comprise 'livelihood'. Carney (1998) provides a simpler vision of sustainable livelihood which also has resonance with that of Chambers and Conway:

> A livelihood comprises the capabilities, assets (including both material and social resources) and activities required for a means of living.

and, when merged with sustainability

> A livelihood is sustainable when it can cope with and recover from stresses and shocks and maintain or enhance its capabilities and assets both now and in the future, while not undermining the natural resource base.

Like so many of the other sustainability topics covered in this book, SLA did not arise out of a vacuum, but was instead the product of an evolution from a number of older trends and ideas. For example, there are echoes to the work of Nobel Prize-winning economist Amartya Kumar Sen and his writing on the importance of capital and optionality as a way of people lifting themselves out of poverty (Sen, 1984, 1985). The United Nations sponsored Human Development Reports (HDR), which began in 1990, were heavily influenced by the writing of Sen and took as their starting point an unambiguous focus on the wellbeing of people, albeit with a nod towards environment:

> The development process should meet the needs of the present generation without compromising the options of future generations. However, the concept of sustainable development is much broader than the protection of natural resources and the physical environment. It includes the protection of human lives in the

future. After all, it is people, not trees, whose future options need to be protected.
(United Nations Development Programme HDR (1990, pages 61–62))

The 'phrase it is people, not trees, whose future options need to be protected' in the HDR can be misleading, as it may imply that the environment is of secondary importance, but the aim is not to seek to facilitate human development at the expense of the environment. Indeed, as Carney puts it:

> *However, while it [sustainable livelihood] starts with people, it does not compromise on the environment. Indeed one of the potential strengths of the livelihoods approach is that it 'mainstreams' the environment within an holistic framework.* Carney (1998)

> *Short-term survival rather than the sustainable management of natural capital (soil, water, genetic diversity) is often the priority of people living in absolute poverty. Yet DFID believes in sustainability. It must therefore work with rural people to help them understand the contribution (positive or negative) that their livelihoods are making to the environment and to promote sustainability as a long-term objective. Indicators of sustainability will therefore be required.* (Carney (1998))

It is sometimes said that human development as espoused by UNDP has more in common with much earlier 'basic needs' approaches to poverty alleviation than to Sen's capabilities (Srinivasan, 1994; Ravallion, 1997), and Sen himself makes a clear distinction between them (Sen, 1984). But even so, the influence of the UN's vision of human development on SLA is clear. Going even further back in time there is an overlap with economics, or more precisely what was called 'new household economics', in the 1980s:

> *The major shortcoming of structural-functional and economic approaches to the household is the neglect of the role of ideology. The socially specific units that approximate 'households' are best typified not merely as clusters of task-oriented activities that are organized in variable ways, not merely as places to live/eat/ work/reproduce, but as sources of identity and social markers. They are located in structures of cultural meaning and differential power.* (Guyer and Peters (1987, page 209). Cited in de Haan (2005, page 3))

There are also resonances from the more macro-scale field of 'integrated rural development', which was in vogue during the 1960s and 1970s amongst major funders such as the World Bank.

SLA takes us some distance away from purely economic approaches to linking people with the environment, as epitomised by EDP and EKC. In SLA we have terms such as identity and power, and phrases such as 'cultural meaning' which are variable over time even

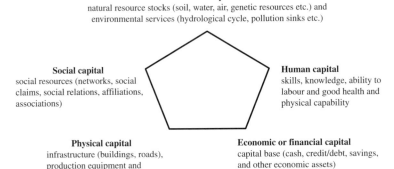

Natural capital
natural resource stocks (soil, water, air, genetic resources etc.) and
environmental services (hydrological cycle, pollution sinks etc.)

Social capital
social resources (networks, social
claims, social relations, affiliations,
associations)

Human capital
skills, knowledge, ability to
labour and good health and
physical capability

Physical capital
infrastructure (buildings, roads),
production equipment and
technologies

Economic or financial capital
capital base (cash, credit/debt, savings,
and other economic assets)

Figure 5.10 The 'capital pentagon' employed as the basis for sustainable livelihood analysis.

for the same community. We have moved from a purely quantitative approach, where everything is measured, to a far more complex and nuanced qualitative position. Also, SLA is an example of a 'multiple capital' approach where sustainability is seen in terms of all available capital (natural, human, social, physical and financial) and not only productive and natural capital (de Haan, 2000). They are often presented as a pentagon (Figure 5.10). Physical capital equates to the 'produced' capital we covered in Section 5.2. Interestingly, the contribution of 'natural capital' to household livelihood can readily be extended beyond the obvious productive and tangible assets such as land for farming to what are often referred to as 'ecosystem goods and services' (Aylward and Barbier, 1992; Boyd and Banzhaf, 2005). The following is a broad definition of such ecosystem goods and services, and some examples are shown in Table 5.3:

> *Ecosystem services are the conditions and processes through which natural ecosystems, and the species which make them up, sustain and fulfill human life. They maintain biodiversity and the production of ecosystem goods, such as seafood, forage, timber, biomass fuels, natural fiber, and many pharmaceuticals, industrial products, and their precursors . . . In addition to the production of goods, ecosystem services are the actual life-support functions, such as cleansing, recycling, and renewal, and they confer many intangible aesthetic and cultural benefits as well. (Daily (1997, page 3)).*

Here we have a clear distinction between 'goods', such as availability of water from streams, but also 'services', such as the cleansing of that water by an ecosystem (Norberg, 1999). Those 'services' are a human

Table 5.3 *Some examples of ecosystems goods and services.*

	Goods	Services
Non-renewable	Renewable	
Rocks and minerals	Water	Purification of air and water (particles, micro-organisms, chemicals)
Fossil fuels (oil, gas)	Air	
	Plants and animals (food, medicine, fodder, fibre, fuel wood)	Maintenance and renewal of soil and soil fertility; pollination of crops and other useful plants; dispersal of seeds; provision of fodder and food for useful animals; control of pests and diseases
	Soil	Control of soil erosion; stabilisation of climate (including rainfall patterns); reduction of incidence of floods and drought

Note that ecosystem 'services' refer to those that are of benefit to humans. Ecosystem processes (functions) and characteristics (such as biodiversity) help to generate these services.

interpretation of our gain from a complex set of components and processes in the ecosystem (Costanza *et al.*, 1997; de Groot *et al.*, 2002; Boyd and Banzhaf, 2005). While the 'goods' may be relatively clear, the problem often rests with the identification of components and processes that deliver the services. This may not be straightforward. For example, some argue that biodiversity is important for maintaining ecosystem services, while others disagree (Mertz *et al.*, 2007). A further complication is one that resonates with the rest of this chapter and, indeed, with the discussion of total factor productivity in Chapter 2 in that the 'ecosystems goods and services' approach to natural capital often goes hand in hand with attempts to cost it in economic terms (Miller, 2003; Curtis, 2004; Winkler, 2006a, 2006b; Barbier, 2007). Thus, taking agricultural production as an example, we would cost not only the inputs provided by the farmer

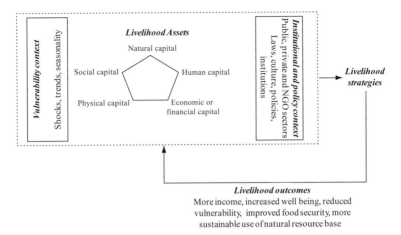

Figure 5.11 Outline of the Sustainable Livelihoods approach.

(labour and so on), but also any materials he or she utilises from the environment, which are typically seen as 'free' (O'Hara, 1997). The discussion in Chapter 2 and indeed earlier in this chapter has already highlighted the complexities involved with costing nature (Chee, 2004; Straton, 2006). Such 'goods and services' are not 'traded' as such, so determining economic value is not easy and neither is ownership. Indeed ecological processes can provide services for people living many miles away. Clearly we have a long way to go. An interesting development proposed by Hau and Bakshi (2004b) is to employ exergy as the basis for an analysis of ecosystem goods and services as one could do for any industry. As well as an expansion of what comprises 'natural capital', the list in Figure 5.10 can be added to. Odero (2006), for example, has made the suggestion that 'information' should be included as a sixth asset.

The logic behind SLA is set out diagrammatically in Figure 5.11. Once the capitals have been identified and assessed, it is necessary to explore the vulnerability context in which the assets exist; what are the trends, shocks and stresses? Thus, it's not only a matter of knowing what is there now, but also what are the trends and what could happen in the future. From here it is necessary to look at the policy and institutional context within which livelihoods are situated, and only then can it be possible to develop strategies which can help enhance livelihood. The assumption is that these planned outcomes would feed back so as to enhance livelihood assets and make them less vulnerable to shocks etc. One of the outcomes often called for as a result of applying an SLA is a diversification of livelihood, for example by enhancing the human capital base through learning and education (Butler and Mazur, 2007).

While SLA has an appeal precisely because it tries to take a more holistic perspective towards the interaction of people with their 'environment' (in its broadest sense of also including a socio-economic dimension), it has not been without its critics. While the language is certainly more holistic and qualitative, in practice it is still very much a capital-based approach to sustainability as indeed is 'green accounting'. The danger is that SLA can become a rather mechanical and quantitative cataloguing exercise of capital and pre-dictions as to what could happen to that capital rather than an analysis which encompasses dimensions such as 'cultural meaning'. Also, while a more holistic stance towards capital is to be welcomed, the reality is often complex, and using this knowledge to interpret livelihood is not straightforward. The pentagon in Figure 5.10 may indeed be a neat representation of important capitals, but each could contain many elements, such as the ecosystem goods and services mentioned under 'natural capital', and the question becomes one of identification as to what are important and how they are to be assessed? Obviously there is an element of 'context specificity' here, as the mix of capitals as well as the stresses and shocks that apply to them could be quite different, even between villages located but a few miles apart. At one level it might sound fairly obvious. For example, the physical asset of significant importance for a rural household is clearly land, and surely land area can be easily meas-ured? We can also assess its quality in terms of supporting crop production and thus begin to estimate parameters such as total factor productivity discussed in Chapter 2. For households dependent on fishing, we can do the same thing in terms of access to fish stocks and trends of effort and landings. But land ownership can be complex, as a household may own many irregular parcels of land which can be spatially scattered at varying distances from the place of residence. Also, of course, there is a difference between ownership and access to land through rent or gift. The latter can be highly volatile. Finally, we are heavily reliant upon the participation of those at the centre of the analysis, yet the key questions being asked over capital ownership and access can be highly sensitive for all sorts of reasons. It would not be surprising if households withhold information that they feel may compromise them in some way. Again, taking land ownership as a seemingly straightforward example, in many countries tax payments are related to land area and/or sales of produce. It would thus not be surprising if a household withheld information about the area of land it owned or the income they generate from that land, or indeed from any other livelihood activity. Finally, as we have seen with the Peruvian Anchovy example in Chapter 3, there is much uncertainty in any well-meaning attempt to assess trends let alone vulnerability to any shocks that might happen. No one foretold the collapse of the Anchovy fishery, or if they did no one seemed to listen, and the impacts on livelihoods of the fisher families was immense. Such shocks can have massive impacts at household scales, including abandonment of villages and migration, but are impossible to predict, except at relatively short timescales. As a result of all this, there is much complexity in SLA. The diagram of the process in Figure 5.11 maybe a neat and simple representation, but people's lives are complex. An attempt to make a 'quick' analysis as the basis for policy change could also result in a 'dirty' one driven by the needs of those doing the SLA and not necessarily those meant to benefit.

5.5 CONCLUSION

Sustainability has economic and social dimensions which don't just sit alongside biological concerns, but have to be fully integrated. In this chapter we have looked at a number of ways in which this has been attempted. Putting aside concerns as to whether we can really place an economic value on the environment, the 'green' GDP approach does build from a well-established methodology and measure of economic activity and thus has the advantage of starting from a place recognised by politicians, policy-makers, managers and indeed the media. Trends in national income over time and, indeed, comparisons across different countries and regions are typically achieved by employing GDP as a measure, and such trends do receive a great deal of publicity in the national and international press. Thus, starting from that established point of reference and introducing a 'green' flavour would appear to have a reasonable chance of influencing those with power to bring about change. Both the EDP and GPI, the two examples discussed here, have been designed with adoption in mind. They are not purely academic exercises, but attempts to change behaviour or at least help with transparency as to what is happening to society and the environment. But have they been successful in this objective? Unfortunately, the jury is still out as there are surprisingly few studies of the 'use' of GDP and GPI in policy. The verb 'use' of course does have many connotations, so we will leave a fuller discussion till the last chapter of the book. What has to be stressed is the subjectivity of the GPI. It represents a vision of what is desirable and thus reflects the value judgements of its creators.

The EKC is not so much a device to influence policy in a specific sense, but is instead a means of envisaging the relationship which exists between wealth and impact on the environment. The hypothesis of an increase in environmental degradation with an increase in wealth as countries industrialise, followed by an improvement as better legal protection, enforcement and technology emerge is an appealing one. The hypothesis certainly has repercussions for policy. The 'good news' of the quadratic form of the EKC implies that, while there may be pain along the way, the pursuance of wealth creation eventually results in a de-coupling between environmental damage and national wealth. This is not to say that a country should not try and 'tunnel' its way through the curve and avoid as much of the peak in environmental damage as possible, but there is a light at the end. The problem with this message for policy is that empirical evidence for the 'good news' form of the EKC has been highly elusive. Many have looked, but so far the evidence is far from being conclusive. Maybe there is no 'good news' for the environment as we continue to increase our wealth. Maybe there is no de-coupling, only a lessening of the degree of environmental degradation which occurs.

The final example covered in the chapter is the Sustainable Livelihood approach (SLA). This is in marked contrast to 'green accounting' in a number of respects. Firstly SLA was designed for much smaller scales of human community; the household rather than the nation. Secondly, SLA goes beyond economics and takes us in the much wider domains of the social and cultural aspects to human existence. Inevitably this means a move away from expressing the relationship between people and environment as numbers, but into a richer and more qualitative appreciation. Indeed it would not be an exaggeration to say that SLA is about analysing human life; our existence, dreams and ambitions. SLA is thus by far the most complex of any of the approaches covered in this chapter. Thirdly, unlike 'green accounting', SLA was designed as an approach to be applied primarily in the developing world. It was conceived as a way of helping people to improve their lives, albeit with externally mediated facilitation, so as to derive an understanding of 'what is present' and what can be done. Thus, like 'green accounting', SLA is meant to be a catalyst for change, but which takes on board a much wider view of people's lives beyond monetary transactions. However, the generic nature of the methodology implies that it can be applied in any context, including those of the developed world. The problem with SLA is its breadth. While the capital available to a household can be identified and its resilience to stress can be assessed, putting all of this together into a picture of 'livelihood', let alone what can be done to improve matters, is far from being easy. Inevitably, the story will vary a great deal between different places and, indeed, households in the same place, so trying to arrive at something that works in terms of a successful intervention for many without disadvantaging others is quite a challenge. The granularity of livelihoods does tend to resist generalisation.

6

The 'doing' of sustainability

6.1 INTRODUCTION

Chapters 2 to 5 have set out theories and approaches to sustainability. Some of these are focused primarily on maintenance of production over time and what needs to be done to achieve that. Total factor productivity attempts to view production through the lens of all that is needed to produce an output, including man-made and natural inputs. Maximum sustainable yield is a theoretical basis for maintaining harvests from a dynamic population resource such as a fishery. In Chapter 4 we looked at industrial production and how we can envision production or the provision of a service in terms of energy and related concepts of emergy and exergy. We also explored ways in which industrial processes can be analysed through material flows and life cycles. In Chapter 5 we encountered economic approaches and the valuation of both man-made and natural resources, their consumption and degradation. The chapter ended with an introduction to the concept of sustainable livelihoods.

Therefore, in this book we have encountered a mixture of approaches employed to better understand sustainability and more applied studies intended to help with the achievement of sustainability through management or policy formulation. The two overlap of course; research designed to analyse the life cycle of a GM crop will add to human knowledge and give us a better understanding of the environmental costs associated with production of GM and non-GM varieties at farm level, but the findings can also feed into policy. Indeed, some of the approaches covered so far are unashamedly geared towards influencing policy. Thus, while the EDP and GPI provide some interesting insights into valuation of social and environmental costs, they were designed to influence decision-making processes. Similarly, while SLA provides new insights into understanding livelihoods through capital and resilience to shocks, it was designed to help facilitate change. Sustainability research is really a mix of those old and often maligned terms – pure and applied.

In this chapter we will focus more explicitly on the applied nature of sustainability and provide further examples of putting the fruits of knowledge into practice. In particular we will discuss some of the limitations involved in making that translation from research into practice. In addition we will take a different slant to the earlier chapters and present sustainability not so much in terms of production, but via consumption. To some extent, of course, we have already done this as each of the chapters has looked at the inputs needed to sustain a production process, livelihood or, indeed, an economy. We also mentioned consumers and 'desired use' of a product or services in the context of material intensity in Chapter 4, but here we will go further by looking explicitly at the ramifications of consumption on a global scale. We will do this by exploring the ecological footprint and its relative – 'food miles'. From here we will discuss one of the tools that is widely applied to make sustainability a reality, namely indicators. The chapter will end with a section on stakeholder participation; how we can engage those who have an interest in a sustainability initiative so as to enhance the prospects of success.

6.2 ECOLOGICAL FOOTPRINT: THE GLOBAL REPERCUSSION OF DEMAND

The ecological footprint (EF) is an attempt to describe the impact a country, region, city etc. has in terms of the land area required to support it (Wackernagel and Rees, 1996; Holmberg et al., 1999; Ferguson, 2002; Wackernagel et al., 2002; Haberl et al., 2004b; Global Footprint Network, 2005; Kitzes and Wackernagel, 2009). This is not to be confused with the 'physical footprint'; the physical land area occupied by the spatial unit. A city may occupy but a few square kilometres in physical terms, yet have an EF of thousands of square kilometres as this is the area required to support the population of that city given current consumption patterns. It is the bioproductive land supporting our populations that is one of our most significant natural resources, given that the surface area of our planet is finite (Haberl et al., 2004a). Once converted to a per capita basis, the EF can be used to compare different populations, with larger EFs being interpreted as being more wasteful and inefficient. The underlying implication, although not overtly stated by the creators of the EF, is a need for egalitarianism in terms of resource use (Vanderheiden, 2008). The ecological footprint is sometimes regarded as another example of 'green accounting' discussed in Chapter 5 (Lawn, 2007), and, given that it can be a proxy measure of 'impact' on the environment, it has been used as a variable in searches for the quadratic form of the environmental Kuznets curve, albeit with limited success (Caviglia-Harris *et al.*, 2009).

In the latest EF results (2005) available from the 'Global Footprint Network', individuals living in the UK have an average EF of 5.33 global ha (gha), while an average resident of the USA has an EF of 9.42 gha. We will come to the meaning of 'global hectares' later, but the implication from these results is that a resident of the USA appears to require almost double the resources of someone living in the UK. Why should this be so? Is it because the quality of life of someone living in the USA is twice as good as that of someone living in the UK or are they simply more wasteful? These are the sort of questions that EF is meant to generate and thus lead people to question their patterns of consumption. As a result, the EF has provided a powerful means of comparing consumption and, indeed, production across nation states.

EF begins with a consideration of six land-use types which are important:

(1)   Crop land
(2)   Forest land
(3)   Fishing grounds
(4)   Grazing land
(5)   Carbon uptake land
(6)   Built-up land (urban areas and dams).

They can be thought of as mutually exclusive demands on a finite global surface area. If land is planted to forest then it can't be used for crops or grazing and built-up land is lost to agriculture and forestry. This is a simplification, of course. In Chapter 2 we explored agroforestry systems, which do involve both trees and crops, and there is a growing interest in urban and peri-urban agriculture, but let us run with it for now. In order to allow aggregation to a single value, these land types are expressed in a common unit – the global hectare (gha), equal to one hectare of 'average' productivity calculated on a global basis. In this system global hectares are used as a unit of output (yield). Thus, one hectare of highly productive crop land will be the equivalent of more than one global hectare, while one hectare of poorly producing crop land will equate to less than one global hectare. Thus, each of

Figure 6.1 Location of Hungary in Europe.

these six land-use types are converted to a consumption of global
bioproductive land; the ecological footprint. This consumption is balanced against the ability of a spatial unit, often a nation, to meet some
of its own demand; so-called biocapacity. The ecological balance is
found by subtracting the EF from biocapacity. This can be positive
(the unit can more than meet its demands) or negative (the unit has
to import to meet its consumptive demands).

Calculation of the EF is a complex process and it is tempting not
to repeat it here. But, as with MSY, it can help the reader to appreciate
the logic and key assumptions behind the device and any associated
problems. A practical example will help, and the one employed here is
based on the EF for Hungary. Hungary is a land-locked country of
Europe (Figure 6.1), with a land area of 93 030 km^2 and a population
estimated to be 10 098 000 in 2005. Not all of the process will be given
here, and instead I will focus primarily on crop land.

The 'crop land' consumption calculation is one of the more complicated elements of EF so it is as well to start here. For Hungary, it is assumed that there are 81 crops produced in the country, and for each of these crops we know the national production (tonnes) and national hectarage, and thus can calculate the yield (tonnes/ha). In the case of alfalfa (also known as Lucerne; *Medicago sativa*), for example, the figures are as follows:

National production: 3 625 731 tonnes
National hectares: 153 290 ha
Yield: 23.65 tonnes/ha (production / area).

Alfalfa is a leguminous crop (a member of the pea family) largely used as a feed for dairy and beef cattle, sheep, goats and horses. It was mentioned in Chapter 2 when discussing some of the problems attributed to GM crops. However, while a yield in Hungary of 23.65 tonnes/ha for alfalfa sounds good, the yield of crops will vary from country to country for a variety of reasons, such as climate, agricultural practices and the presence of economic incentives. Indeed, the average global yield of alfalfa is actually 29.81 tonnes/ha; a little higher than the average yield in Hungary. The ratio between the yield of alfalfa in Hungary and the global yield is called the yield factor (YF):

$$YF_{alfalfa} = \frac{23.65}{29.81}$$
$$YF_{alfalfa} = 0.79$$

Therefore, the yield of alfalfa in Hungary is 79% that of the world average, or put another way, the production of alfalfa in Hungary would take place on 121 618 ha rather than the actual area of 153 290 hectares if a global yield average of 29.81 tonnes/ha was assumed to apply.

We can do the same arithmetic based on these assumptions for the remaining 80 crops, although in some cases the crop yield in Hungary will be higher than the global average. Maize, for example, is widely grown on a global scale and has an average yield of 4.9 tonnes/ha. Maize yields can be much lower than this for subsistence farmers in Africa, for example, but in Hungary the average yield is 7.6 tonnes/ha. Thus the 'yield factor' for Maize in Hungary is:

$$YF_{maize} = \frac{7.6}{4.9}$$
$$YF_{maize} = 1.55$$

We can sum up the areas for all crops in Hungary, if a global average yield is assumed, and it comes to 6 146 497 ha. The real figure for crop

Table 6.1 *Bioproductive global areas and equivalent factors used to calculate ecological footprint.*

Bioproductive unit	Actual area (billion ha)	Equivalence factor (gha/ha)	Equivalent area (billion gha)
Fisheries	2.89	0.4	1.15
Land			
Crop land	1.6	2.64	4.22
Forest	3.95	1.33	5.25
Grazing land	4.8	0.5	2.4
Built-up area	0.165	2.64	0.44
Total	**13.41**		**13.46**

Note: equivalent area (ha) is found by multiplying actual area (ha) by equivalence factor.

Source of data: Global Footprint Network (2005).

land in Hungary (not including unharvested crops), based upon agricultural returns, is 4 292 638 ha. Thus, Hungary would have to have some 43% more crop land than it does in order to maintain its total crop production, if global average yields were assumed to apply.

The next complication is one of comparing land-use types. One hectare of crop land will differ from say one hectare of grazing land in terms of biological productivity; crop land is typically more productive in a year than is grazing land. Table 6.1 lists the biological productivity equivalences of the six different land-use types. Crop land is considered to be 2.64 times as biologically productive as all land combined, while fisheries are only 40% as productive. These equivalences are important assumptions, of course, even though the architects of the EF do provide a rationale for these relative weightings. Therefore the 121 618 ha of alfalfa in Hungary needed to produce 3 625 731 tonnes (based upon the average global yield of that crop) equates to 321 570 gha of biologically productive land (= 121 618 × 2.64). This can be thought of as the global 'footprint' of the alfalfa production in Hungary (note how 'ha' has been replaced by 'gha'). Repeating this for all of the crop land in Hungary gives a 'footprint' of 6 146 497 ha (based upon global average yield of each crop) × 2.64 = 16 251 981 gha. This transition from a crop area to a bioproductive equivalent area needed to generate a production is a key step within EF estimation and the transition is presented graphically as Figure 6.2.

The remaining steps to finding the EF for crop land in Hungary essentially involve making various adjustments to this bioproductive

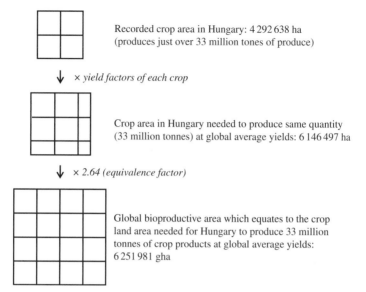

Recorded crop area in Hungary: 4 292 638 ha
(produces just over 33 million tones of produce)

↓ × *yield factors of each crop*

Crop area in Hungary needed to produce same quantity
(33 million tonnes) at global average yields: 6 146 497 ha

↓ × *2.64 (equivalence factor)*

Global bioproductive area which equates to the crop
land area needed for Hungary to produce 33 million
tonnes of crop products at global average yields:
6 251 981 gha

Figure 6.2 Conversion of crop land areas for Hungary.

area equivalent. The adjustments are needed in part because of the flows
in produce and pollution that take place across porous national boundaries. Thus, to begin with, we need to move from a focus on production to
one on consumption. Hungary does not necessarily consume all of the
crops it produces and some will be exported. Indeed, the country may also
import crop products if its own production fails to meet domestic demand.
Thus the 16 251 981 gha needs to be adjusted to allow for exports and
imports. Once we know the quantities of the crops exported and imported
we can follow the same logic as above and convert to bioproductive land
(assuming the conversion value of 2.64 applies for all crops). I will not do
this here, but the values for all crops imported and exported come out as 1
396 870 gha (imports) and 5 361 443 gha (exports). The balance of these
figures provides the consumption which took place in Hungary.

$$\text{Consumption} = \text{national production} + \text{imports} - \text{exports}$$
$$\text{Consumption} = 16\,1251\,981 + 1\,396\,870 - 5\,361\,443$$
$$= 12\,287\,408 \text{ gha}$$

There are yet more complications that need to be addressed. First, we
have to make an allowance for crop land which exists in Hungary, but
was not harvested, and thus would not show up in the production and
area figures used to calculate national yield. This can happen for a
number of reasons, perhaps because some farmers regard the yield as

too low to warrant the expenditure on harvest. The 'unharvested' crop land figure for Hungary in 2005 was estimated after adjustment to be 2 729 005 gha; by no means an insignificant value.

Another complication regarding the crop land global hectares for Hungary is the inclusion of animal imports and exports where those animals are fed on crop products (maize, soybean, wheat etc.) rather than grazing. Thus, the crop is converted to animal products before import–export and would not show up in the import–export records for crop products. Thus, movement of animal products can result in an underestimation of 'crop land' consumption. In terms of the crop land equivalents these animal product figures are 547 313 gha (imports) and 610 348 gha (exports). These are notably smaller than the area of unharvested crop land, but are certainly not insignificant. Taking all of this into account the new figure for consumption in Hungary is:

$$
\begin{aligned}
\text{Crop land consumption} = {} & 12\,287\,408 + \text{unharvested crop land} \\
& + \text{animal product imports} \\
& - \text{animal product exports} \\
\text{Crop land consumption} = {} & 12\,287\,408 + 2\,729\,005 \\
& + 547\,313 - 610\,384 \\
= {} & 14\,953\,379 \text{ gha}
\end{aligned}
$$

This new figure for bioproductive land equivalent has to be adjusted for population size (assumed to be 10 098 000 in 2005) to provide an EF for crop land:

$$
\begin{aligned}
\text{EF}_{\text{crop land}} &= \frac{14\,953\,379}{10\,098\,000} \\
\text{EF}_{\text{crop land}} &= 1.48 \text{ gha/copita}
\end{aligned}
$$

Thus, every citizen in Hungary consumes the equivalent of 1.48 gha of global bioproductive land each year, just in terms of crops. But, of course, Hungary has the potential to meet some of this consumption via its own resources and not all of that 1.48 gha has to be 'consumed' outside Hungary. What potential does Hungary have to meet this demand? In other words, what is the biopotential for crop land in Hungary?

The total area under crops in Hungary in 2005 according to the CORINE 2000 land-cover dataset is 5 163 078 ha. More details on the CORINE 2000 land-cover mapping project, an EU sponsored initiative, can be found at etc-lusi.eionet.europa.eu. This figure is based upon satellite imagery and is notably higher than the figure of 4 292 638 ha given earlier, based upon agricultural return data. Why the difference? Well some of it may be because of errors in reporting, and some crop land is unharvested as mentioned above and/or perhaps not reported. Thus the CORINE 2000 figure can be thought of as the potential crop land which existed at that time, although, of course, such figures can change dramatically, depending upon factors such as economic incentive. With the right incentives even highly marginal land may be cultivated. The average 'yield factor' for all of the 81 crops employed in the ecological footprint for crop land in Hungary is 1.47. Thus, on average, crop yields in Hungary are actually 47% higher than the global average. This figure is calculated from national and global yields available in 2005. Thus, the CORINE figure of 5 163 078 ha for Hungary equates to 7 584 875 ha if a global average yield is employed. Multiplying by the equivalence factor of 2.64 for crop land gives a bioproductive land equivalent of 20 055 202 gha. Once adjusted for population we have

$$\text{Bioproduction}_{\text{crop land}} = \frac{20\,055\,202}{10\,098\,000}$$
$$\text{Bioproduction}_{\text{crop land}} = 1.99 \text{ gha/capita}$$

This figure represents what Hungary could produce and can be compared with the $\text{EF}_{\text{crop land}}$ of 1.48 gha/capita. The difference between these figures is $+0.51$ gha/capita. Thus each citizen in Hungary actually consumed less in 2005 than the country could produce. In global terms that country does not, at least in theory for the crop land component of EF, need to consume any bioproductive land outside its own borders.

But crop land is but one element of consumption for each of the citizens in Hungary. What about the other elements? Given the length of the above explanation for crop land there is little point in repeating the same detail for all of the other components of EF, but it is worth highlighting some important aspects. I will do this for fishing grounds and carbon uptake land.

For fishing grounds, the calculation is a little simpler given that Hungary is land-locked and thus we only have to consider inland water bodies, including fish farms. For example, the production of Silver Carp (*Hypophthalmichthys molitrix*) in Hungary is 1 143 tonnes/annum and the global yield of this species is assumed to be 3.01 tonne/ha. Note that while fish are obviously harvested within a volume of water, unlike crops, pasture or forest which grow on a more or less two-dimensional surface, the adjustment is still made in terms of a surface area of water. Therefore the 1 143 tonnes/annum of Silver Carp equates to a relatively small global surface area of 378 ha, once a global average yield of 3.01 tonnes/ha is assumed. Applying the equivalence factor of 0.4, these 378 ha convert to just 151 gha of bioproductive surface area. There are only 12 fish and other species in total which are 'produced' in Hungary, so this calculation is repeated for all of them, giving a total bioproductive surface equivalent of 19 657 gha. We again have to include imports of fish products (which can, of course, be very significant for a land-locked country) and exports, as we did with crops, and the results are:

$$\text{Fishing ground consumption} = 19\,657 \text{ (production)}$$
$$+\,49\,998 \text{ (imports)}$$
$$-\,4\,603 \text{ (exports)}$$
$$=\,65\,052 \text{ gha}$$

Once divided by the population size of 10 098 000 this gives a relatively small EF for fishing grounds of just 0.01 gha/capita; much lower than the corresponding value for crop land.

The CORINE 2000 assessment of inland water in Hungary is 173 752 ha. The architects of the EF assume that the average production of fish and other harvested species for inland water is 1.0 tonne/ha (on a global scale) and, thus, after adjusting for biocapacity (0.4), we have 69 010 gha of global bioproductive surface. Adjusting for population size as before gives us a value of 0.01 gha. Thus, consumption and biocapacity per capita in Hungary for 'fishing grounds' are both small and are, in fact, identical. Hungary is able to meet its 'fishing consumption footprint' from its own resources.

The 'Carbon uptake land' component of EF is different to the crop and fishing ground components. Rather than being founded on the notion of a global area required for production, the 'carbon-uptake land' represents the area required to sequester (via photosynthesis) the carbon dioxide emissions from fossil-fuel combustion. Some of the CO_2 will be sequestered by the oceans and some by land plants, notably pristine (unharvested) forest. The first step to estimating this component of EF is to find the CO_2 emissions, or equivalent, for the various sectors in Hungary (energy generation, manufacturing, transport etc.). The conversion from production of CO_2 to the bioproductive equivalent follows the same underlying logic as employed for crop land and fishing. It is assumed that the global production of CO_2 from these sectors is 3.59 tonnes CO_2/ha/year. It is also assumed that the ocean sequestration (capture) of CO_2 is approximately 25% of this production. Thus, of the 18.1 million tonnes gross output of CO_2 produced by the electricity and heat-production sector in Hungary, a proportion of this (4.56 million tonnes) would be sequestered by the oceans. The remaining 13.54 tonnes of CO_2 represents the net output from Hungary. On a global scale this equates to 13.54 / 3.59 = 3.77 million ha, and once converted to equivalent area of bioproductive land (multiply by 1.33; the biological

Table 6.2 *Main sources and production of CO_2 in Hungary*

Source of CO_2	Production (million tonnes CO_2 per year)	Bioproductive equivalent (gha)
Electricity and heat production	18.1	5 021 882
Other energy industries	1.9	527 159
Manufacturing industries and construction	8.46	2 347 244
Transport	11.92	3 307 228
Other sectors	17.3	4 799 920
Totals	57.69	16 003 433

Source of data: Global Footprint Network (2005)

Table 6.3 *Components of the Ecological Footprint for Hungary*

	EF (gha/ capita)	Biocapacity (gha/ capita)	Balance (gha/ capita)
Crop land	1.48	1.99	+0.51
Forest land	0.38	0.47	+0.09
Fishing grounds	0.01	0.01	0
Grazing land	0	0.15	+0.15
Carbon-uptake land	1.49	0	−1.49
Built-up land	0.2	0.2	0
Totals	3.55	2.82	−0.73

Source of data: Global Footprint Network (2005)

productivity equivalence for forest) this is just over 5 million gha. Across all major CO_2-emitting sectors in Table 6.3, this comes to just over 16 million gha, and 16.5 million gha, once other emissions of CO_2 besides the sectors in Table 6.3 are taken into account. Further allowance has to be made for imports and exports of emissions (i.e. products generated by the burning of fossil fuel) as we have done with crop land and fishing grounds, and the result is the following balance:

$$
\begin{aligned}
\text{Carbon uptake land} = {} & 16\,527\,224 \text{ (production)} \\
& + 24\,650\,241 \text{ (import)} \\
& - 26\,180\,211 \text{ (export)} \\
= {} & 14\,997\,254 \text{ gha}
\end{aligned}
$$

Once divided by population, the footprint for carbon uptake is 1.49 gha/capita. There is no biocapacity (unharvested forest) in Hungary for sequestering this carbon, to provide an offset, and the result is a balance of −1.49 gha/capita. This more than wipes out the favourable balances for the other components of EF.

The final results for EF and biocapacity for Hungary are shown in Table 6.2. The total EF is 3.55 gha/capita and the total biocapacity is 2.82 gha/capita. Therefore, the crop land footprint is some 42% of the overall footprint and 71% of the biocapacity. Interestingly, the biocapacity of Hungary is greater than its crop land and forest land consumption footprints. The overall ecological balance of 2.82−3.55 = −0.73 gha/capita is largely down to the EF of −1.49 gha/capita for carbon-uptake land. The pattern of EF components can be quite different across countries and some examples of this are provided as Table 6.4. The UK has negative ecological balances for almost all of the land-use types, with the exception of fishing grounds. By way of contrast, the USA actually has positive ecological balances for the majority of the land-use types and, like Hungary, it is the carbon footprint which mostly accounts for the negative balance of −4.4 gha/capita. Gabon and Mongolia have relatively large and positive ecological balances, largely because of their forest and grazing biocapacity, respectively.

Looking at Table 6.4, it is probably of no surprise that there is a great deal of variation in how global EF is distributed between nations (Hammond, 2006; White, 2007), and there is a relationship between EF and wealth. Figure 6.3 is a plot of EF as a function of GDP/capita (based on purchasing power parity $). Sure enough, as GDP increases so does EF, yet for each value of GDP/capita there is something of a range in EF, and this is particularly so for higher values of GDP/capita. Incidentally, Figure 6.3 suggests that EF keeps increasing with GDP/capita, at least over the ranges shown here, and does not have a levelling off or eventual decline (Boutaud *et al.*, 2006; Bagliani *et al.*, 2008; Caviglia-Harris *et al.*, 2009). Is there scope to reduce the EF while still maintaining GDP/capita? If we rearrange these same data in terms of EF/GDP plotted against EF we can see that the ratio (sometimes called the EF intensity or EFI; York *et al.*, 2004) increases as EF increases (Figure 6.4). Thus, at higher values of EF there is more EF being consumed for every dollar of national wealth and there is no sign of this levelling off.

Each country does have biocapacity to meet at least part of its EF. Intuitively it might seem that biocapacity will be broadly related to land area (larger countries could, in theory, have a greater biocapacity), but this is not necessarily so, as shown in Figure 6.5. The spread of data

Table 6.4 *Some example calculations of ecological deficit based upon ecological footprint (EF) and biocapacity.*

	EF	Biocapacity	Difference
(a) UK			
Crop-land footprint	0.87	0.64	−0.23
Grazing footprint	0.21	0.17	−0.04
Forest footprint	0.46	0.09	−0.37
Fishing ground footprint	0.08	0.55	0.47
Carbon footprint	3.51		−3.51
Built-up land	0.20	0.20	0.00
Totals	**5.33**	**1.65**	**−3.68**
(b) USA			
Crop-land footprint	1.38	2.30	0.92
Grazing footprint	0.30	0.29	−0.01
Forest footprint	1.02	1.78	0.76
Fishing ground footprint	0.10	0.55	0.44
Carbon footprint	6.51		−6.51
Built-up land	0.10	0.10	0.00
Totals	**9.42**	**5.02**	**−4.40**
(c) Gabon			
Crop-land footprint	0.43	0.55	0.12
Grazing footprint	0.04	4.65	4.61
Forest footprint	0.60	15.86	15.25
Fishing ground footprint	0.15	3.86	3.71
Carbon footprint	0.01		−0.01
Built-up land	0.06	0.06	0.00
Totals	**1.30**	**24.97**	**23.68**
(d) Mongolia			
Crop-land footprint	0.21	0.25	0.04
Grazing footprint	1.91	11.12	9.20
Forest footprint	0.12	3.25	3.12
Fishing ground footprint	0.00	0.00	0.00
Carbon footprint	1.22		−1.22
Built-up land	0.03	0.03	0.00
Totals	**3.50**	**14.65**	**11.15**

Source of data: Global Footprint Network (2005)

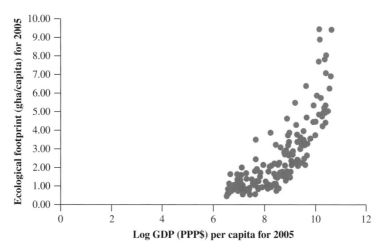

Figure 6.3 The relationship between ecological footprint for some nation states and GDP/capita (adjusted for purchasing power). Data are for 2005. GDP has been adjusted by taking the logarithm (base e). It seems that EF increases with national wealth.

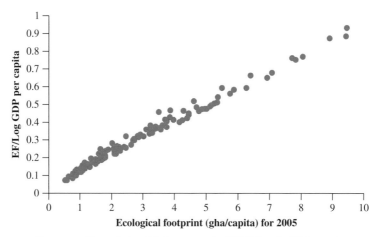

Figure 6.4 The relationship between the EF/GDP ratio (EF intensity, or EFI) for some nation states and EF. Data are for 2005. GDP has been adjusted by taking the logarithm (base e). More EF is 'consumed' per dollar national income as EF increases.

points is very 'messy' with no discernible pattern. We should also consider ecological balance as a function of GDP/capita, and this is shown as Figure 6.6. The pattern of data points is again 'messy', but there is a discernible trend towards more negative deficits with

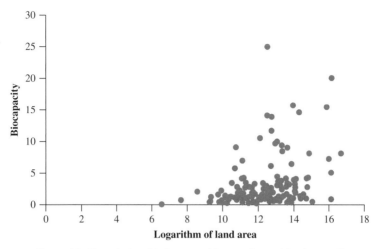

Figure 6.5 The relationship between biocapacity and land area of some nation states. There is none – no clear relationship exists!

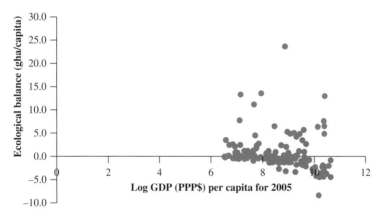

Figure 6.6 The relationship between ecological balance (biocapacity – ecological footprint) for some nation states and GDP/capita (adjusted for purchasing power). Data are for 2005. GDP has been adjusted by taking the logarithm (base e). Slight downward trend in ecological balance with increasing wealth, but not as powerful a message as that seen in Figure 6.3.

increasing wealth. This implies that even when we allow for capacity within the nation state, there is still a trend towards the wealthier countries taking up a greater share of the planet's bioproductive area. The same sort of analysis can be achieved by using wider measures of the 'quality of life' rather than just GDP/capita (Moran *et al.*, 2008). Similarly, it is possible to compare values of the EF for the same place over time (Wackernagel *et al.*, 2004). Indeed, it is possible to make a

Table 6.5 *Some countries having very different ecological balances,*
but similar GDP/capita.

Country	Ecological balance (gha/capita)	GDP/capita (PPP US$, 2005)
Switzerland	−3.7	35 633
Ireland	−2.0	38 505
Norway	−0.8	41 420
USA	−4.4	41 890

number of predictions based upon what future populations could do
(Kitzes *et al.*, 2008), but the clear message presented by the EF is that we
need to manage our consumption of resources and enhance productivity, while recognising that there are limits to what technology can do to
alleviate the problems we face (Rees, 1996, 2002; York *et al.*, 2003).

In essence, this is the advantage of the EF. It is a highly intuitive
device, given that it is expressed in units we can see and experience –
area – and therefore a large EF/capita can readily be imagined as being
'bad' (i.e. an indicator of greed). It is this clear connotation that has
led some to criticise the EF for being anti-competition or anti-trade.
Indeed, it is perhaps ironical given the central ethos upon which EF
has been founded, but this link between wealth and share of bioproductive land can be interpreted as a positive attribute in a neoliberal context. After all, can it not be argued that greater wealth has occurred
because of better ability to compete for resources and thus ecological
balance almost becomes an indicator of international competitiveness?
However, this would not explain how it is that some countries can have
very similar values of GDP/capita, but quite different ecological balances.
For example, in Figure 6.6 the two worst-performing countries in terms
of ecological balance were Saudi Arabia and Kuwait (both −8.4 gha/
capita), but there is a group of countries with similar GDP/capita and
yet quite different ecological balances. For example, Table 6.5 is a list of
only four countries from the same dataset that generated Figure 6.5.
These countries have similar GDP/capita of between $35 000 and
$42 000, yet ecological balances from −0.8 to −4.4 gha/capita. Do these
figures really suggest that the USA economy is that much more competitive than that of Norway, given that wealth/capita is so similar?

The EF is but a tool; a presentation of the state of consumption defined in standardised units to allow cross-comparison.
Modifications to the basic methodology have been suggested, including approaches based on emergy (Chen and Chen, 2006) and exergy

(Chen and Chen, 2007). There have also been efforts to include a monetary valuation dimension to EF (Zhao *et al.*, 2009) and to include it as a component of corporate social responsibility (Herva *et al.*, 2008). However, while I've only skimmed the surface of the EF calculation, I'm sure the reader can gain a feel as to the complexity involved and the assumptions upon which it is all built. As a result of the complexity and numerous simplifying assumptions it is perhaps not surprising that the EF concept has received some criticism (van den Bergh and Verbruggen, 1999, 2000; Ayres, 2000; van Kooten and Bulte, 2000). Underlying it all, of course, is the availability of good-quality data, both on national and global scales (Monfreda *et al.*, 2004; Hammond, 2006; Kitzes *et al.*, 2009). Global yields, used to convert national areas to global areas, are highly variable, across both space and time, and all of that variability in any one year becomes subsumed into a single value. Another major assumption is that of the equivalence factors. A single value of 2.64 to convert from any crop land to global bioproductive land does seem simplistic in the extreme, but one can easily imagine the complexities involved in determining this separately for all different species of crop. The use of global average yields to calculate global hectares discounts intensification of agricultural production (Fiala, 2008). Another issue is the exclusion of open oceans and less-productive land from biocapacity (Venetoulis and Talberth, 2008). Walsh *et al.* (2009) have made the point that methane (CH_4), another potential greenhouse gas, should also be included alongside CO_2. However, perhaps most important of all is whether the EF is actually being employed to influence management and policy, and it has to be said that the jury is still out (McManus and Haughton, 2006; Stoeglehner and Narodoslawsky, 2008). Why this should be so will be returned to at the end of this chapter. Nonetheless, some argue that EF as a measure of the balance between consumption and production should be seen as but one of a suite of assessments which are needed in any appraisal of sustainable development (Lawn, 2007).

6.3 FOOD MILES

EF can be viewed as a measure of consumption to augment the discussions we have had on sustainability of production in Chapters 2, 3 and 4. But EF is by no means the only attempt to explore sustainability through consumption, and another approach has been the use of 'food miles'. Food transportation burns up much fossil fuel, generates pollution (noxious gases and heavy metals) and contributes to global

This poster indicates roughly how much energy each form of transportation uses and how much carbon dioxide it produces. As any car driver knows, these figures depend a great deal on how the vehicle is driven, the vehicle's condition and technology, and the weather. These are some of our best guesses of industry-wide averages based upon the existing literature.

Figure 6.7 The evocative imagery of food miles (Farmscape Ecology Program, Hawthorne Valley Farm, USA).

warming via release of CO_2, especially as much of that now takes place across the globe. A walk around your local supermarket, or indeed corner, shop will quickly illustrate the distances that food must have travelled to arrive there, be it from farms just outside the cities where we live or from farms, fishing grounds and plantations on the other side of the world. Hence the notion of 'food miles', the total distance in miles the food item is transported from field to plate, has gained some popularity since the 1990s as a convenient indicator of sustainability (Iles, 2005). Like EF, it has the immediate appeal of logic; people can readily understand what it means and it is expressed in units (distance) that can be experienced and thus appreciated. The imagery is clear and evocative, and an example is provided as Figure 6.7; a poster produced as a part of the Farmscape Ecology Program of Hawthorne Valley Farm in the USA (www.hawthornevalleyfarm.org).

A report published in the UK in July 2005 explored the use and trend of food miles as an indicator of sustainability. The authors of the report estimated that all food transport to, from and within the UK reached 30 billion kilometres in 2002, and the vast majority (82%) of these food miles actually took place within the UK itself, with the remaining 18% accounted for as food transport to and from the UK. All of these food miles generated 19 million tonnes of CO_2, with 10 million tonnes of this within the UK. However, these emissions of CO_2 from food miles accounted for less than 2% of the UK's total emissions of

CO_2. The report estimated the economic impact of road transport of food within the UK at over £9 billion each year, largely due to additional congestion on the roads from HGV transportation and accidents (£7 billion per year). The remaining £2 billion is attributed to impacts of pollution, and wear and tear on the infrastructure. This cost is significant when compared with the gross value of the agricultural sector (£6.4 billion) and the food and drink manufacturing sector (£19.8 billion). Thus, the increase in transportation imposes a set of externalities (pollution, congestion) which society has to pay for (Jones, 2002; Pretty *et al.*, 2005). These figures are certainly substantial, but how did we manage to arrive at this situation? The report identified a number of reasons for the trend in increasing food miles:

(1)   Globalisation of the food industry; an increase in the volume of imports and exports of food
(2)   Concentration of the food supply base into fewer, larger suppliers, so as to handle distribution and storage in bulk
(3)   Changes in delivery patterns, with goods increasingly being routed through supermarket regional distribution centres using HGVs. Since 1978 to the time of publication of the report, the annual amount of food moved by HGVs in the UK had increased by 23% with the average distance for each trip also up by 50%
(4)   Centralised and concentrated sales in supermarkets. The pattern changed from one or more frequent visits to a local corner shop, often on foot, to fewer, but larger shop visits by car.

Given these trends in food miles and the associated negative impacts these have both economically and environmentally, the typical response has been to advocate a more local production and sourcing of food; a trend towards 'localism' (Jones, 2002; Hilson, 2008). However, it is interesting to note that one of the main conclusions of the 2005 report, and indeed a number of researchers working in this field, is that food miles by itself is not an adequate measure of sustainability (Edwards-Jones *et al.*, 2008). What is needed instead is a suite of indicators of which the food miles indicator is but one component. Why did they come to this conclusion? Well largely because sustainability is so complex and multi-faceted and a measure of food miles by itself is simply not enough. For example, the concept of food miles does not include the energy used to prepare food. It doesn't include cooking, for example, or processing and neither does it include energy employed to produce the food at farm level and the CO_2 emissions that could result. The latter can be far more significant than the transportation emissions of CO_2 and, given the differences between various products, a more effective choice may be to change household consumption patterns (Weber and Mathews, 2008). Thus while 'food miles' may be a useful and evocative headline, it does not present the complete picture. For that we require a range of indicators and/or a life-cycle analysis which includes transportation as but one element (Heller and Keoleian, 2003).

6.4   SUSTAINABILITY INDICATORS AND INDICES

Perhaps the most popular approach to helping us gauge progress in sustainable development has been the employment of indicators and indices (where an index is a composite number arising from the combination of more than one indicator). The terminology employed with indicators is rather varied, although terms such as sustainability indicators (SIs) and indicators of sustainable development (ISDs) are perhaps the most common. So far in this book we have come across a number of indicators, some of which could be regarded as SIs. EF and food miles, for example, can be regarded as indicators of consumption, while TFP and MSY have been employed as indicators of sustainable production. There are many other examples and reviews of SIs, including examples and discussions of issues involved are provided by Parris and Kates (2003), Mayer *et al.* (2004) and Moffatt (2008). The popularity of SIs should not be surprising, given the widespread use of indicators in biology (Burger, 2006; Pereira and Cooper, 2006) and economics. It has long been known that the presence of certain species is a good indicator of environmental conditions (Hilty and Merenlender, 2000; Carignan and Villard, 2002; Buchs, 2003; Diekmann, 2003). Einoder (2009), for example, provides a review of the use of seabirds as indicators of abundance of fish stocks, where they could clearly have some value in helping to address some of the problems we discussed in Chapter 3. It has also long been known that biodiversity is related to environmental 'quality', with the general assumption that higher biodiversity is 'better', even if there is some ambiguity in the meaning of the term 'biodiversity' and how it should best be measured (Haila and Kouki, 1994; Ricotta, 2005). A well-known example of a biodiversity index is the Shannon index (H; also called the Shannon–Wiener and Shannon–Weaver index). The index has a rather novel origin in information theory rather than biology where 'bits' of data (0 or 1) were translated into 'presence' and 'absence'. The technical formula for H is as follows:

$$H = -\sum_{i=1}^{i=s} p_i \log_2 p_i$$

where Σ = 'sum of' (sum over all species from 1 to S)

  S = the number of species in the community

  $\log_2$ = logarithm to the base 2 ('presence' or 'absence')

  p_i = the proportion of total sample belonging to the ith species
    such that:

$$p_i = \frac{n_i}{N}$$

where n_i is the number of individuals in species i and N is the total sample size.

The negative sign in H converts the results of the calculation from negative to positive (e.g. $-(-0.5) = +0.5$). It is required because the logarithm to the base 2 of values less than 1 are always negative ($\log_2$ of 1 = 0). In basic terms, the higher the value of H then the greater the biodiversity of the sample. However, finding the value of H for a particular community is not as easy as it may at first appear, given that species may be present in patches or have other unknown distribution patterns and, strictly speaking, H should be found over all of the species present and not just the ones which can easily be observed (Dallot, 2001).

Biodiversity and indicator species are not unrelated. A degradation in an environment is typically associated with a decline in biodiversity, and an increasing dominance from a relatively few tolerant species. But as we have already seen with our discussion of the environmental Kuznets curve in Chapter 5, words such as 'degradation' are subjective and can also be somewhat emotive. After all, it could be argued that farmers purposely 'degrade' their fields by reducing biodiversity and ensuring the dominance of one or relatively few plant species of economic or nutritional importance. That may be true in a technical sense, but is hard to imagine a farmer agreeing to use that term to describe what they do.

In an ecological context, a representative example of the derivation of a list of SIs can be found in a paper written by Rowland *et al.* (2004). These authors set out to create a set of indicators for a 'sustainable ecosystem', specifically a site located on a Canadian Forces Base at Shilo (CFB Shilo, Manitoba, 200 km west of Winnipeg).

The base has been used for training Canadian troops and indeed troops from other nations since 1910. The training area of CFB Shilo covers almost 40 000 ha and comprises a unique mix of open prairie, sand dunes and woodlands which makes it ecologically valuable. However, as can be imagined, the site is under pressure from military land use and the aim of the research was to develop a set of SIs which would help management to reduce ecological degradation. Therefore, the objective is clear and the boundary of the site is also defined. I certainly do not wish to imply that this is the only such example that could have been chosen of SI development or indeed necessarily is the best. I have selected it because their SIs provides a number of points of general interest that are often encountered with SI initiatives.

The Rowland *et al.* (2004) list of 12 SIs is provided in Table 6.6, and at first glance comprises a majority of indicators that one would expect in terms of ecological 'quality' (tree growth, changes in land cover, burnt area) and even numbers of the largest herbivore (Moose; *Alces alces*). These are termed 'state' indicators; they provide a snapshot of the environment. There are two other indicators – intensity of use of the site for military training and temperature – that are termed 'pressure' indicators; they measure the main forces that will change the values of the state indicators. Also shown in Table 6.6 are examples of what are termed 'response' indicators; indicators that measure what we are doing to try and manage a situation. In this case the 'response' is largely centred on environmental training. The relationship between pressure, state and response (PSR) indicators is shown in Figure 6.8. Pressure indicators influence state indicators, while response indicators are influenced by the value of the state indicators and in turn seek to influence the pressure indicators. The result is a circle of influence. Alongside descriptions of the indicators there are targets. Indicators are of little use unless we also have some idea as to what we want, even if it was only a matter of specifying direction (increase or decrease). Note how all the indicators are quantitative: they can be measured. Indeed these SIs have to be continually monitored and this requires an ongoing commitment and of course allocation of resources to do this. All too often indicator projects are seen as a 'once off'.

The first point to consider in the Rowland *et al.* (2004) case study is perhaps the most obvious – why have the indicators in Table 6.6 been selected and not others? Herein lies the essence of most SI lists, as they are, after all, human constructs and not laws of nature. Most SI lists reflect the background and interests of those that create them, although great care is often taken to justify the selection. Thus, it should

Table 6.6 *Example list of sustainability indicators (after Rowland* et al.*, 2004).*

	Indicators	Notes and targets
1	Amount and intensity of military training	Deemed to be satisfactory as long as ecosystem is not degraded as shown by any of the indicators below
2	Mean temperature (1 March to 1 August)	8.5 ± 2.3 °C (based on measurements over 1985 to 2001)
3	Amount of environmental training given to troops	
4	Number of moose in GHA 30 base area	318
5	% cover of coniferous tree growth	% pixel coverage in 1988 = 10.4%
6	% cover of riparian, fen and marsh	Riparian = 8.8%; fen and marsh = 6%
7	% cover of burnt area	0.4%
8	Change in cover of leafy spurge compared to 1988	Leafy spurge is an invasive non-native plant, so a reduction is preferable. Figure in 1988 = 11.8%
9	Change in cover of poor health grass compared to 1988	Reduction is preferable. Should be $\leq 6\%$
10	Change in cover of medium health grass compared to 1988	Reduction is preferable. Should be approximately 4.4%
11	Change in cover of bare ground compared to 1988	Reduction is preferable. Should be $\leq 10.2\%$
12	Whether soil was well graded in top 10–20 cm	Majority of sites should be well graded at this depth

Two other indicators recommended by the authors were: cover of healthy mixed grass prairie (percentage of healthy mixed grass should be $\geq 8.8\%$) and number of endangered species (should not increase). This is a Canadian priority and hence has to be included.

be noted that environmental 'quality' is defined by the indicators in Table 6.6 and there is potential for bias. This dilemma has long been acknowledged in indicator projects, although perhaps not stressed as often as it should be. The Rowland *et al.* (2004) study is no different in that regard, but is unusual in the way they have attempted to address the problem. Most SI studies usually comprise a list of indicators and lengthy rationales as to why the author(s) feel that their selection is the most appropriate. Rowland *et al.* (2004) have taken a different approach in that

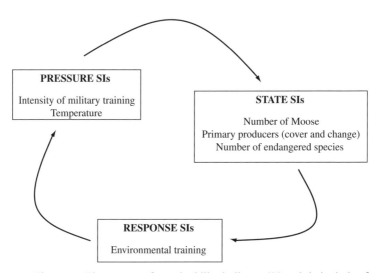

Figure 6.8 Three types of sustainability indicator (SI) and their circle of influence.

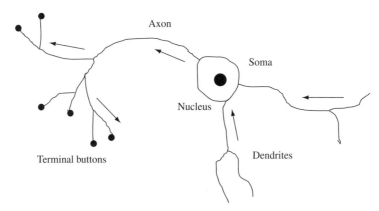

Figure 6.9 Simplified diagram of a biological neuron. Arrows indicate direction of signal – from dendrites which receive chemical signals from other neurons through the main body of the cell to the terminal buttons on to the dendrites of other neurons.

they employed an artificial neural network (ANN) to select the 12 SIs in Table 6.6. Thus the researchers could claim that the SI selection process was 'objective' in the sense that they emerged from the ANN, but how is that possible? In order to illustrate the logic it is necessary to explain how ANNs work and that in turn requires an explanation as to how they are grounded within biological processes.

An ANN is a model of a biological nervous system comprising a set of neurons (Figure 6.9). Neurons collect signals from other nerve cells

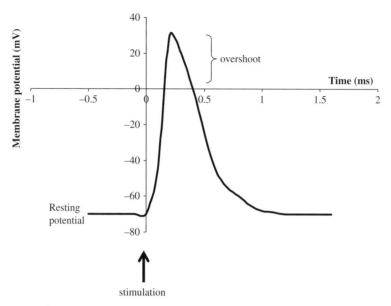

Figure 6.10 The nature of the nerve impulse.

along their dendrites, and once the aggregate input from these connections exceeds a certain threshold the cell 'fires' a signal through its
terminal buttons. The size of the signal is the same at the end point of
each of the buttons; there is no dilution effect. The signal, represented in
Figure 6.10, is carried by a potential difference across the cell wall of the
axon. In the resting neuron the difference is maintained by the active
pumping of positively charged ions out from the cell. During the signal
the permeability of the cell wall to these ions increases so the inside of
the cell becomes positive with respect to the exterior. Once the signal
reaches the terminal button the signal is carried across the synaptic gap
by a chemical neurotransmitter such as acetylcholine (Figure 6.11). The
neurotransmitter is released and activates a receptor site in the dendrite
of another neuron. In effect this is an 'all or nothing' process as the
signal either is or isn't transmitted'; there is no half-way state.

   Given the 'all or nothing' firing of a neuron and the fact that
there can be many of them, the human brain alone can have approximately 10 000 000 000 neurons, with each one having as many as a
1000 inputs from other neurons, the result can be highly complex. It is
this potential for handling complex information that makes an ANN so
attractive in sustainability. This is particularly so with the ability of the
ANN to extract patterns from complex data. As a simple example, the
ANN could be 'trained' to generate an output when a certain pattern of

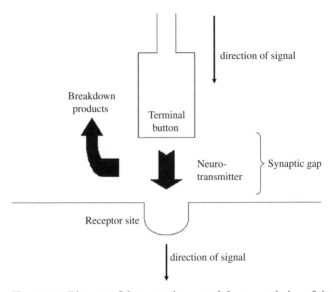

Figure 6.11 Diagram of the synaptic gap and the transmission of signals across the gap.

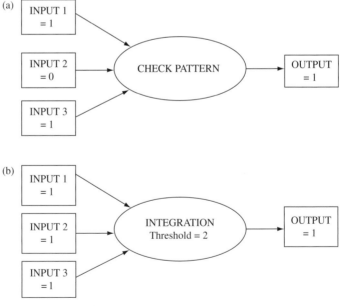

Figure 6.12 Two different approaches to the use of an artificial neural network (ANN): (a) pattern recognition: output is 1 when a series of inputs occurs (in this case 1, 0, 1); (b) integrating input values.

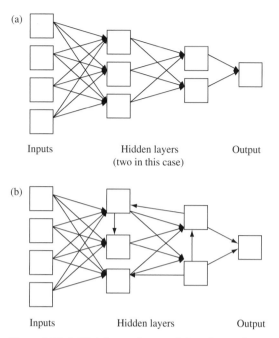

Figure 6.13 Artificial neural network based upon integration of input values with four layers: (a) feed-forward network; (b) dynamic network.

inputs occurs. In this case the ANN is trained to recognise a pattern of 1 0 1 in the three inputs and if this happens to generate an output value of '1' (Figure 6.12a). The neuron can also be trained to output a '0' or '1' if a number of input patterns occur. These are 'firing rules' based on pattern recognition. Indeed, so far there is nothing that a conventional computer algorithm using IF AND THEN operators could not do (IF input1 = 1 AND input 2 = 0 AND input 3 = 1 THEN output = 1).

A more complex approach would be to make this model mirror biological neurons by integrating input values and only generating a specific output once a threshold has been exceeded. In that case, the model is shown in Figure 6.12b. Only if the combined signals from the three inputs match or exceed the threshold (in this case '2') will there be an output. The three inputs do not have to have an identical weighting in the process of integration. Input 1, for example, may have a higher weighting than inputs 2 and 3. This may sound like a minor modification from the character-recognition example, but imagine an ANN with four layers, as shown in Figure 6.13. This is a network with a 4 – 3 – 2 – 1 architecture. There are four input units (nodes) which comprise the raw data for the network and these feed into a hidden layer of three nodes followed by a further hidden layer of two nodes. The output layer consists of just one node. While there are only 10 nodes in this network, the connections are complex. The 20 interactions could all be weighted differently, and, as a result, the output could vary substantially, depending upon the values of the inputs and the weightings applied throughout. Figure 6.13a is an example of a 'feed-forward' network, as at each layer the nodes do not interact with each other. A more complex network could include feedback between the hidden layers as shown in Figure 6.13b. This is a dynamic network, as values within the hidden layers will change constantly until for any set of inputs the network will arrive at equilibrium. If the inputs (or weightings) change, the network will shift to a new equilibrium state. Weightings can either be fixed or allowed to change (adaptive networks) with time.

Because of this flexibility ANNs are sophisticated systems and are particularly useful in the identification of patterns in input data, and have been applied in a wide variety of disciplines, including medicine, to identify disease, and in the estimation of fish abundance. The extension of ANNs into selecting SIs is a logical progression, and was chosen by Rowland *et al.* (2004) because the ANN will ensure 'a more scientifically sound plan, with indicators chosen involving little human bias' (page S130). They employed a 20–3–1 architecture and an initial suite of 62 potential indicators 'deemed potentially important in determining the overall health of the ecosystem'. There is still some potential for bias, of course, in terms of the initial selection of 62 SIs to be fed into the ANN and in the selection of criteria for the screening. From this ANN emerged the 12 SIs listed in Table 6.6. It should also be noted that there are two indicators at the foot of Table 6.6 which did not emerge from the ANN, but were nonetheless deemed to be important by the authors. One of them is the number of endangered species and was included as 'the preservation of species is a priority of Canada and therefore must be monitored'. This might seem like a dilution of a scientific process, but such compromises are not unusual with SI lists and, if anything, it represents the norm.

The final point of general interest arising from the Rowland *et al.* (2004) case study is their use of the year 1988 as the base point for comparison with the 'change' indicators. Clearly some sort of reference is required, but why 1988? Why not 1987 and 1989, or indeed why not 1978? Perhaps surprisingly, although not unusual with such lists of SIs, there is relatively little justification for 1988 as the reference year in their paper. One simple reason typical in such cases is the availability of existing good quality baseline data. As can be imagined the choice of a reference condition, which implies a state of the ecosystem that was deemed to be sustainable, is of critical importance. The same ecosystem can be labelled as 'sustainable' or 'unsustainable' depending upon the reference condition that has been used. In this example, the reference condition is a year, but it could equally be another ecosystem separated by space from the one under consideration, but which has received little human interference.

Despite all of these issues, it should be noted that SIs do have a major advantage in being tangible. The SIs in Table 6.6 can be measured and they do help frame an understanding of what these authors mean by sustainability in that context. We are not looking at abstract ideas expressed in a complex language but in variables that can be seen, touched and measured. The same conclusion has been reached in a number of SI projects operating in very different geographical and social contexts to that of the Rowland *et al.* (2004) case study. Rydin (2007), for example, also talks about tangible SIs helping to formulate a vision of sustainable development amongst community groups in London. Indeed, the usefulness of indicators as a means of facilitating interaction between experts and the public is an often claimed advantage of such tools.

6.5   PARTICIPATORY SUSTAINABILITY

The Rowland *et al.* (2004) example of the use of artificial neural networks to select a list of SIs is a classic example of an essentially top-down and technocentric process, i.e. a process conceived and created entirely by experts. The list of SIs are no doubt relevant and applicable within the specific context for which they were developed, and it can also be reasonably assumed that the same ANN process for selecting indicators could be applied in any context. Socio-economic and cultural SIs could well be part of this, even if some have to based on a quantification of inherently subjective feelings. While the use of an ANN is a good (in a technical sense) means of selecting SIs, there are situations where people may differ significantly in terms of their vision of sustainability and how it should be assessed. In such situations there are, quite literally, thousands of potential SIs that could form the starting point in an ANN, so who makes the decision over what to include and how they are to be weighted in terms of relative importance? Can basic human bias ever be removed from such a choice? Indeed, does it matter if there is bias?

The notion of including those meant to both benefit and be integrally involved in the achievement of sustainability, typically referred to as stakeholder participation, has become an important theme and has spawned a host of different approaches (Bell and Morse, 2003; Stringer *et al.*, 2006; Welp *et al.*, 2006; Newig *et al.*, 2008; Reed, 2008; Reed *et al.*, 2009; Schwilch *et al.*, 2009), including efforts within the private sector as a part of corporate social responsibility to bring companies and stakeholders together (Bhattacharya *et al.*, 2009; Muthuri *et al.*, 2009), and the interesting hybridisation of stakeholder participation and life-cycle assessment (Thabrew *et al.*, 2009). Unsurprisingly, there has been a substantial interest in bringing together stakeholder participation within the more ecologically based fishery management models outlined in Chapter 3 (Gray and Hatchard, 2008; Mikalsen and Jentoft, 2008; Varjopuro *et al.*, 2008). The principle which underlies all of this interest is enshrined within Principle 10 of the 1992 Rio Declaration of Environment and Development:

> *One of the fundamental prerequisites for the achievement of sustainable development is broad public participation in .decision-making. Furthermore, in the more specific context of environment and development, the need for new forms of participation has emerged. This includes the need of individuals, groups and organizations to participate in environmental impact assessment procedures and to know about and participate in decisions.* (UNCED (1992). Earth Summit. Preamble of Chapter 23, 'Strengthening the role of major groups')

This was stressed again five years after the 1992 Earth Summit:

> *Democracy, respect for all human rights and fundamental freedoms, including the right to development, transparent and accountable governance in all sectors of society, as well as effective participation by civil society, are also an essential part of the necessary foundations for the realization of social and people-centred sustainable development.* (UNCED (1997). Earth Summit+5. Paragraph 23)

Participation is as much a matter of human dignity as ensuring that sustainability is achieved most efficiently and at lowest cost (Miller *et al.*, 2005). Of course, in countries with a democratic tradition, participation is integral to the fabric of the society, but may be expressed at time periods (every four, five years or so, when elections take place) that may be unsuitable for regular intervention in sustainability. Also, participation in elections can vary and people are voting for a whole raft of issues and reasons and not just those important in sustainability. Thus, stakeholder participation is meant to supplement the usual democratic processes; not to supplant them. Even so, stakeholder

Table 6.7 *Sherry Arnstein's 'Ladder of Participation'.*

Type of participation	Characteristics
Passive	People are told about a decision related to sustainability, or what they have to do or what has happened, with no ability to change the decision
Functional	Participation is seen by managers or policy makers as the best way to achieve their goals or to reduce costs. The people have little control over what needs to be done, but may have some control over how it is to be done
Consultative	People are consulted about what needs to be done to achieve sustainability, but the way in which they are asked is set by external agents and this group also controls the analysis and presentation of the results
Manipulative	People are given limited representation on a committee, board or panel charged with implementing or managing sustainability. However, they have no real power as they may be easily outvoted by other members. As a result participation is a pretence, and the public has no real power
Interactive	People are involved in the analysis of condition, development of action plans etc., as part of sustainability. Public participation is seen as a right and not just a means of making implementation more effective
Self-mobilisation	People mobilise themselves and initiate actions without the involvement of any external agency, although the latter can help with an enabling environment.

After Arnstein (1969)

participation is a complex subject, largely because, like sustainability, it can mean many things to many people. Thus, in a section as short as this, all I can do is provide a brief overview of some of the key issues. Sherry Arnstein (1969), referring specifically to community development in the USA, derived what she referred to as a 'ladder of participation' that presents some of these different meanings (Table 6.7). They can extend from a 'passive' situation, where people may not be consulted at all (except perhaps in elections) to the other extreme, where the public mobilise themselves into action. In practice, it seems reasonable to assume that most sustainability projects which include an element of public participation probably operate towards the top end of Table 6.7.

During the 1960s there was a gradual disenchantment amongst social scientists with macro-economic policies as perhaps the main tool for development intervention by the richer parts of the world in helping those perceived as poorer (Sellamna, 1999). Their response was to move away from macro-scale interventions at the level of the nation state and regions towards what was called 'grassroots' initiatives where the engagement was at more micro-scale (village and household) levels. We have already touched upon some of this momentum when we discussed the sustainable livelihood approach in Chapter 5. Moving to these smaller scales made development more personal, but this was also founded upon a series of trends within the social sciences from the 1940s (Hoben, 1982). The writings of Kurt Lewin (1948) and others regarding organisational structures and management were highly influential. Lewin coined the term 'action research', based upon the notion that in the social sciences, where people research other people, there is no separation between researcher and researched. The very act of doing social science research can influence what people do, and Lewin harnessed this to create a philosophy of action research which embraced this inter-locking. Today we often use the term problem-solving methodologies (PSMs; Checkland, 1981; Checkland and Scholes, 1990) and they have increasingly become incorporated within sustainability projects (Bell and Morse, 2003; Conroy and Berke, 2004; Jonasson, 2004; Vantanen and Maritunen, 2005). Another important influence in the rise of participation was liberation theology and the writings of Paulo Freire (1972) primarily in Latin America (Aldunate, 1994).

One of the first formalised forms of stakeholder participation in a development context was referred to as rapid rural appraisal (RRA; Chambers, 1983). RRA emerged in the mid- to late-1970s with a focus on more local scales and founded primarily upon a rejection of the questionnaire survey approach which had dominated social science up to that point. Instead, the emphasis in RRA was upon qualitative approaches to collecting information; unstructured or partly structured conversations, use of diagrams and maps, transect walking and observation and so on. In themselves, these were not necessarily new techniques, but the way in which they were being used was new. In RRA the aim was to extract information as quickly as possible in order to provide the basis for a development intervention. In the 1970s most of the development interventions were still rooted within rural areas, based on an old and somewhat stubborn assumption that most of the poor were subsistence farmers and their families. Hence the term 'rapid' (to arrive at an analysis quickly) 'rural' (the groups being engaged were in rural areas) 'appraisal' (rather than research).

During the 1980s RRA evolved from being an essentially 'information extraction' process into a more action research and problem-solving orientation (Chambers, 1993, 1997). The new approach was termed participatory rural appraisal (PRA; the rural bit was later dropped in favour of the term participatory learning and action, PLA). PRA sought to facilitate change within a community in an 'action research' sense, with the stakeholders themselves taking some responsibility for change rather than expecting an external agency to bring it about. Thus PRA was not solely about collecting information in a one-way direction as was RRA, but a learning process amongst all those involved, with an aim of making things 'better'. Even the very meaning of the term 'better' was negotiable in this process rather than being imposed from outside. The 'tools' of PRA were ironically much the same as those of RRA and continued to borrow from the social sciences. It was more the philosophy (or epistemology) of PRA which was different from RRA.

Following the popularity of RRA-PRA in the developing-country context, some began to question whether the same approaches would enhance community development in the developed countries (see, for example, Sultana et al., 2008). This represents one of those rare examples where approaches and thinking originally created by researchers and workers in the developed world for implementation in the developing world began to be re-exported back to their point of origin! There has been a growing emphasis on participation as a means to facilitate 'knowledge rights' in scientific decision-making (Leach et al., 2002) and citizenship (Williams, 2004; Hickey and Mohan, 2005). The philosophy here is towards engendering a wider sense of emancipation or empowerment rather than immediate change (Chhotray, 2004). In order to achieve this, there is a plethora of different techniques and methods favoured by individuals and organisations, but all sharing a valuation of 'localism' which mirrors the emphasis we saw with the 'food miles' measure discussed earlier (Mohan and Stokke, 2000). Given this emphasis on the 'local', it is of no great surprise that sustainability has embraced participation as a core ideal (Rockloff and Moore, 2006), although the reality is often far removed from the theory (Eversole, 2003). There is also something of a tension between matching demands of local communities and experts (Lundqvist, 2001; Alberts, 2007). Based upon topography, wind speeds and so on, an expert may highlight an area as being ideal for the location of wind turbines, but the local community may want none of it. Thus, stakeholder participation is part of a complex mix of concerns within any planning process (Evans and Klinger, 2008). However, if the views of local communities are regularly over-ruled as a result of other considerations, then it is not difficult to imagine a rapid and growing disenchantment setting in, which would be detrimental.

Given the increased emphasis placed on stakeholder participation we have progressed to the stage where a project proposal may have little chance of success unless an element of stakeholder participation is included, even if the meaning of 'participation' let alone the practice within such proposals is somewhat nebulous (Poolman and Van de Giesen, 2006). Indeed, such has been the popularity of stakeholder participation in development that one writer (Francis, 2001) has claimed that it has taken on almost mystic undertones. Unfortunately, participation is often assumed to be another word for 'panacea' (Bevan, 2000; King, 2003); all a project need do is include an element of participation and success is guaranteed. However, while the need for stakeholder participation as a human right is laudable, there is surprisingly little evidence to support the contention that stakeholder participation generates positive benefits (Cleaver, 2001; Beard, 2005). One empirical study where a participatory approach was shown to provide benefits in terms of natural resource management in Bangladesh is provided by Sultana et al. (2007). Understandably, a number of critiques emerged of participatory approaches within development (Cooke and Kothari, 2001; Mansuri and Rao, 2004) and these were countered by proponents of the participation (Mutamba, 2004; Parfitt, 2004; Williams, 2004). But why would participation not succeed?

To begin with, it should be noted that employing participatory methods to help identify problems that need to be addressed does not necessarily mean that those problems can, or indeed will, be addressed. Maybe the community simply doesn't have the resources or power to bring about a required change (Mohan and Stokke, 2000). For example, a fishing community may argue that one of their major problems is a decline in fish yields, but if that common property resource is also being fished by other communities, some of whom may even live in a different country, doing something about this issue may be difficult. The outcome may perhaps be a somewhat bland set of conclusions that the community should make representation to perhaps distant politicians and hope for the best. But policy-makers and managers have many agenda, and frankly the concerns of a relatively small community having little power may not rank high on a list of priorities. Thus participation can become a corrupted term and achieve nothing more than highlight or even reinforce marked differences in power (Nuijten, 2004; Parkins, 2006). Indeed, at one extreme this so-called 'participation' provides a mirage for the state to claim that it has listened to the concerns of the community (after all the state paid for the project didn't it?), so therefore has 'done something', while in practice little has actually been achieved. Thus, it can be a way for the state to side-step its responsibilities (Mohan and Stokke, 2000).

Secondly, participation does assume that a consensus can be achieved within a community as to what needs to be done and how (Peterson *et al.*, 2005). The notion of consensus is often allied with an assumption that the community is both homogeneous and harmonious (Guijt and Shah, 1998; Mohan and Stokke, 2000). Thus, the community is assumed to be comprised of 'fishermen and their families' as a more or less homogeneous group, and to be at one (harmonious) in its analysis of the problem (e.g. declining fish yield) and how that problem can be solved. As a result of this apparent consensus, any potential solution(s) have legitimacy; they carry the weight of the community behind them (Heysse, 2006). Indeed, techniques such as multi-criteria analysis (MCA), integrated assessment (IA) and risk analysis have been designed to help elicit a pattern amongst the inevitable diversity of opinion that may exist within a community (Marjolein and Rijkens-Klomp, 2002; Willis *et al.*, 2004; Mendoza and Prabhu, 2005). But any community, even a relatively small one, encompasses a wide range of individuals and social units, spanning gender, age, ethnic, experience and wealth spectra, and a priori one would expect to find plurality rather than consensus (Hibbard and Lurie, 2000). For example, while the majority within a community may be fishermen, they might well have different capabilities and different skill sets. Thus, not all of them may be suffering from a decline in fish yield, as prices may increase and some can travel further or perhaps be able to fish in a different way. Also, of course, perhaps some households are engaged in a range of subsistence and income-generating activities. Thus diversity of perspective is not a bad thing (Dryzek and Niemeyer, 2006) and the participatory process may draw this out (van de Kerkhof, 2006), but this plurality may be reflected in quite different aspirations and visions as to what needs to be achieved and how (Holden, 1998; Castro, 2004; Peterson *et al.*, 2005). The complications which may arise provide a temptation on behalf of those facilitating the participation to play down the diversity and play up an apparent consensus which may not exist (Mendoza and Prabhu, 2005; Parkins, 2006). At the other extreme, the participatory exercise may do no more than draw out the views and wishes of those with the loudest voices and simply reinforce and exacerbate existing power inequalities (Mosse, 2001; Cornwall, 2003; Williams, 2004; Forde, 2005; Peterson *et al.*, 2005; Faysse, 2006; Few *et al.*, 2007; Soma and Vatn, 2009).

Stakeholder participation needs to be handled with care.

6.6   CONCLUSION

Consumption is as important a consideration within sustainability as is production. Any analysis of sustainability purely through the means of production will miss the driving force of demand. Production and consumption are the two sides of the sustainability coin. Ecological footprint (EF) is one way in which the impact of demand can be represented, and it certainly makes for a powerful projection onto our mindset. Representing consumption in terms of the area of the globe's finite surface required to sustain our lifestyle does make a strong statement. Questions can be raised as to why some countries have a higher EF than others, yet also have very similar wealth or indeed quality of life. EF is an evocative tool which can be employed to make a change. Much the same applies to the concept of 'food miles'. This is also a clearly grasped measure of consumption in the sense that it articulates the distances that food has to travel to reach our table. It highlights the globalised nature of food these days and points out the environmental and economic costs of that transport. Both EF and food miles point us in the same direction and cry out for a re-thinking of consumption patterns. With food miles the answer is to source food more locally, and with EF one answer is to increase efficiency of resource use so less is required.

EF and food miles are often referred to as sustainability indicators (SIs). SIs are fashionable for a number of reasons. At one level they can help frame what we mean by sustainability and thus what we need to do in order to achieve it. They provide a means by which we can present the somewhat nebulous concept of sustainability in ways in which it can be touched, tasted and smelt. Once framed like this then we can measure and assess. At another level SIs can help us track our progress (or not) towards sustainability. They can act as measures of performance and, indeed, provide the basis for accountability and communication. The history of indicators in economics, environmental science and ecology is a long one, so SIs provide a neat extension of this experience.

But SIs also have their downside. They simplify by definition (not accident) and inevitably this means that some important aspects of sustainability may be left out. Food miles, for example, as an SI completely misses important considerations such as the costs associated with food preparation (e.g. processing and cooking). Any collection of SIs will miss aspects that some consider important and will thereby reflect the power of those who were able to make the decisions as to what to include, the targets to aim for and how the indicators should best be measured. What may look like science, as in the artificial neural network case study described in this chapter, is in fact an edifice built upon subjectivity and bias.

Including the voices of those meant to benefit from a sustainability project or be involved in its implementation would seem to be a logical step. After all, this would give stakeholders a sense of 'ownership' and thereby enhance the chances of success. It is surely also a fundamental human right to involve those who will be affected by any change. There is certainly no shortage of efforts spanning a host of different participatory approaches to engage stakeholders in this way. However, the handling of the inevitable diversity of opinion – the many voices – is the crux of the matter. Unfortunately, all too often the many voices become condensed into but one, perhaps reflecting those with power in the community or the desire of those who want a predetermined change and thus seek to only look for those voices that match a desired agenda. Stakeholder participation does need to be handled with care.

7

Sustainability science?

We have covered a great deal of ground in this book, but given the breadth of sustainability, even if the perspective is biological, this was inevitable. Figure 7.1 sets out the territory we have surveyed and mapped. I have grouped related topics together under broad themes, but it is important to recognise that everything listed in Figure 7.1 is related to everything else and a two-dimensional diagram does not do full justice to all of the linkages. After all, in the book there is a separation of production and consumption as themes for chapters. This has logic, as consumption drives further demand for goods and services and in turn this feeds into production, but the two are also inversely related, as demand can also be created through clever marketing and this will in turn drive consumption and production. As a result of this inexorable relationship, production and consumption appear in all of the chapters, even if the emphasis might happen to be on one or the other. Also, while the left-hand side of Figure 7.1 is perhaps more 'biological' than topics to the right-hand side, biology pervades it all. Similarly, while policy appears at the bottom of Figure 7.1 it has to be noted that much of what is in the diagram was developed with the motive of operationalising a concept of sustainability. Hence, MSY, green accounting, GPI, ecological footprint, food miles and so on were all intended to have an influence on policy and/or behaviour.

While each of the topics in Figure 7.1 is covered by its own literature and has a group of specialists who work in the field, there are also overlaps. Primary production via photosynthesis as a means of harnessing energy from the sun underpins the whole of Figure 7.1, and energy flows through managed ecosystems provides us with much of our food. We have explored various ways of looking at production (TFP,

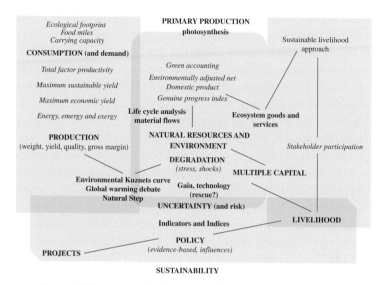

Figure 7.1 Summary of topics covered in the book.

MSY, MEY etc.) including economic perspectives and through life-cycle analysis and material flows. Energy provides an alternative set of units and perspective to that of money. Ecological footprint and food miles are but two ways of assessing the impact of consumption on the planet, but that is also linked to production. If we can produce more on a unit area for fewer inputs then we can reduce our footprint, and techniques such as genetic modification can arguably provide an answer, but this is contested as it raises other concerns over the technology, including ethical ones, as well as impacts arising from the production of artificial inputs such as machinery, fertilizer and pesticide. While we can 'trade' any technical concerns surrounding a technology with its benefits, providing we have the scientific evidence, this is not possible when an ethical dimension is added as is so often the case when genetic modification is involved. Carrying capacity is central to this notion of ecological footprint as a measure of consumption, but is also a component of production measures such as the MSY.

Production and consumption are related to the 'green accounting' approach to sustainability. There are various ways in which the environment has been integrated with economic measures and only two have been covered here: the environmentally adjusted net domestic product (EDP) and the genuine progress indicator (GPI). They come at the issue from two separate directions, but both aim to assess the economic cost of environmental degradation and the consumption of natural capital. Degradation and consumption of human and natural capital occurs as a result of production, which in turn is driven by demand and the prices which can be realised by goods and services which are traded. Some goods and services are not traded, and setting a value for them, as in the components of the GPI, is difficult. Principles such as those set out by the 'Natural Step' are meant to provide a guidance to limit this damage and thereby lead us towards sustainability. Specific techniques such as life cycle analysis, material-flow analysis and 'ecosystems goods and services' are designed to help take on board the full costs of production and losses to natural capital. LCA links back in part to broader views of TFP where all inputs to production are costed, but LCA takes a broader perspective by including goods and services, such as clean water provision, and environmental impacts. The environmental Kuznets curve is yet another way of looking at this complex relationship between environmental quality and human wellbeing, even if the latter is only assessed somewhat narrowly as income.

The sustainable livelihood approach (SLA) also attempts to integrate the multiple dimensions of sustainability, but this time through a broader sense of capital that extends beyond the 'natural' of EDP and ecosystem goods and services. In SLA 'capital' includes social, human, physical and financial, and these are explored within the context of stresses and shocks which the socio-economic and natural environment provides. Capitals are not necessarily translated into monetary terms, but the intention is to see how they provide the basis for supporting and enhancing livelihood. There are links here to LCA and, indeed, back to consumption and production, as these all support livelihood. Indeed, the 'natural' capital of SLA has resonance with the ecosystems goods and services approach, even if the latter attempts to put these in monetary terms, while the former does not. The stresses and shocks looked at within SLA can emerge, of course, through environmental degradation as a result of other activities. Thus global warming can provide a long-term and growing stress on capital that requires households to adapt. SLA was designed to provide evidence for planned intervention, either from outside (government etc.) or from within the community.

Some claim that life will save us – that there is, for example, a Gaia that dampens swings in our environment to make sure that it remains conducive to life – but, while appealing, the evidence is not convincing. We will not be saved from our excesses by Gaia. Some also say that technology can provide an answer, as, for example, with genetic modification or the 'seeding' of oceans with limiting nutrients, and thereby boost primary productivity, but there are always risks and uncertainties. We are often dealing in terms such as 'likelihood' rather than 'definite'. The extensive scientific evidence to date suggests that global warming is being driven, at least in part, by the activities of humans, but this has not been proven in the sense of being 'definite' (100% certainty). This leaves space for some to dispute the science and hence argue against mitigation which they perceive as being both economically and socially damaging. Similarly, the science to date suggests that the GM crops currently being grown do not present a hazard to human health, but there is always the doubt that some negative impacts might be found at some time in the future.

Given the need to operationalise the topics in Figure 7.1, some have suggested the development and use of sustainability indicators (SIs) to help translate the vast and growing body of research related to sustainability so policy-makers and others can make informed decisions. SIs pervade many of the topics in Figure 7.1 like the roots of a plant and help bring them together into packages of information or even single indices, but, by definition, they cannot cover every nuance of these topics and so compromises have to be made as to what to include and what to leave out. Who makes those choices and how the indicators are to be assessed are critical questions, and can present quite different perspectives on the same system. As a result, SIs have a very objective and hard face which can mask a very subjective and soft base. Even attempts to employ technology, such as artificial neural networks, to help us make these choices, do not remove the subjectivity.

Each of the topics presented in Figure 7.1 needs further research. For example, how we can include common pool resources in TFP or improve our management regimes for fisheries that break out of an over-reliance on simple yet unrealistic models. Even fundamental processes such as photosynthesis still require more elucidation, especially in terms of how the process can be made more efficient in providing yield. Some of the inter-connections in Figure 7.1 have also been explored, but much more needs to be done. Methodologies such as LCA and SLA may look quite different in some ways, but both seek to achieve a holistic assessment. In a sense they come at the same target, but from different directions. Perhaps there is scope to bring them together. Maybe SLA can help handle some of the geographical and social differentiation in impacts that LCA misses? Other examples could be the meshing of TFP and LCA using exergy, bringing together ecosystems goods and services and SLA and the use of indicators in policy. Allied to that is the need for a better understanding of the impacts of shocks and stresses, including conflict, on the topics in Figure 7.1. The agenda is certainly full.

Thus, while we know much about all the components and linkages shown in Figure 7.1, there is also much we don't know. In science, of course, that is not a 'problem', but a challenge; we want to throw light into dark areas! Even with our existing knowledge we are often dealing with uncertainty. We simply don't know all there is to know about life, its interaction with the environment and how we are influencing the processes involved. Whether we ever will is a moot point. Will it ever be possible to predict environmental fluctuations over large spatial and temporal scales with 100% certainty? Maybe, but I doubt it. In science we have no difficulty in claiming that existing knowledge points to the likelihood of 'A' happening in a given set of circumstances or that our current theories predict 'X' and so far our models fit available data. Phrases like 'so far', 'likelihood' and 'probability' are accepted parlance and science builds upon knowledge to make it wider and deeper. In biological science we routinely apply statistical techniques that speak of the likelihood of an outcome being less than 5% or 1% ($P < 0.05$ and $P < 0.01$, respectively) by chance. Scientific journal papers and reports are full of these phrases, and reviewers and readers know what they mean. But as we move towards the foot of Figure 7.1 these phrases do become an issue. Here we are looking at the translation of existing knowledge into policy and managerial interventions, and this can create both winners (those who benefit from a change) and losers (those who lose out from a change). Scientists are interacting not with other scientists who are used to the same language, but with policy-makers, managers and politicians, and these groups have responsibilities to others, notably the general public. At this place in Figure 7.1 uncertainty translates into risks and trade-offs, as we see all too clearly with the current debates over global warming. If ever there was a threat to sustainability it is wholesale climatic change and the havoc it could force onto our socio-economic systems. The repercussions are immense. The language employed by scientists is again one of likelihood of something happening – of the planet's temperature rising by X °C, if we carried on as we are doing now, and what could happen to sea levels and climatic systems. But bringing about the necessary changes to our society entails substantial costs (loss of income, increased unemployment etc.) and these are perhaps underestimated by those who readily call for the changes to happen without considering the nature and depth of sacrifices that have to be made and, indeed, who will make them. Thus, at one level we can speak of the science which underpins sustainability, but not of a 'sustainability science'.

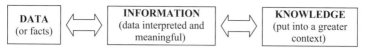

Figure 7.2 Translation of data to knowledge (after Bruckmeier and Tovey, 2008).

In this final chapter of the book we will explore the processes of interaction between scientists and policy. How can scientists make their voices heard by those who have the power to bring about change? This is by no means a new question, it is perhaps as old as science itself, but are we anywhere nearer a resolution? Indeed, and in a provocative vein, is this a question that concerns scientists far more than it does policy-makers?

7.2 MAKING IT MATTER: INFLUENCING LIVES

There has been something of a growing trend in recent years towards making policy more 'evidence based'. Figure 7.2 is an example of a flow from data at one end through to information and knowledge. Note how the creators of the model make a distinction between these three. Indeed, the authors of this model also suggest that the flow can go the other way, as 'knowledge' can help determine what data we still need to fill gaps. After all, it is society through its public funding bodies in particular which pays for research. This contradicts the common perception of Figure 7.2 as a one-way process, with those involved at the left-hand side of the diagram being largely independent of those at the right-hand side. Thus, as some have put it:

> A modern perception of 'evidence-based policy making' is sometimes characterized as a process whereby the 'evidence' is assembled almost independently of the policy options and then through a process of analysis and distillation the policy options and then the preferred policy choice emerge. (Holt (2008; page 324))

> The ideal of value free science is still very dominant, for example when you look at what is expected of science and at how divisions of labor between science and policy are organized. Science is supposed to produce facts and policy then makes value-laden decisions. (Turnhout et al. (2007, page 218))

Whether these two groups really are so separate as they might believe is a matter of conjecture, but problems with communication are almost inevitable when the two collide. Scientists see themselves as seeking the truth, while policy-makers look for feasibility, relevance etc. and are typically conservative and risk-avoiding. After all, politicians as one group of policy-makers ultimately have the next election in mind and that will understandabley influence their policy priorities. As a result of this collision, Turnhout *et al* (2007; page 221) state:

> In the case of ecological indicators, science and policy enter in some kind of joint knowledge production. Scientific knowledge is used in ecological indicators but so is political knowledge. Ecological indicators are shaped by political preferences and considerations to protect certain species, certain types of nature, etc. Development and use of indicators go hand in hand and are hard to distinguish empirically.

Indicators, discussed in Chapter 6, are one tool designed to bridge the gap between knowledge and policy. They are meant to be easily digested 'bite-size' summaries of key information and can be presented in ways that non-specialists can follow. Some have called them 'exchange tools', as they are designed to facilitate an exchange of knowledge between quite disparate groups (Bruckmeier and Tovey, 2008). But, surprisingly, much of the indicator research to date has been focused on what indicators to choose and how best to measure and present them, as we saw earlier with the Rowland *et al.* (2004) case study. There has been almost nothing on the effectiveness of indicators to influence policy. Blair (2005) provides a rare example of this in terms of a community indicator programme (CIP) and its influence on policy. The CIP is based in Santa Monica (USA) and Blair (2005) concludes that the programme was successful in its connection with policy, but why should that be? A number of reasons are given, including:

- Transparency of the process and use of numerical targets. Numerical information remains popular in policy (Neylan, 2008)
- Intended use of the programme from the very start as a strategic tool for governance
- Adequate provision of resources
- Recognition of the vital link provided between processes and policy by all of those involved.

But transparency also has its problems in the competitive politics of a democracy where trade-offs are almost inevitable, and will the other points mentioned above always be present or will there only be lip service? After all, it is easy to claim that the commitment and resources are there, but are they? In addition, we also have the contestable meaning of the term 'success'. Does success have to be seen in terms of a tangible and measurable change being made, or is it enough for indicators to simply raise awareness?

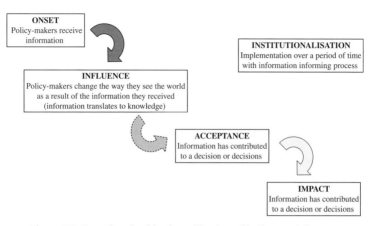

Figure 7.3 Steps involved in the utilisation of indicators (after Hezri, 2004).

Governments have often called for policy to be evidence-based. New Labour in the UK, for example, were vocal in the support for this (Sorrell, 2007), very much in the 'modernist-rationalist' approach of Sanderson (2002, page 6) where 'policymakers seek to manage economic and social affairs "rationally" in an apolitical, scientized manner such that social policy is more of less an exercise in social technology'. Hezri (2004, 2005) suggests that the utilisation of indicators (or indeed information in a general sense) to bring about a change follows a number of steps (Figure 7.3). The information has first to be presented to policy-makers who then need to incorporate it into their worldview. In terms of the model in Figure 7.2, this equates to information becoming knowledge. From here it arguably becomes fuzzier as we consider whether the knowledge has been translated into change. The next step is acceptance; in other words that the knowledge has influenced a decision or set of decisions designed to bring about change. The final stage of Figure 7.3 is a decision or decisions bringing about a change. This is more complex as, of course, it will depend upon many factors, including the resources that have been allocated as we have seen with the Blair (2005) example discussed above. Thus, a decision may be well intentioned, but fail to bring about a required change, not because the information upon which it was founded was poor, but other constraints have entered the fray. A side issue is the institutionalisation of the process; that the chain from information acceptance through to decisions is a regular one rather than a 'once off'. This can work against you, of course, as we have seen with the all too ready institutionalisaton of MSY in Chapter 3 and the damage that can result from an unquestioning acceptance of an apparent 'truth'.

Table 7.1 *Different categories of indicator use (after Hezri, 2004, 2005).*

Type of use	Notes
Instrumental	Direct link between information and decision outcomes as implied in Figure 7.3. This equates to the modernist-rationalist perspective of Sanderson (2002) and the positivist-empiricist label employed by Greenhaigh and Russell (2009).
Conceptual	Information sensitises or changes understanding of a problem or situation without going on to make a direct cause–effect impact as implied in Figure 7.3.
Tactical	Information used as a delaying tactic, substitute for action or to deflect criticisms.
Symbolic	Information used to provide ritualistic assurances rather than decisions intended to bring about a change.
Political	Information used to provide ammunition to support a predetermined position.

Thus, the word 'use', like 'success', can also mean many things in the context of Figure 7.3 (Innvaer *et al.*, 2002). It could be interpreted as the influencing of policy-makers' world view (i.e. helping to frame their knowledge) or indeed as a direct influence into decisions. Inevitably there is much 'greyness' in here and an influence of world view could perhaps be equally as important, if not more so, than a direct impact in the short term. Indeed proving an instrumental use of information may not necessarily be an easy matter (Hezri, 2005).

Overlapping the model in Figure 7.3 Hezri (2004, 2005) has suggested that there are different types of 'use' in the diagram which are partly driven by the motives of those involved. Thus, we have the categories in Table 7.1 from instrumental use of indicators at one end of the scale to political use at the other. This is a simplification and there are overlaps between these classifications. Indeed, the same information can pass through a number of categories over a period of time, perhaps beginning as a symbolic use (lip service), followed by a tactical use (delaying) and eventually be instrumental in helping to bring about change. The same indicator might also be used in different ways within the same organisation. Still, some of the categories towards the foot of Table 7.1 do not exactly inspire researchers to try and feed the information they create into policy (Wilson *et al.*, 2007). As one writer puts it:

> *Most social scientists believe that strong evidence should lead policymakers to adopt effective programs and to eschew those that are demonstrably ineffective, but*

policies sometimes seem to fly in the face of data. The unpredictable and volatile world of social policy has led some researchers to renounce efforts to inform it because they believe that decisions are entirely political and that data are invoked at best only to support a position that someone has already decided to endorse.
(Huston (2008, page 1))

There are indeed strong forces that can work against an instrumental use of information, and like it or not this does include environmental policy (Juntti *et al.*, 2009). According to Black (2001), Romsdahl (2005), Greenhaigh and Russell (2009) and others these include:

- Policy-makers have goals other than effectiveness (social, financial, strategic development of service, terms and conditions of employees, electoral)
- Research evidence dismissed as irrelevant (from different sector or specialty, practice depends on tacit knowledge, not applicable locally)
- Lack of clarity on research questions and/or policy objectives
- Lack of consensus about research evidence (complexity of evidence, scientific controversy, different interpretations). Includes disagreement on findings, i.e. a lack of consistent or cumulative research results on a given subject. The global warming debate mentioned in Chapter 4 provides a classic example
- Failure to produce results in the form of generalised principles or politically feasible recommendations
- Other types of competing evidence (personal experience, local information, eminent colleagues' opinions, reports)
- Social environment not conducive to policy change
- Limited time and resources available to policy-makers to allow them to access research findings. This is in part what Howlett (2009) refers to as 'policy analytical capacity'. Therefore one cannot assume that good science published in a good journal will be read by a policy-maker, even if that is the main criterion of quality employed by scientists and their funders.

How do we bridge this gap and thereby help make policy more evidence based? Some have called for much greater personal contact between scientists and policy-makers, or perhaps to have intermediaries ('knowledge brokers' or 'knowledge purveyors') who can facilitate the exchange of information (Black, 2001; Choi *et al.*, 2005), although much depends upon the quality of these individuals and there are dangers inherent in allowing choices as to what information to exchange. In short, evidence-based policy is a complex subject – far more complex than many may think – but there has to be realism on the part of scientists as to what can be achieved within a certain spatial and time frame. As Pawson (2006, page 178) tellingly puts it with regard to his 'realist' vision of evidence-based policy:

> Part of the enlightenment ethos is also about scepticism. My own impression of my own efforts to get my own reviews noticed is that much of the recent governmental head-nodding to evidence-based policy is mere lip service. As one moves up the policy-making ladder through 'analytic divisions' to 'policy divisions' the appetite for evidence dwindles. As one ascends the intervention hierarchy from practitioners to managers to bureaucrats to the political classes, the capacity to absorb complex information dwindles by the bullet point. Evidence can inform policy but it can also be used as a tool to 'park' policy in much the same way as indecision is disguised by the need to await review and committee reports. It can, of course, also be used to misinform policy through sifting, selection and simplification.

Frustrating indeed, but does this mean we should give up trying to bring together all of the research outlined in Figure 7.1 so as to achieve sustainability? Far from it, given the importance of sustainability, as after all ultimately we are speaking of nothing less than the survival of the human race, but it will require perseverance and imagination. Forms of presentation of information are important, and there is much that biologists working in the broad field of sustainability can learn from other biologists working in health care, where evidence-based policy has received far more attention and the topic is widely aired in the literature (Pullin and Knight, 2009). Of far greater value to publications may be face-to-face and follow-up interactions, between researchers and decision-makers (Romsdahl, 2005), but this requires commitment from all.

7.3   CHALLENGES AHEAD: SOME CONCLUSIONS

> Achieving sustainable development is possibly the largest change challenge in human history ... Several cultural blockages to change for sustainable development are identified. These include behavior that is unnecessarily competitive, insular and secretive and that suppresses moves towards useful cooperation. (Ballard (2000, page 53))

The Ballard (2000) quotation above sets out both the challenge and one of the reasons why meeting that challenge is difficult, as many of the examples discussed in this book have shown. While there are 'cultural blockages' to making sustainability a reality, I will suggest that we have two goals. Firstly, much more needs to be done in terms of our understanding of sustainability, but secondly we need to know how we can best translate that knowledge into practice. Both of these are important and those of us engaged in sustainability-relevant research also have a responsibility to consider how best to make our findings available to policy-makers. Publishing in journal papers is a fundamental requirement for researchers. It acts as a convenient measure of output and thus provides an all too easy means of enforcing accountability and judging 'worth' by those charged with managing research. But this is not enough as it cannot be assumed that policy-makers will have access to the journals or indeed the time and expertise to prise them apart and extract the nuggets. We have to engage in 'publishing plus'. This can be difficult, given the immense pressures to publish in peer-reviewed journals as a key part of career progression, and indeed accountability to funders, and all too often the temptation is to leave the 'influence' agenda to someone else. Indeed, governments and other research funders are good at paying lip service to the need for researchers to make their findings more widely available as a means of influencing policy, while with the other hand (the one often in the iron glove unfortunately) they continue to insist on measuring performance by the tried and trusted indicators of refereed journal papers and journal impact factors. Real incentives beyond lip service for scientists to engage in trying to make their results more widely available to those that could use them are often lacking. Perhaps this is yet another example of the numerous trade-offs that pervade sustainability. Unfortunately, this is not the first time this issue has been raised and it will not be the last. It can, indeed, be difficult, and perhaps even risky, for scientists working at the 'coal face' of deepening our knowledge to look to a second frontier and consider how they can help influence policy, but try we must.

Neither is the onus only upon scientists. Indeed, as important as science is in terms of helping us achieve sustainability, there are limits to what it can do:

> Sustainable development is a moving target. It has multiple dimensions, scientific, economic and political, many of which are not amenable to scientific illumination.
> (Salwasser (1993, page 588))

Politicians and policy-makers also have a responsibility and must recognise the constraints within which scientists have to work. It is all too easy to call for more resources – there are never enough – but there has to be acknowledgement, given the complexity of sustainability and the imperfect state of our knowledge regarding many of its facets, that complete consensus amongst all scientists on the interpretation of a set of data may not be possible. The debates over global warming provide an excellent example. Instead there will be differences in opinion and majority views, although that is not to say that those who find themselves in a minority will not occasionally and ultimately be proved right. Greater cognisance needs to be taken of this and not used as a convenient excuse for discarding the hypothesis as 'unproven', even when what emerges may be unpopular amongst the electorate. Ideally, there should also be much more inter-party co-operation on sustainability (Meadowcroft, 1999) although that could be just wishful thinking, given the political sensitivities associated with many of the required actions.

The topics covered in this book have been wide-ranging and I make no apologies for that. It is the nature of the beast we call sustainability. Indeed, while this book is entitled *Sustainability: A Biological Perspective*, it is simply not possible to take any one subject and view sustainability only with that lens. By definition and necessity we have to take on board other sciences, as well as economics and social science. Hence, the reader will have been pulled in many directions. While we can begin with primary production as the basis for agriculture, we are immediately thrust into the realm of appreciating why farmers do what they do with regard to cropping systems and that is not always with the aim of maximising yield. Crop production has to be placed within the environmental and socio-economic context of farmer's lives, and ultimately within livelihoods. This trajectory takes us from photosynthesis, the niche, cropping systems, natural capital, other capitals and ultimately to culture and politics. Biologists can help with that trajectory, but they cannot do it all themselves.

I have also made much of the gaps that exist in our knowledge and the mistakes which have been made in attempting to manage complexity with an often incomplete bank of knowledge. As Kates *et al.* (2000) have put it:

> It is clear that incomplete knowledge, and limitations in our ability to utilize it, will permanently challenge sustainability science as it tries to link research to action and to reconcile scientific excellence with social relevance. (page 2)

> The idea of sustainable development emerged in the early 1980's from scientific perspectives on the relationship between nature and society. Over the last 15 years, however, with few exceptions, science and technology have not been active partners in the societal and political process of sustainable development. Scientists helped construct an agenda for science but had little impact on subsequent action. (page 4)

This may sound like criticism, and indeed it is to an extent, given the devastating impacts that can arise when we arrogantly think we know all the answers and single-mindedly force through changes which can cause substantial damage. But at the same time, it is far from being a call to do nothing. Perhaps the dilemma is that sustainability has become an issue for us almost before we are ready for it. Hence, we are often forced to do what we can with incomplete knowledge of the systems we are trying to manage and the impacts we are having within it; we are having to run before we have really figured out how to walk. As mentioned earlier, these gaps and uncertainties can be exploited by those who wish to pursue other agendas.

If nothing else I hope this book has helped provide the reader with an overview of some of the issues we face in sustainability and conveyed the urgent need for us all to work together towards our goal of improving the human existence, while at the same time ensuring that we don't spoil the home upon which that existence depends. I also hope it will inspire a drive to keep adding to our knowledge and look for new insights, as well as a desire to engage with others who can use the knowledge to make change happen.

Given the 'Perfect Storm' referred to at the start of the book, we certainly need that change.

References

Adams W. M. (2001). Green development. *Environment and sustainability in the Third World*, 2nd Edn, London and New York: Routledge.

Agegnehu G., Ghizaw A. and Sinebo W. (2008). Yield potential and land-use efficiency of wheat and faba bean mixed intercropping. *Agronomy for Sustainable Development* 28(2), 257–263.

Aikman D. P. (1989). Potential increase in photosynthetic efficiency from the redistribution of solar radiation in a crop. *Journal of Experimental Botany* 40(217), 855–864.

Alberts D. J. (2007). Stakeholders or subject matter experts, who should be consulted? *Energy Policy* 35(4), 2336–2346.

Aldunate J. (1994). Human-rights as the rights of the poor. The perspective from Liberation-Theology. *Journal of Moral Education* 23(3), 297–303.

Alfsen K. H. and Greaker M. (2007). From natural resources and environmental accounting to construction of indicators for sustainable development. *Ecological Economics* 61(4), 600–610.

Ali Y., Aslam Z., Rafique T. and Hussain F. (2005). Economical use of land and agricultural resources under different cropping system, *International Journal of Biology and Biotechnology* 2(1), 223–225.

Al-Jufaili S. M. (2007). Conceptual model for sardine and anchovy inverse cyclic behavior in abundance. *Journal of Food Agriculture & Environment* 5(1), 317–327.

Allen P., Van Dusen D., Lundy L. and Gliessman S. (1991). Integrating social, environmental and economic issues in sustainable agriculture. *American Journal of Alternative Agriculture* 6, 34–39.

Ambec S. and Lanoie P. (2008). Does it pay to be Green? A systematic overview. *Academy of Management Perspectives* 23(4), 45–62.

Andow D. A. (1991). Yield loss to arthropods in vegetationally diverse agro-ecosystems. *Environmental Entomology* 20(5), 1228–1235.

Andow D. A. and Zwahlen C. (2006). Assessing environmental risks of transgenic plants. *Ecology Letters* 9(2), 196–214.

Anon (2002). PVC industry encouraged to take the natural step to sustainability. *Materials World* 10(6), 5.

Apaiah R. K., Linnemann A. R., van der Kooi H. J. (2006). Exergy analysis: A tool to study the sustainability of food supply chains. *Food Research International* 39(1) 1–11.

Aras, G. and Crowther, D. (2009). Corporate Sustainability Reporting: A Study in Disingenuity? *Journal of Business Ethics* 87, 279–288.

Arnstein S. (1969). A ladder of citizen participation. *Journal of the American Institute of Planners* 35(4), 216–224.

Aslanidis N. and Iranzo S. (2009). Environment and development: Is there a Kuznets curve for CO_2 emissions? *Applied Economics* 41(6), 803–810.

Auty R. M. (2007). Natural resources, capital accumulation and the resource curse. *Ecological Economics* 61(4), 627–634.

Aylward B. and Barbier E. B. (1992). Valuing environmental functions in developing-countries. *Biodiversity and Conservation* 1(1), 34–50.

Ayres R. U. (2000). Commentary on the utility of the ecological footprint concept. *Ecological Economics* 32(3), 347–349.

Ayres, R. U. (1978), *Resources, Environment and Economics*, New York: John Wiley & Sons, Inc.

Ayres R. U. (2008). Sustainability economics: Where do we stand? *Ecological Economics* 67(2), 281–310.

Bagliani M., Bravo G. and Dalmazzone S. (2008). A consumption-based approach to environmental Kuznets curves using the ecological footprint indicator. *Ecological Economics* 65(3), 650–661.

Ballard, D. (2000). The cultural aspects of change for sustainable development. *Eco-Management and Auditing* 7, 53–59.

Barbier E. B. (2007). Valuing ecosystem services as productive inputs. *Economic Policy Issue* 49, 178–229.

Bartelmus P. (2007). SEEA-2003: Accounting for sustainable development? *Ecological Economics* 61(4), 613–616.

Bartelmus P. (2009). The cost of natural capital consumption: Accounting for a sustainable world economy. *Ecological Economics* 68, 1850–1857.

Bartelmus P., Richmond A. and Kumar S. (Topic Eds) (2008). Green accounting. In *Encyclopedia of Earth* ed. Cutler J. Cleveland, Washington, DC: Environmental Information Coalition, National Council for Science and the Environment. [First published in the Encyclopedia of Earth August 9, 2006; last revised September 17, 2008; eetrieved July 26, 2009]. www.eoearth.org/article/Green_accounting

Bazin D. (2009). What exactly is corporate responsibility towards nature? Ecological responsibility or management of nature? A pluri-disciplinary standpoint. *Ecological Economics* 68(3), 634–642.

Beard V. A. (2005). Individual determinants of participation in community development in Indonesia. *Environment and Planning C: Government and Policy* 23(1), 21–39.

Becchetti L., Di Giacomo S. and Pinnacchio D. (2008). Corporate social responsibility and corporate performance: Evidence from a panel of US listed companies. *Applied Economics* 40(5), 541–567.

Bell S. and Morse S. (2003). *Measuring Sustainability: Learning by Doing*, Earthscan: London.

Bellamy D. and Barrett J. (2007). Climate stability: an inconvenient proof. *Proceedings of the Institution of Civil Engineers-Civil Engineering* 160(2), 66–72.

Bevan P. (2000). Who's a goody? Demythologizing the PRA agenda. *Journal of International Development* 12(5), 751–759.

Bhattacharya C. B., Korschun D. and Sen S. (2009). Strengthening Stakeholder-Company relationships through mutually beneficial corporate social responsibility initiatives. *Journal of Business Ethics* 85(2), 257–272.

Biabani A., Hashemi M. and Herbert S. J. (2008). Agronomic performance of two intercropped soybean cultivars. *International Journal of Plant Production* 2(3), 215–221.

Black N. (2001). Evidence based policy: proceed with care. *British Medical Journal* 323, 275–278.

Blair J. M. (2005). Community indicator programs: Their construction, logic and consistency based on a program evaluation of the Santa Monica CIP, California. *Journal of Environmental Assessment Policy and Management* 7(4), 597–617.

Block M. D., Botterman J., Vandewiele M., *et al.* (1987). Engineering herbicide resistance in plants by expression of a detoxifying enzyme. *Journal of the European Molecular Biology Organization (EMBO)* 6, 2513–2518.

Blowfield M. (2007). Reasons to be cheerful? What we know about CSR's impact. *Third World Quarterly* 28(4), 683–695.

Blutstein H. (2003). A forgotten pioneer of sustainability. *Journal of Cleaner Production* 11(3), 339–341.

Boerema L. K. and Gulland J. A. (1973). Stock assessment of the Peruvian anchovy (Engraulis ringens) and management of the fishery. *Journal Fisheries Research Board of Canada* 30, 2226–2235.

Bolton J. R. and Hall D. O. (1991). The maximum efficiency of photosynthesis. *Phytochemistry and Photobiology* 53(4), 545–548.

Bousquet A. and Favard P. (2005). Does S. Kuznets's belief question the Environmental Kuznets Curves? *Canadian Journal of Economics* 38(2), 604–614.

Boutaud A., Gondran N. and Brodhag C. (2006). (Local) environmental quality versus (global) ecological carrying capacity: what might alternative aggregated indicators bring to the debates about environmental Kuznets curves and sustainable development? *International Journal of Sustainable Development* 9(3), 297–310.

Boyd J. (2007). Nonmarket benefits of nature: What should be counted in green GDP? *Ecological Economics* 61(4), 716–723.

Boyd, J. W. and Banzhaf, H. S. (2005). Ecosystem services and government: the need for a new way of judging nature's value. *Resources* 158, 16–19.

Boyd P. W., Jickells T., Law C. S., *et al.* (2007). Mesoscale iron enrichment experiments 1993–2005: Synthesis and future directions, *Science* 315 (5812), 612.

Bradbury H. and Clair J. A. (1993). Promoting Sustainable Organizations with Sweden's Natural Step. *The Academy of Management Executive* 13(4), 63–74.

Broman G., Holmberg J., Robert K. H. (2000). Simplicity without reduction: Thinking upstream towards the sustainable society. *Interfaces* 30(3), 13–25.

Bruckmeier K. and Tovey H. (2008). Knowledge in sustainable rural development: From forms of knowledge to knowledge processes. *Sociologia Ruralis* 48(3), 313–329.

Buchs W. (2003). Biodiversity and agri-environmental indicators – general scopes and skills with special reference to the habitat level. *Agriculture Ecosystems & Environment* 98(1–3), 35–78.

Buesseler K. O., Doney S. C., Karl D. M., *et al.* (2008). Ocean iron fertilization. Moving forward in a sea of uncertainty, *Science* 319 (5860), 162.

Burger J. (2006). Bioindicators: A review of their use in the environmental literature 1970–2005. *Environmental Bioindicators* 1(2), 136–144.

Burns S. (1999). The Natural Step: A Compass for Environmental Management Systems. *Corporate Environmental Strategy* 6(4), 329–342.

Butler L. M. and Mazur R. E. (2007). Principles and processes for enhancing sustainable rural livelihoods: Collaborative learning in Uganda. *International Journal of Sustainable Development and World Ecology* 14(6), 604–617.

Byerlee D. and Murgai R. (2001). Sense and sustainability revisited: the limits of total factor productivity measures of sustainable agricultural systems. *Agricultural Economics* 26(3), 227–236.

Carignan V. and Villard M. A. (2002). Selecting indicator species to monitor ecological integrity: A review. *Environmental Monitoring and Assessment* 78(1), 45–61.

Carney D. (Ed) (1998), *Sustainable Rural Livelihoods: What Contribution Can We Make?* Department of International Development. Nottingham: Russell Press Ltd.

Carson R. (1962) *Silent Spring*, London: Penguin.

Castro C. J. (2004). Sustainable development – Mainstream and critical perspectives. *Organization and Environment* 17(2), 195–225.

Caterina M. and Lorenzo-Molo F. (2009). Why corporate social responsibility (CSR) remains a myth: The case of the Philippines. *Asian Business & Management* 8(2), 149–168.

Caviglia-Harris J. L., Chambers D. and Kahn J. R. (2009). Taking the 'U' out of Kuznets A comprehensive analysis of the EKC and environmental degradation. *Ecological Economics* 68(4), 1149–1159.

Cerdeira A. L. and Duke S. O. (2006). The current status and environmental impacts of glyphosate-resistant crops: A review. *Journal of Environmental Quality* 35(5), 1633–1658.

Chambers R. (1983). *Rural Development: Putting the Last First*, London: Longman.

Chambers R. (1993). *Challenging the Professionals: Frontiers for Rural Development*, London: Intermediate Technology.

Chambers R. (1997). *Whose Reality Counts? Putting the Last First*, London: Intermediate Technology.

Chambers R. and Conway G. R. (1992). *Sustainable Rural Livelihoods: Practical Concepts for the 21st Century*, IDS Discussion Paper No. 296, Brighton: IDS.

Chang D.-S. and Kuo, L.-C. R. (2008). The effects of sustainable development on firms' financial performance – an empirical approach. *Sustainable Development* 16(6), 365–380.

Checkland P. and Scholes J. (1990). *Soft Systems Methodology in Action*, Chichester: John Wiley & Sons, Ltd.

Checkland P. (1981). *Systems Thinking, Systems Practice*, Chichester: John Wiley & Sons, Ltd.

Chee Y. E. (2004). An ecological perspective on the valuation of ecosystem services. *Biological Conservation* 120(4), 549–565.

Chen C. C., Westcott M., Neill K., Wichman D. and Knox M. (2004). Row configuration and nitrogen application for barley-pea intercropping in Montana. *Agronomy Journal* 96(6), 1730–1738.

Chen B. and Chen G. Q. (2006). Ecological footprint accounting based on emergy – A case study of the Chinese society. *Ecological Modelling* 198(1–2), 101–114.

Chen B. and Chen G. Q. (2007). Modified ecological footprint accounting and analysis based on embodied exergy – a case study of the Chinese society 1981–2001. *Ecological Economics* 61(2–3), 355–376.

Chen G. Q., Jiang M. M., Yang Z. F., *et al.* (2009). Exergetic assessment for ecological economic system: Chinese agriculture. *Ecological Modelling* 220(3), 397–410.

Chhotray V. (2004). The negation of politics in participatory development projects, Kurnool, Andhra Pradesh. *Development and Change* 35(2), 327–352.

Choi B. C. K., Pang T., Lin V., *et al.* (2005). Can scientists and policy makers work together? *Journal of Epidemiology and Community Health* 59, 632–637.

Christensen V. (1995). Ecosystem maturity – Towards quantification. *Ecological Modelling* 77(1), 3–32.

Christou P., Capell T., Kohli A., Gatehouse J. A. and Gatehouse A. M. R. (2006). Recent developments and future prospects in insect pest control in transgenic crops. *Trends in Plant Science* 11(6), 302–308.

Chu G. X., Shen Q. R. and Cao J. L. (2004). Nitrogen fixation and N transfer from peanut to rice cultivated in aerobic soil in an intercropping system and its effect on soil N fertility. *Plant and Soil* 263(1–2), 17–27.

Ciegis R., Streimikiene D. and Zavadskas E. K. (2008). The use of the environmental Kuznets curve: environmental and economic implications. *International Journal of Environment and Pollution* 33(2–3), 313–335.

Clapp J. (2008). Illegal GMO releases and corporate responsibility: Questioning the effectiveness of voluntary measures. *Ecological Economics* 66(2–3), 348–358.

Clark M. R. and Tracey D. M. (1994). Changes in a population of Orange Roughy, Hoplostethus atlanticus, with commercial exploitation on the Challenger Plateau, New Zealand. *Fishery Bulletin* 92(2), 236–253.

Clarke M. and Lawn P. (2008). Is measuring genuine progress at the sub-national level useful? *Ecological Indicators* 8(5), 573–581.

Cleaver F. (2001). Institutions, agency and the limitations of participatory approaches to development. In *Participation the New Tyranny*, ed. B Cooke and U. Kothari, Zed Books, 36–55.

Cole M. A. (2003). Development, trade and the environment: How robust is the Environmental Kuznets Curve? *Environment and Development Economics* 8(4), 557–580.

Conroy M. M. and Berke P. R. (2004). What makes a good sustainable development plan? An analysis of factors that influence principles of sustainable development. *Environment and Planning A* 36(8), 1381–1396.

Cooke B. and Kothari U. (Eds.) (2001). *Participation the New Tyranny*, London: Zed Books.

Cornwall A. (2003). Whose voices? Whose choices? Reflections on gender and participatory development. *World Development* 31(8), 1325–1342.

Corten A. (1996). The widening gap between fisheries biology and fisheries management in the European Union. *Fisheries Research* 27(1–3), 1–15.

Costanza R., Erickson J., Fligger K., *et al.* (2004). Estimates of the Genuine Progress Indicator (GPI) for Vermont, Chittenden County and Burlington, from 1950 to 2000. *Ecological Economics* 51(1–2), 139–155.

Costanza R., d'Arge R., de Groot R., *et al.* (1997). The value of the world's ecosystem services and natural capital. *Nature* 387, 253–260.

Costanza R., Graumlich L., Steffen W., *et al.* (2007). Sustainability or collapse: What can we learn from integrating the history of humans and the rest of nature? *Ambio* 36(7), 522–527.

Craig J. L. (2004). Science and sustainable development in New Zealand. *Journal of the Royal Society of New Zealand* 34(1), 9–22.

Craig W., Tepfer M., Degrassi G. and Ripandelli D. (2008). An overview of general features of risk assessments of genetically modified crops. *Euphytica* 164(3), 853–880.

Curtis I. A. (2004). Valuing ecosystem goods and services: a new approach using a surrogate market and the combination of a multiple criteria analysis and a Delphi panel to assign weights to the attributes. *Ecological Economics* 50(3–4), 163–194.

Curwell S. and Cooper I. (1998). The Implications of Urban Sustainability. *Building Research and Information*, 26(1) 17–28.

Cury P., Roy C., and Faure V. (1998). Environmental constraints and pelagic fisheries in upwelling areas: The Peruvian puzzle. *South African Journal of Marine Science* 19, 159–167.

Dagg J. L. (2002). Unconventional bed mates: Gaia and the selfish gene. *Oikos* 96 (1), 182–186.

Daily G. C. (1997). Introduction: what are ecosystem services? In *Nature's Services: Societal Dependence on Natural Scosystems*, ed. G. C. Daily, Washington, DC: Island Press, 1–10.

Dallot S. (2001). Sampling properties of biodiversity indices. *Oceanis* 24(4), 89–105.

Daniels P. L. and Moore S. (2002). Approaches for quantifying the metabolism of physical economies. Part I: Methodological overview. *Journal of Industrial Ecology*, 5 (4), 69–93.

Danielsson A. (2005). Methods for environmental and economic accounting for the exploitation of wild fish stocks and their applications to the case of Icelandic fisheries. *Environmental & Resource Economics* 31(4), 405–430.

de Groot R. S., Wilson M. A. and Boumans R. M. J. (2002). A typology for the classification, description and valuation of ecosystem functions, goods and services. *Ecological Economics* 41(3), 393–408.

de Haan L. J. (2000). Globalization, localization and sustainable livelihood. *Sociologia Ruralis* 40(3), 339–365.

de Haan L. J. (2005). How to research the changing outlines of African livelihoods. Paper presented at the 11th General Assembly of CODESRIA, 6–10 December 2005, Maputo 2005.

Department for International Development (DFID) (1997). *Eliminating World Poverty: A Challenge for the 21st Century. White Paper on International Development*. HMSO, London. Available at www.dfid.gov.uk/Pubs/files/whitepaper1997.pdf

Deroba J. J. and Bence J. R. (2008). A review of harvest policies: Understanding relative performance of control rules. *Fisheries Research* 94(3), 210–223.

Devinney T. M. (2009). Is the socially responsible corporation a myth? The good, the bad, and the Ugly of Corporate Social Responsibility. *Academy of Management Perspectives* 23(2), 44–56.

Dewulf J., Van Langenhove H., Muys B., *et al.* (2008) Exergy: Its potential and limitations in environmental science and technology. *Environmental Science & Technology* 42(7), 2221–2232.

Diekmann M. (2003). Species indicator values as an important tool in applied plant ecology – a review. *Basic and Applied Ecology* 4(6), 493–506.

Dietz S. and Neumayer E. (2007). Weak and strong sustainability in the SEEA: Concepts and measurement. *Ecological Economics* 61(4), 617–626.

Dincer I. (2007). Exergetic and sustainability aspects of green energy systems. *Clean-Soil Air Water* 35(4), 311–322.

Dinda S. (2005). A theoretical basis for the environmental Kuznets curve. *Ecological Economics* 53(3), 403–413.

Dona A. and Arvanitoyannis I. S. (2009). Health Risks of Genetically Modified Foods. *Critical Reviews in Food Science and Nutrition* 49(2), 164–175.

Dryzak J. S. and Niemeyer S. (2006). Reconciling pluralism and consensus as political ideals. *American Journal of Political Science* 50(3), 634–649.

Dutta D. and Bandyopadhyay P. (2007). Productivity, economics and competition functions of groundnut (Arachis hypogaea) plus pigeonpea (Cajanus cajan) intercropping system under various plant density and fertilizer management in rainfed uplands of West Bengal. *Advances in Plant Sciences* 20(1), 181–184.

The Ecologist (1972). Blueprint for survival 2(1). Available at www.theecologist. info/key27.html. Also published by Penguin Books.

Edwards-Jones G., Canals L. M. I., Hounsome N., *et al.* (2008). Testing the assertion that 'local food is best': the challenges of an evidence-based approach. *Trends in Food Science & Technology* 19(5), 265–274.

Ehrlich P. and Ehrlich A. (1990). *The Population Explosion*, Pymble: Simon & Schuster Australia.

Ehui S. K. and Spencer D. S. C. (1993). Measuring the sustainability and economic viability of tropical farming systems – a model from sub-Saharan Africa. *Agricultural Economics* 9(4), 279–296.

Einoder L. D. (2009), A review of the use of seabirds as indicators in fisheries and ecosystem management. *Fisheries Research* 95(1), 6–13.

Ekins P. (1997). The Kuznets curve for the environment and economic growth: Examining the evidence. *Environment and Planning A* 29(5), 805–830.

Elton C. S. (1927). *Animal Ecology*, New York: Macmillan.

Espinoza P. and Bertrand A. (2008). Revisiting Peruvian anchovy (Engraulis ringens) trophodynamics provides a new vision of the Humboldt Current system. *Progress in Oceanography* 79(2–4), 215–227.

Evans K. E. and Klinger T. (2008). Obstacles to bottom-up implementation of marine ecosystem management. *Conservation Biology* 22(5), 1135–1143.

Eversole R. (2003). Managing the pitfalls of participatory development: Some insights from Australia. *World Development* 31(5), 781–795.

Faysse N. (2006). Troubles on the way: An analysis of the challenges faced by multi-stakeholder platforms. *Natural Resources Forum* 30(3), 219–229.

Ferguson A. R. B. (2002). The assumptions underlying eco-footprinting. *Population and Environment* 23(3), 303–313.

Few R., Brown K. and Tompkins E. L. (2007). Public participation and climate change adaptation: Avoiding the illusion of inclusion. *Climate Policy* 7(1), 46–59.

Fiala N. (2008). Measuring sustainability: Why the ecological footprint is bad economics and bad environmental science. *Ecological Economics* 67(4), 519–525.

Field F. R., Isaacs, J. A. and Clark, J. P. (1994). Life-cycle analysis of automobiles – a critical review of methodologies. *Journal of the Minerals Metals & Materials Society* 46(4), 12–16.

Fielding A. (1991). Chaotic biology. *Biologist* 38(5), 185–188.

Florides G. A. and Christodoulides P. (2009). Global warming and carbon dioxide through sciences. *Environment International* 35(2), 390–401.

Forde C. (2005). Participatory democracy or pseudo-participation? Local government reform in Ireland. *Local Government Studies* 31(2), 137–148.

Francis C. A. (1986). Introduction: distribution and importance of multiple cropping. In *Multiple Cropping Systems*, ed. C. A. Francis, New York: Macmillan, 1–19.

Francis C. A. (1989). Biological efficiencies in multiple-cropping systems. *Advances in Agronomy* 42, 1–42.

Francis P. (2001). Participatory development at the World Bank: The primacy of process. In *Participation the New Tyranny*, ed. B. Cooke and U. Kothari, Londond: Zed Books, 72–87.

Francis R. I. C. C. and Clark M. R. (2005). Sustainability issues for Orange Roughy fisheries. *Bulletin of Marine Science* 76(2), 337–351.

Free A. and Barton N. H. (2007). Do evolution and ecology need the Gaia hypothesis? *Trends in Ecology & Evolution* 22(11), 611–619.

Freire P. (1972). *Pedagogy of the Oppressed*, London: Sheed and Ward.

Funke T., Han H., Healy-Fried M.L., Fischer M. and Schönbrunn E. (2006). Molecular basis for the herbicide resistance of Roundup Ready crops. *Proceedings of the National Academy of Science USA* 103, 13010–13015.

Gaichas S.K. (2008). A context for ecosystem-based fishery management: Developing concepts of ecosystems and sustainability. *Marine Policy* 32(3), 393–401.

Galeotti M. and Lanza A. (2005). Desperately seeking environmental Kuznets. *Environmental Modelling and Software* 20(11), 1379–1388.

Garcia S.M., Zerbi A., Aliaume C., Chi T.D. and Lasserre G. (2003). The ecosystem approach to fisheries: Issues, terminology, principles, institutional foundations, implementation and outlook. *FAO Fisheries Technical Paper Issue* 443, i-vii, 1–71.

Garcia-Serna J., Perez-Barrigon L. and Cocero M.J. (2007). New trends for design towards sustainability in chemical engineering: Green engineering. *Chemical Engineering Journal* 133(1–3), 7–30.

Gari L. (2002). Arabic treatises on environmental pollution up to the end of the thirteenth century. *Environment and History* 8(4), 475–488.

Gause G.F. (1934). *The Struggle for Existence*, Baltimore: Williams and Wilkins.

Ghosh P.K., Bandyopadhyay K.K., Wanjari R.H., *et al.* (2007). Legume effect for enhancing productivity and nutrient use-efficiency in major cropping systems – An Indian perspective: A review. *Journal of Sustainable Agriculture* 30(1), 59–86.

Giljum S. (2006). Material flow-based indicators for evaluation of eco-efficiency and dematerialisation policies. In *Sustainability Indicators in Ecological Economics*, ed. P. Lawn, Cheltenham: Edward Elgar, 376–398.

Glantz M.H. (1990). Does history have a future – forecasting climate change effects on fisheries by analogy. *Fisheries* 15(6), 39–44.

Glendining M.J., Dailey A.G., Williams A.G., *et al.* (2009). Is it possible to increase the sustainability of arable and ruminant agriculture by reducing inputs? *Agricultural Systems* 99(2–3), 117–125.

Global Footprint Network (2005). National Footprint Accounts, 2005 Edition. Available online at www.footprintnetwork.org).

Goodland R. (1995). The concept of environmental sustainability. *Annual Review of Ecology and Systematics* 26, 1–24.

Gopinath M. and Roe T.L. (1997). Sources of sectoral growth in an economy wide context: The case of US agriculture. *Journal of Productivity Analysis* 8(3), 293–310.

Gordon H.S. (1954). The economic theory of a common-property resource: the fishery. *Journal of Political Economy*, 62, 124–42.

Graciano J.D., Zarate H., Antonio N., *et al.* (2007). Yield and gross income of radish and lettuce in monocrop and intercrop system. *Acta Scientiarum Agronomy* 29(3), 397–401.

Gray T. and Hatchard J. (2008). A complicated relationship: Stakeholder participation and the ecosystem-based approach to fisheries management. *Marine Policy* 32(2), 158–168.

Greenhalgh T. and Russell J. (2009). Evidence-based policy making a critique. *Perspectives in Biology and Medicine* 52(2), 304–318.

Grinnell J. (1904). The origin and distribution of the chestnut-backed chickadee. *Auk* 21,364–82.

Guarnieri V., Benessia A., Camino E. and Barbiero G. (2008). The Myth of Natural Barriers. Is transgene introgression by genetically modified crops an environmental risk? *Rivista Di Biologia-Biology Forum* 101(2), 195–214.

Guijt I. and Shah M. (1998). *The myth of community: Gender issues in participatory development*, London: IT Publications.

Guvenc I. and Yildirim E. (2005). Intercropping with eggplant for proper utilisation of interspace under greenhouse conditions. *European Journal of Horticultural Science* 70(6), 300–302.

Haberl H., Wackernagel M. and Wrbka T. (2004a). Land use and sustainability indicators. *An introduction. Land Use Policy* 21(3), 193–198.

Haberl H., Wackernagel M., Krausmann F., Erb K. H. and Monfreda C. (2004b). Ecological footprints and human appropriation of net primary production: a comparison. *Land Use Policy* 21(3), 279–288.

Haila Y. and Kouki J. (1994). The phenomenon of biodiversity in conservation biology. *Annales Zoologici Fennici* 31(1), 5–18.

Hamilton C. (1999). The genuine progress indicator methodological developments and results from Australia. *Ecological Economics* 30(1), 13–28.

Hammond G. P. (2006). People, planet and prosperity: The determinants of humanity's environmental footprint. *Natural Resources Forum* 30(1), 27–36.

Harbaugh W. T., Levinsom A. and Wilson D. M. (2002). Re-examining the empirical evidence for an Environmental Kuznets Curve. *The Review of Economics and Statistics* 84(3), 541–551.

Hardi P., Barg S., Hodge T. and Pinter L. (1997). Measuring Sustainable development: review of current practice, Occasional Paper no. 17, Ottawa: Industry Canada.

Hardin G. (1968). The tragedy of the commons. *Science* 162, 1243–1248.

Hatch M. D. (1992). C4 Photosynthesis: An unlikely process full of surprises. *Plant and Cell Physiology,* 33(4), 333–342.

Hau J. L. and Bakshi B. R. (2004a). Promise and problems of emergy analysis. *Ecological Modelling* 178(1–2), 215–225.

Hau J. L. and Bakshi B. R. (2004b). Expanding exergy analysis to account for ecosystem products and services. *Environmental Science & Technology* 38(13), 3768–3777.

Heller M. C. and Keoleian G. A. (2003). Assessing the sustainability of the US food system: a life cycle perspective. *Agricultural Systems* 76(3), 1007–1041.

Hepbasli A. (2008). A key review on exergetic analysis and assessment of renewable energy resources for a sustainable future. *Renewable & Sustainable Energy Reviews* 12(3), 593–661.

Herdt R. W. (2006). Biotechnology in agriculture. *Annual Review of Environment and Resources* 31, 265–295.

Herendeen R. A. (2004). Energy analysis and EMERGY analysis – a comparison. *Ecological Modelling* 178(1–2), 227–237.

Hertwich E. G. (2005). Life cycle approaches to sustainable consumption: A critical review. *Environmental Science & Technology* 39(13), 4673–4684.

Herva M., Franco A., Ferreiro S., Alvarez A. and Roca E. (2008). An approach for the application of the Ecological Footprint as environmental indicator in the textile sector. *Journal of Hazardous Materials* 156(1–3), 478–487.

Heysse T. (2006). Consensus and power in deliberative democracy. *Inquiry – An Interdisciplinary Journal of Philosophy* 49(3), 265–289.

Hezri A. A. (2004). Sustainability indicator system and policy processes in Malaysia: a framework for utilisation and learning. *Journal of Environmental Management* 73, 357–371.

Hezri A. A. (2005). Utilisation of sustainability indicators and impact through policy learning in the Malaysian policy processes. *Journal of Environmental Assessment Policy and Management* 7(4), 575–595.

Hibbard M. and Lurie S. (2000). Saving land but losing ground. Challenges to community planning in the era of participation. *Journal of Planning Education and Research* 20(2), 187-195.

Hickey S. and Mohan G. (2005). Relocating participation within a radical politics of development. *Development and Change* 36(2), 237-262.

Hilborn R., Annala J. and Holland D. S. (2006). The cost of overfishing and management strategies for new fisheries on slow-growing fish: Orange Roughy (Hoplostethus atlanticus) in New Zealand. *Canadian Journal of Fisheries and Aquatic Sciences* 63(10), 2149-2153.

Hilborn R., Walters C. J. and Ludwig D. (1995). Sustainable exploitation of renewable resources. *Annual Review of Ecology and Systematics* 26, 45-67.

Hilson C. (2008). Going local? EU Law, localism and climate change. *European Law Review* 33(2), 194-210.

Hilty J. and Merenlender A. (2000). Faunal indicator taxa selection for monitoring ecosystem health. *Biological Conservation* 92(2), 185-197.

Hinterberger F., Luks F. and Schmidt-Bleek F. (1997). Material flows vs. natural capital. *What makes an economy sustainable? Ecological Economics*, 23 (1), 1-14.

Holden E. (1998). Planning theory: Democracy or sustainable development? Both (but don't bother about the bread please). *Scandinavian Housing and Planning Research* 15(4), 227-247.

Holmberg J., Lundqvist U., Robert K. H. and Wackernagel M. (1999). The ecological footprint from a systems perspective of sustainability. *International Journal of Sustainable Development and World Ecology* 6(1), 17-33.

Holt T. (2008). Official statistics, public policy and public trust. *Journal of the Royal Statistical Society Series A - Statistics in Society* 171(2), 323-346.

Holt S. (2009). Sunken billions - But how many? *Fisheries Research* 97(1-2), 3-10.

Holub H. W., Tappeiner G. and Tappeiner U. (1999). Some remarks on the 'System of Integrated Environmental and Economic Accounting' of the United Nations. *Ecological Economics* 29(3), 329-336.

Hoben A. (1982). Anthropologists and development. *Annual review of Anthropology* 11, 349-375.

Hooks C. R. R. and Johnson M. W. (2003). Impact of agricultural diversification on the insect community of cruciferous crops. *Crop Protection* 22(2), 223-238.

Howlett M. (2009). Policy analytical capacity and evidence-based policy-making: Lessons from Canada. *Canadian Public Administration* 52(2), 153-175.

Hulten C. R. (2000). Total Factor Productivity: A short siography. NBER Working Paper No. W7471. Available at SSRN: http://ssrn.com/abstract=213430.

Hunter C. M. and Runge M. C. (2004). The importance of environmental variability and management control error to optimal harvest policies. *Journal of Wildlife Management* 68(3), 585-594.

Huston A. C. (2008). From research to policy and back. *Child Development* 79(1), 1-12.

Hutchinson G. E. (1957). Concluding remarks. *Cold Spring Harbour Symposium* 22, 415-27.

Ibarra A. A., Reid C. and Thorpe A. (2000). The political economy of marine fisheries development in Peru, Chile and Mexico. *Journal of Latin American Studies* 32, 503-527.

Idyll C. P. (1973). *The anchovy crisis, Scientific American.* 228(6), 22-29.

Iles A. (2005). Learning in sustainable agriculture: Food miles and missing objects. *Environmental Values* 14(2), 163-183.

Innvaer S., Vist G., Trommald M. and Oxman A. (2002). Health policy-makers' perceptions of their use of evidence: a systematic review. *Journal of Health Services Research Policy* 7(4), 239-244h.

Intergovernmental Panel on Climate Change (2007). Synthesis Report. Summary for Policymakers. Available at www.ipcc.ch/pdf/assessment-report/ar4/syr/ar4_syr_spm.pdf

Izac A.-M. N. and Swift M. J. (1994). On agricultural sustainability and its measurement in small-scale farming in sub-Saharan Africa. *Ecological Economics* 11, 105–125.

Jahansooz M. R., Yunusa I. A. M.., Coventry D. R., Palmer A. R. and Eamus D. (2007). Radiation- and water-use associated with growth and yields of wheat and chickpea in sole and mixed crops. *European Journal of Agronomy* 26(3), 275–282.

James C. (2006). *Global status of commercialized biotech/GM crops: 2006*. (ISAAA Briefs No. 35). New York: International Service for the Aquisition of Agri-Biotech Applications (ISAAA).

Jennings S., Kaiser M. J. and Reynolds J. D. (2001). *Marine Fisheries Ecology*, Malden MA: Blackwell Publishing.

Johnston P., Everard M., Santillo D., Robert K.-H. (2007). Reclaiming the definition of sustainability. *Environmental Science and Pollution Research* 14(1), 60–66.

Jonasson B. L. (2004). Stakeholder participation as a tool for sustainable development in the Em River Basin. *International Journal of Water Resources Development* 20(3), 345–352.

Jones A. (2002). An environmental assessment of food supply chains: A case study on dessert apples. *Environmental Management* 30(4), 560–576.

Jones P., Comfort D. and Hillier D. (2007). Sustainable development and the UK's major retailers. *Geography* 92(1), 41–47.

Jonsson A. (2000). Tools and methods for environmental assessment of building products – methodological analysis of six selected approaches. *Building and Environment* 35(3), 223–238.

Juntti M., Russel D. and Turnpenny J. (2009). Evidence, politics and power in public policy for the environment. *Environmental Science & Policy* 12(3), 207–215.

Kallio T. J. (2007). Taboos in corporate social responsibility discourse. *Journal of Business Ethics* 74(2), 165–175.

Karnani M. and Annila A. (2009). Gaia again. *Biosystems* 95(1), 82–87.

Kates R. W., Clark W. C., Corell R., *et al.* (2000). *Sustainability Science*. Cambridge MA: Belfer Center for Science and International Affairs, Harvard University.

Katz S. L., Zabel R., Harvey C., Good T. and Levin P. (2001). Ecologically sustainable yield, *American Scientist* 91(2), 150.

Keller C. F. (2007). Global warming 2007. An update to global warming: the balance of evidence and its policy implications. *The Scientific World Journal* 7, 381–99.

Keller C. F. (2009). Global warming: a review of this mostly settled issue. *Stochastic Environmental Research and Risk Assessment* 23(5), 643–676.

Kelling K. A. and Klemme R. M. (1989). Defining 'sustainable'. *Agrochemical Age*, May, 32.

Key S., Ma J. K. C. and Drake P. M. W. (2008). Genetically modified plants and human health. *Journal of the Royal Society of Medicine* 101(6), 290–298.

Kidd C. V. (1992). The evolution of sustainability, *Journal of Agricultural and Environmental Ethics* 5 (1), 1–26.

King C. A. (2008). Community resilience and contemporary agri-ecological systems: Reconnecting people and food, and people with people. *Systems Research and Behavioral Science* 25(1), 111–124.

King G. (2003). The role of participation in the European demonstration projects in ICZM. *Coastal Management* 31(2), 137–143.

Kirchner J. W. (2002). The Gaia hypothesis: Fact, theory, and wishful thinking. *Climatic Change* 52(4), 391–408.

Kirchner J. W. (2003). The Gaia hypothesis: Conjectures and refutations. *Climatic Change* 58(1–2), 21–45.

Kitzes J. and Wackernagel M. (2009). Answers to common questions in Ecological Footprint accounting. *Ecological Indicators* 9(4), 812–817.

Kitzes J., Wackernagel M., Loh J., *et al.* (2008). Shrink and share: humanity's present and future Ecological Footprint. *Philosophical Transactions of the Royal Society B-Biological Sciences* 363(1491), 467–475.

Kitzes J., Galli A., Bagliani M., *et al.* (2009). A research agenda for improving national Ecological Footprint accounts. *Ecological Economics* 68(7), 1991–2007.

Krotscheck C. (1997). Measuring eco-sustainability: Comparison of mass and/or energy flow based highly aggregated indicators. *Environmetrics* 8(6), 661–681.

Kuznets S. and Simon P. (1955). Economic growth and income inequality American Economic Review 45, 1–28.

Landon J. R. (Ed.) (1984). *Booker tropical soil manual*. Harlow, UK: Longman.

Lange G. M. (2007). Environmental accounting: Introducing the SEEA-2003. *Ecological Economics* 61(4), 589–591.

Larkin P. A. (1977). An epitaph for the concept of Maximum Sustainable Yield, *Transactions of the American Fisheries Society* 106 (1), 1–11.

Lawlor D. W. and Mitchell R. A. C. (1991). The effects of increasing CO_2 on crop photosynthesis and productivity – a review of field studies. *Plant Cell and Environment* 14(8), 807–818.

Lawn P. A. (2003). A theoretical foundation to support the Index of Sustainable Economic Welfare (ISEW), Genuine Progress Indicator (GPI), and other related indexes. *Ecological Economics* 44, 105–118.

Lawn P. (2007). A stock-take of green national accounting initiatives. *Social Indicators Research* 80(2), 427–460.

Laws E. A. (1997). *El Nino and the Peruvian Anchovy Fishery*, Sausalito, CA: University Science Books.

Leach M., Scoones I. and Thompson L. (2002). Citizenship, science and risk: Conceptualising relationships across issues and settings. *IDS Bulletin* 33(2), 40.

Lee J. J., Ocallaghan P. and Allen D. (1995). Critical-review of life-cycle analysis and assessment techniques and their application to commercial activities. *Resources Conservation and Recycling* 13(1), 37–56.

Lee M.-D. P. (2008). A review of the theories of corporate social responsibility: Its evolutionary path and the road ahead. *International Journal of Management Reviews* 10(1), 53–73.

Lehman H., Clark E. A. and Weise S. F. (1993). Clarifying the definition of sustainable agriculture. *Journal of Environmental Ethics* 6(2), 127–143.

Leibold M. A. (1995). The niche concept revisited – mechanistic models and community context. *Ecology* 76(5), 1371–1382.

Lenton T. M. and van Oijen M. (2002). Gaia as a complex adaptive system. *Philosophical Transactions of the Royal Society of London Series B – Biological Sciences* 357(1421), 683–695.

Levins R. (1968). *Evolution in Changing Environments*. Princeton, NJ: Princeton University Press.

Lewin K. (1948). *Resolving Social Conflicts: Selected Papers on Group Dynamics*, New York: Harper & Brothers.

Lo S.-F. and Sheu H.-J. (2007). Is corporate sustainability a value-increasing strategy for business? *Corporate Governance-An International Review* 15(2), 345–358.

Long S. P., Zhu X.-G., Naidu S. L. and Ort D. R. (2006). Can improvement in photosynthesis increase crop yields? *Plant, Cell and Environment* 29, 315–330.

Long N. and Long A. (1992). *Battlefields of Knowledge: Interlocking of Theory and Practice in Social Research and Development*. London: Routledge.

Lopez M. V., Garcia A. and Rodriguez L. (2007). Sustainable development and corporate performance: A study based on the Dow Jones Sustainability Index. *Journal of Business Ethics* 75(3), 285–300.

Lovelock J. E. (1987).*Gaia: A New Look at Life on Earth*, Oxford, UK: Oxford University Press.

Lovelock J. E. (1988). *The Ages of Gaia. A Biography of Our Living Earth*, Oxford, UK: Oxford University Press.

Lovelock J. E. and Margulis L. (1974). Atmospheric homeostasis by and for biosphere – Gaia hypothesis. *Tellus* 26(1–2), 2–10.

Lynam J. K. and Herdt R. W. (1989). Sense and sustainability: Sustainability as an objective in international agricultural research. *Agricultural Economics* 3, 381–398.

MacDonald M. and Peters K. (2007). *The Sustainability Report: A Review of Corporate Sustainability Reporting*, York, UK: York Centre for Applied Sustainability, York University, www.sustreport.org/business/report/intro.html. Accessed 10/9/09.

Mace P. M. (2001). A new role for MSY in single-species and ecosystem approaches to fisheries stock assessment and management. *Fish and Fisheries* 2, 2–32.

Malezieux E., Crozat Y., Dupraz C., *et al.* (2009). Mixing plant species in cropping systems: concepts, tools and models. *A review. Agronomy for Sustainable Development* 29(1), 43–62.

Mallory-Smith C. and Zapiola M. (2008). Gene flow from glyphosate-resistant crops. *Pest Management Science* 64(4), 428–440.

Manrique L. A. (1993). Crop production in the tropics – a review. *Journal of Plant Nutrition* 16(8), 1485–1516.

Mansuri G. and Rao V. (2004). Community-based and –driven development: A critical review. *World Bank Research Observer* 19(1), 1–39.

Marjolein B. A. V. and Rijkens-Klomp N. (2002). A look in the mirror; reflection on participation in Integrated Assessment from a methodological perspective. *Global Environment, Change-Human and Policy Dimensions* 12(3), 167–184.

Mayer A. L., Thurston H. W. and Pawlowski C. W. (2004). The multidisciplinary influence of common sustainability indices. *Frontiers in Ecology and the Environment* 2(8), 419–426.

McLean I. (2008). Climate change and UK politics: From Brynle Williams to Sir Nicholas Stern. *Political Quarterly* 79(2), 184–193.

McManus P. and Haughton G. (2006). Planning with Ecological Footprints: a sympathetic critique of theory and practice. *Environment and Urbanization* 18(1), 113–127.

Mead R. and Willey R. W. (1980). The concept of a land equivalent ratio and advantages in yields from intercropping. *Experimental Agriculture* 16(3), 217–228.

Meadowcroft J. (1999). The politics of sustainable development: Emergent arenas and challenges for political science. *International Political Science Review* 20(2), 219–237.

Mebratu D. (1998). Sustainability and sustainable development: Historical and conceptual review. *Environmental Impact Assessment Review* 18(6), 493–520.

Meehl G. A., Stocker T. F., Collins W. D., *et al.* (2007). Global climate projections. In *Climate Change 2007: The Physical Science Basis*, Contribution of Working Group I to the Fourth Assessment Report of the Intergovernmental Panel on Climate Change, ed. S. Solomon, D. Qin, M. Manning, Z. Chen, M. Marquis, K. B. Averyt, M. Tignor and H. L. Miller, Cambridge, UK and New York: Cambridge University Press.

Mendoza G. A. and Prabhu R. (2005). Combining participatory modelling and multi-criteria analysis for community-based forest management. *Forest Ecology and Management* 207(1–2), 145–156.

Mertz O., Ravnborg H. M., Lovei G. L., Nielsen I. and Konijnendijk C. C. (2007). Ecosystem services and biodiversity in developing countries. *Biodiversity and Conservation* 16(10), 2729–2737.

Metz, M. (2003). *Baccillus thuringiensis: A Cornerstone of modern agriculture.* Binghampton: Haworth Press.

Mikalsen K. H. and Jentoft S. (2008). Participatory practices in fisheries across Europe: Making stakeholders more responsible. *Marine Policy* 32(2), 169–177.

Miller F. P. (2003). Natural resources management and the second Copernican revolution. *Journal of Natural Resources and Life Sciences Education* 32, 43–51.

Miller R. P. and Nair P. K. R. (2006). Indigenous agroforestry systems in Amazonia: from prehistory to today. *Agroforestry Systems* 66(2), 151–164.

Miller V., VeneKlasen L. and Clark C. (2005). Rights-based development: Linking rights and participation – Challenges in thinking and action. *IDS Bulletin* 36(1), 31.

Mills J. H. and Waite T. A.. (2009). Economic prosperity, biodiversity conservation, and the environmental Kuznets curve. *Ecological Economics* 68(7), 2087–2095.

Mitcham C. (1995). The concept of sustainable development: its origins and ambivalence. *Technology in Society* 17(3), 311–326.

Moffatt I. (2008). A preliminary analysis of composite indicators of sustainable development. *International Journal of Sustainable Development and World Ecology* 15(2), 81–87.

Mohan G. and Stokke K. (2000). Participatory development and empowerment: the dangers of localism. *Third World Quarterly* 21(2), 247–268.

Mohsenabadi G. R., Jahansooz M. R., Chaichi M. R., *et al.* (2008). Evaluation of barley vetch intercrop at different nitrogen rates. *Journal of Agricultural Science and Technology* 10(1), 23–31.

Monfreda C., Wackernagel M. and Deumling D. (2004). Establishing national natural capital accounts based on detailed – Ecological Footprint and biological capacity assessments. *Land Use Policy* 21(3), 231–246.

Montambault J. R. and Alavalapati J. R. R. (2005). Socioeconomic research in agroforestry: a decade in review. *Agroforestry Systems* 65(2), 151–161.

Montiel I. (2008). Corporate social responsibility and corporate sustainability – Separate pasts, common futures. *Organization & Environment* 21(3), 245–269.

Moon J. (2007). The contribution of corporate social responsibility to sustainable development. *Sustainable Development* 15(5), 296–306.

Patil D. H., Pujari B. T. and Mudalagiriyappa B. T. (2007). Fertilizer management in groundnut and sunflower intercropping system for better economics and land utilization. *Crop Research (Hisar)* 34(1–3), 80–83.

Paulsen H. M. (2008). Organic mixed cropping systems with oilseeds 2. Yields of mixed cropping systems of linseed (Linum ustitatissivum L.) with spring wheat, oats or false flax. *Landbauforschung Volkenrode* 58(4), 307–314.

Pava M. L. (2008). Why corporations should not abandon social responsibility. *Journal of Business Ethics* 83(4), 805–812.

Pawson R. (2006). *Evidence-Based Policy: A Realist Perspective*, Londond: Sage Publications.

Pelletier N. L., Ayer N. W., Tyedmers P. H. *et al.* (2007). Impact categories for life cycle assessment research of seafood production systems: Review and prospectus. *International Journal of Life Cycle Assessment* 12(6), 414–421.

Pepper D. (1987). *The Roots of Modern Environmentalism*, London: Routledge.

Pereira H. M. and Cooper H. D. (2006). Towards the global monitoring of biodiversity change. *Trends in Ecology & Evolution* 21(3), 123–129.

Perman R. and Stern D. I. (2003). Evidence from panel unit root and co-integration tests that the Environmental Kuznets Curve does not exist. *Australian Journal of Agricultural and Resource Economics*, 47(3). 325–347.

Peterson M. N., Peterson M. J. and Peterson T. R. (2005). Conservation and the myth of consensus. *Conservation Biology* 19(3), 762–767.

Polacheck T., Hilborn R. and Punt A. E. (1993). Fitting surplus production models: Comparing methods and measuring uncertainty. *Canadian Journal of Fisheries and Aquatic Sciences* 50(12), 2597–2607.

Poolman M. and Van de Giesen N. (2006). Participation: rhetoric and reality. The importance of understanding stakeholders based on a case study in Upper East Ghana. *International Journal of Water Resources Development* 22(4), 561–573.

Popielarz P. A. and Neal Z. P. (2007). The niche as a theoretical tool. *Annual Review of Sociology* 33, 65–84.

Porwal M. K., Agarwal S. K. and Khokhar A. K. (2006). Effect of planting methods and intercrops on productivity and economics of castor (Ricinus communis)-based intercropping systems. *Indian Journal of Agronomy* 51(4), 274–277.

Prager M. H. (1994). A suite of extensions to a non-equilibrium surplus-production model. *Fishery Bulletin* 92(2), 374–389.

Prakash V., Pandey A. K. and Srivastava A. K. (2004a). Relay intercropping of potato (Solanum tuberosum) in maize (Zea mays) under mid-hill condition of north-western Himalaya. *Indian Journal of Agricultural Sciences* 74(2), 64–67.

Prakash V., Pandey A. K., Srivastva A. K. and Gupta H. S. (2004b). Relay intercropping of hybrid tomato (Lyeopersicon esculentum) in maize (Zea mays) under mid-hill condition of North-Western Himalayas. *Indian Journal of Agricultural Sciences* 74(8), 405–408.

Pretty J. N., Ball A. S., Lang T and Morison J. I. L. (2005). Farm costs and food miles: An assessment of the full cost of the UK weekly food basket. *Food Policy* 30(1), 1–19.

Pullin A. S. and Knight T. M. (2009). Doing more good than harm – Building an evidence-base for conservation and environmental management. *Biological Conservation* 142(5), 931–934.

Rahimi M. M. and Yadegari M. (2008). Assessment of product in corn and soybean intercropping. *International Conference on Mathematical Biology 2007, AIP Conference Proceedings* 971, 187–191.

Raji J. A. (2007). Intercropping kenaf and cowpea. *African Journal of Biotechnology* 6(24), 2807–2809.

Raji J. A. (2008). The feasibility of intercropping kenaf with sorghum in a small-holder farming system. *Journal of Sustainable Agriculture* 32(2), 355–364.

Rao S. S., Regar P. L., Jangid B. L. and Chand K. (2009). Productivity and economics of sorghum (Sorghum bicolor) and greengram (Phaseolus radiata) intercropping system as affected by row ratio and nitrogen in and fringes. *Indian Journal of Agricultural Sciences* 79(2), 101–105.

Raugei M. and Ulgiati S. (2009). A novel approach to the problem of geographic allocation of environmental impact in Life Cycle Assessment and Material Flow Analysis. *Ecological Indicators* 9(6), 1257–1283.

Raup D. and Sepkoski J. (1982). Mass extinctions in the marine fossil record. *Science* 215, 1501–1503.

Ravallion M. (1997). Good and bad growth: The Human Development Reports. *World Development* 25(5), 631–638.

Rebitzer G., Ekvall T., Frischknecht R. *et al.* (2004). Life cycle assessment Part 1: Framework, goal and scope definition, inventory analysis, and applications. *Environment International* 30(5), 701–720.

Reed M. S. (2008). Stakeholder participation for environmental management: A literature review. *Biological Conservation* 141(10), 2417–2431.

Reed M. S., Graves A., Dandy N. *et al.* (2009). Who's in and why? A typology of stakeholder analysis methods for natural resource management. *Journal of Environmental Management* 90(5), 1933–1949.

Rees W. E. (1996). Ecological footprints of the future. *Overview. People Planet* 5(2), 6–9.

Rees W. E. (2002). Footprint: our impact on Earth is getting heavier. *Nature* 420(6913), 267–268.

Ricotta C. (2005). Through the jungle of biological diversity. *Acta Biotheoretica* 53 (1), 29–38.

Riley J. (1984). A general-form of the Land Equivalent Ratio. *Experimental Agriculture* 20(1), 19–29.

Robèrt K.-H. (2002). *The Natural Step Story. Seeding a Quiet Revolution.* Gabriola Island BC: New Society Publishers.

Robèrt K.-H., Daly H., Hawken P. and Holmberg J. (1997). A compass for sustainable development. *International Journal of Sustainable Development and World Ecology* (4),79–92.

Rockloff S. F. and Moore S. A. (2006). Assessing representation at different scales of decision making: Rethinking local is better. *Policy Studies Journal* 34(4), 649–670.

Rohde R. A. and Muller R. A. (2005). Cycles in fossil diversity. *Nature* 434, 209–210.

Romsdahl R. J. (2005). Appendix A. *When do environmental decision makers use social science? In Decision Making for the Environment: Social and Behavioural Science Research Priorities,* ed. G. D. Brewer and P. C. Stern Washington DC: National Academies Press.

Rosen M. A., Dincer I. and Kanoglu M. (2008). Role of exergy in increasing efficiency and sustainability and reducing environmental impact. *Energy Policy* 36(1), 128–137.

Rosenberg A. A., Swasey J. H. and Bowman M. (2006). Rebuilding US fisheries: progress and problems. *Frontiers in Ecology and the Environment* 4(6), 303–308.

Rowland J., Andrews W. S. and Creber K. A. M. (2004). A neural network approach to selecting indicators for a sustainable ecosystem. *Journal of Environmental Engineering and Science* 3(Supplement 1), S129-S136.

Rupasingha A., Goetz S. J., Debertin D. L. and Pagoulatos A. (2004). The environmental Kuznets curve for US counties: A spatial econometric analysis with extensions. *Papers in Regional Science* 83 (2), 407–424.

Rydin Y. (2007). Indicators as a governmental technology? The lessons of community-based sustainability indicator projects. *Environment and Planning D: Society and Space* 25, 610–624.

Salazar J. F. and Poveda G. (2009). Role of a simplified hydrological cycle and clouds in regulating the climate-biota system of Daisyworld. *Tellus Series B – Chemical and Physical Meteorology* 61(2), 483–497.

Salwasser H. (1993). Sustainability needs more than better science. *Ecological Applications* 3(4), 587–589.

Sanderson I. (2002). Evaluation, policy learning and evidence-based policy making. *Public Administration* 80(1), 1–22.

Sarkar R. K., Malik G. C. and Pal P. K. (2004). Effect of intercropping lentil (Lens culinaris) and linseed (Linum usitatissimum) under varying plant density and row arrangement on productivity and advantages in system under rainfed upland. *Indian Journal of Agronomy* 49(4), 241–243.

Scales B. R. and Marsden S. J. (2008). Biodiversity in small-scale tropical agroforests: a review of species richness and abundance shifts and the factors influencing them. *Environmental Conservation* 35(2), 160–172.

Schaefer M. B. (1954). Some aspects of the dynamics of populations important to the management of commercial marine fisheries. *Bulletin of the Inter-American Tropical Tuna Commission* 1, 27–56.

Schaefer M. B. (1957). A study of the dynamics of the fishery for yellowfin tuna in the eastern tropical Pacific Ocean. *Bulletin of the Inter-American Tropical Tuna Commission* 2, 245–285.

Scherr S. J. (1991). On-farm research – the challenges of agroforestry. *Agroforestry Systems* 15(2–3), 95–110.

Schmidt-Bleek F. (2000). The Factor 10/MIPS-Concept. Bridging ecological, economic, and social dimensions with Sustainability Indicators. Available for download at factor10-institute.org/files/MIPS.pdf.

Schulthess F., Chabi-Olaye A. and Gounou S. (2004). Multi-trophic level interactions in a cassava-maize mixed cropping system in the humid tropics of West Africa. *Bulletin of Entomological Research* 94(3), 261–272.

Schwilch G., Bachmann F. and Liniger H. P. (2009). Appraising and selecting conservation measures to mitigate desertification and land degradation based on stakeholder participation and global best practices. *Land Degradation & Development* 20(3), 308–326.

Science Council of Canada (1992). *Sustainable Agriculture: The Research Challenge.* Report 43, July, Ottawa, Ontario: Science Council of Canada.

Scott I. M. (2000). Green symbolism in the genetic modification debate. *Journal of Agricultural & Environmental Ethics* 13(3–4), 293–311.

Sellamna N.-E. (1999). *Relativism in Agricultural Research and Development: Is Participation a Post-Modern Concept?* ODI Working Paper 119. Overseas Development Institute: London.

Sen A. K. (1984). *Resources, Values and Development*, Cambridge, MA: Harvard University Press.

Sen A. K. 1985. *Commodities and Capabilities*, Oxford: Oxford University Press.

Sepkoski J. J. (2002). A compendium of fossil marine animal genera. *Bulletin of American Paleontology* 363, 1–560.

Sharma K. C. (2008). Fodder productivity and economics of multi-cut pearlmillet (Pennisetum glaucum) intercropped with clusterbean (Cyamopsis tetragonoloba). *Indian Journal of Agronomy* 53(1), 51–56.

Sharma R. P., Singh A. K., Poddar B. K. and Raman K. R. (2008). Forage production potential and economics of maize (Zea mays) with legumes intercropping under various row proportions. *Indian Journal of Agronomy* 53(2), 121–124.

Shelton P. A. and Sinclair A. F. (2008). It's time to sharpen our definition of sustainable fisheries management. *Canadian Journal of Fisheries and Aquatic Sciences* 65(10), 2305–2314.

Shen C.-H. and Chang Y. (2009). Ambition versus conscience, does Corporate Social Responsibility pay off? The application of matching methods. *Journal of Business Ethics* 88, 133–153.

Shrivastava G. K., Lakpale R., Choubey N. K. and Singh A. P. (2004). Productivity and economics of pigeonpea (Cajanus cajan) plus urdbean (Phaseolus mungo) intercropping system under various planting geometry and fertilizer management in rainfed condition of Chhattisgarh. *Indian Journal of Agronomy* 49(2), 101–103.

Sibbald A. R. (1999). Agroforestry principles – Sustainable productivity? *Scottish Forestry* 53(1), 18–23.

Smith P. J., Francis R. I. C. C. and McVeagh M. (1991). Loss of genetic diversity due to fishing pressure. *Fisheries Research* 10(3–4), 309–316.

Smith H. and McSorley R. (2000). Intercropping and pest management: A review of major concepts. *American Entomologist* 46(3), 154–161.

Smith V. and Langford P. (2009). Evaluating the impact of corporate social responsibility programs on consumers. *Journal of Management & Organization* 15(1), 97–109.

Smithson J. B. and Lenne J. M. (1996). Varietal mixtures: A viable strategy for sustainable productivity in subsistence agriculture. *Annals of Applied Biology* 128(1), 127–158.

Sobhee S. K. (2004). The environmental Kuznets curve (EKC): a logistic curve? *Applied Economics Letters* 11(7), 449–452.

Soma K. and Vatn A. (2009). Local democracy implications for coastal zone management-A case study in southern Norway. *Land Use Policy* 26(3), 755–762.

Sorrell S. (2007). Improving the evidence base for energy policy: The role of systematic reviews. *Energy Policy* 35, 1858–1871.

Spangenberg H., Hinterberger F., Moll S. and Schutz H. (1999). Material flow analysis, TMR and the MIPS concept: a contribution to the development of indicators for measuring changes in consumption and production patterns. *International Journal of Sustainable Development* 2(4), 491–505.

Spector B. (2008). Business Responsibilities in a Divided World: The Cold War roots of the corporate social responsibility movement. *Enterprise & Society* 9(2), 314–336.

Speight M. R. (1983). The potential of ecosystem management for pest control. *Agriculture, Ecosystems and Environment* 10(2), 183–199.

Spencer D. S. C. and Swift M. J. (1992). Sustainable agriculture: Definition and measurement In *Biological Nitrogen Fixation and Sustainability of Tropical Agriculture*, ed. K. Mulongoy, M. Gueye and D. S. C. Spencer Chichester, UK: John Wiley & Sons, Ltd. 15–24.

Srinivasan T. N.. (1994). Human development: A new paradigm or reinvention of the wheel? *The American Economic Review* 84(2), 238–243.

Staley M. (2002). Darwinian selection leads to Gaia. *Journal of Theoretical Biology* 218(1), 35–46.

Steinbeck J. (1939). *The Grapes of Wrath*, London: William Heinemann.

Stern D. I. (2004). The rise and fall of the environmental Kuznets curve. *World Development* 32 (8), 1419–1439.

Stern D. I., Common M. S. and Barbier E. B. (1996). Economic growth and environmental degradation: The Environmental Kuznets Curve and sustainable development. *World Development* 24 (7), 1151–1160.

Stockle C. O., Papendick R. I., Saxton K. E., Campbell G. S. and van Evert F. K. (1994). A framework for evaluating the sustainability of agricultural production systems. *American Journal of Alternative Agriculture* 9(1 and2), 45–50.

Stoeglehner G. and Narodoslawsky M. (2008). Implementing ecological footprinting in decision-making processes. *Land Use Policy* 25(3), 421–431.

Strange P. (1983). Permaculture – practical design for town and country in permanent agriculture. *Ecologist* 13(2–3), 88–94.

Strange A., Park J., Bennett R. and Phipps R. (2008). The use of life-cycle assessment to evaluate the environmental impacts of growing genetically modified, nitrogen use-efficient canola. *Plant Biotechnology Journal* 6, 337–345.

Straton A. (2006). A complex systems approach to the value of ecological resources. *Ecological Economics* 56(3), 402–411.

Stringer L. C., Dougill A. J., Fraser E., Hubacek K., Prell C. and Reed M. S. (2006). Unpacking 'participation' in the adaptive management of social ecological systems: A critical review. *Ecology and Society* 11(2), Article Number: 39.

Stubbs W. and Cocklin C. (2008). Conceptualizing a 'sustainability business model'. *Organization & Environment* 21(2), 103–127.

Suganthi L. and Samuel A. A. (2000). Exergy based supply side energy management for sustainable energy development. *Renewable Energy* 19(1–2), 285–290.

Sultana P., Abeyasekera S. and Thompson P. (2007). Methodological rigour in assessing participatory development. *Agricultural Systems* 94(2), 220–230.

Sultana P., Thompson P. and Green C. (2008). Can England learn lessons from Bangladesh in introducing participatory floodplain management? *Water Resources Management* 22(3), 357–376.

Sunderland K. and Samu F. (2000). Effects of agricultural diversification on the abundance, distribution, and pest control potential of spiders: a review. *Entomologia Experimentalis et Applicata* 95(1), 1–13.

Talberth J., Cobb C. and Slattery N. (2007). *The Genuine Progress Indicator 2006: A Tool for Sustainable Development*, Oakland, CA: Redefining Progress.

Thabrew L., Wiek A. and Ries R. (2009). Environmental decision making in multi-stakeholder contexts: applicability of life cycle thinking in development planning and implementation. *Journal of Cleaner Production* 17(1), 67–76.

Thirtle C. and Bottomley P. (1992). Total factor productivity in UK agriculture, 1967–90. *Journal of Agricultural Economics* 43(3), 381–400.

Thompson C. J., Movva N. R., Tizard R. *et al.* (1987). Characterization of the herbicide-resistance gene bar from Streptomyces hygroscopicus. *Journal of the European Molecular Biology Organization (EMBO).* 6, 2519–2523.

Torquebiau E. (1992). Are tropical agroforestry home gardens sustainable? *Agriculture Ecosystems & Environment* 41(2), 189–207.

Torras M. and Boyce J. K. (1998). Income, inequality and pollution: A reassessment of the Environmental Kuznets Curve. *Ecological Economics* 25 (2), 147–160.

Tripathi H. N., Chand S. and Tripathi A. K. (2005). Biological and economical feasibility of chickpea (*Cicer arietinum*) plus Indian mustard (*Brassica juncea*) cropping systems under varying levels of phosphorus. *Indian Journal of Agronomy* 50(1), 31–34.

Tukker A. and Jansen B. (2006). Environment impacts of products – A detailed review of studies. *Journal of Industrial Ecology* 10(3), 159–182.

Turnhout E., Hisschemoller M. and Eijsackers H. (2007). Ecological indicators: Between the two fires of science and policy. *Ecological Indicators* 7, 215–228.

Tyteca D. (1996). On the measurement of environmental performance of firms – A literature review and a productive efficiency perspective. *Journal of Environmental Management* 46(3), 281–308.

United Nations Development Programme (1990). *Human Development Report 1990*, , New York: UNDP, Human Development Report Office.

Upham P. (2000a). Scientific consensus on sustainability: The case of the Natural Step. *Sustainable Development* 8(4), 180–190.

Upham P. (2000b). An assessment of The Natural Step theory of sustainability. *Journal of Cleaner Production* 8(6), 445–454.

van Beurden P. and Gossling T. (2008). The Worth of Values – A Literature Review on the Relation Between Corporate Social and Financial Performance. *Journal of Business Ethics* 82(2), 407–424.

Van de Kerkhof M. (2006). Making a difference: On the constraints of consensus building and the relevance of deliberation in stakeholder analysis. *Policy Studies* 39(3), 279–299.

van den Bergh J. C. J. M. and Verbruggen H. (1999). Spatial sustainability, trade and indicators: an evaluation of the 'ecological footprint'. *Ecological Economics* 29(1), 61–72.

van den Bergh J. and Verbruggen H. (2000). An evaluation of the 'ecological footprint': reply to Wackernagel and Ferguson. *Ecological Economics* 31(3), 319–321.

van Kooten G. C. and Bulte E. H. (2000). The ecological footprint: useful science or politics? *Ecological Economics* 32(3), 385–389.

Vanderheiden S. (2008). Two conceptions of sustainability. *Political Studies* 56(2), 435–455.

Vanhamme J. and Grobben B. (2009). 'Too Good to be True!' The Effectiveness of CSR history in countering negative publicity. *Journal of Business Ethics* 85, 273–283.

Vantanen A. and Maritunen M. (2005). Public involvement in multi-objective water level regulation development projects – evaluating the applicability of public involvement methods. *Environmental Impact Assessment Review* 25(3), 281–304.

Varga M. and Kuehr R. (2007). Integrative approaches towards Zero Emissions regional planning: synergies of concepts. *Journal of Cleaner Production* 15(13–14), 1373–1381.

Varjopuro R., Gray T., Hatchard J., Rauschmayer F. and Wittmer H. (2008). Introduction: Interaction between environment and fisheries – The role of stakeholder participation. *Marine Policy* 32(2), 147–157.

Venetoulis J. and Talberth J. (2008). Refining the ecological footprint. *Environment Development and Sustainability* 10(4), 441–469.

Verkerk R. H. J., Leather S. R. and Wright D. J. (1998). The potential for manipulating crop-pest-natural enemy interactions for improved insect pest management. *Bulletin of Entomological Research* 88(5), 493–501.

Verma S. S., Joshi Y. P. and Saxena S. C. (2005). Effect of row ratio of fodder sorghum (*Sorghum bicolor*) in pigeonpea (*Cajanus cajan*) intercropping system on productivity, competition functions and economics under rainfed conditions of north India. *Indian Journal of Agronomy* 50(2), 123–125.

Vilanova M., Lozano J. M. and Arenas D. (2009). Exploring the nature of the relationship between CSR and competitiveness. *Journal of Business Ethics* 87, 57–69.

Villanueva A. and Wenzel H. (2007). Paper waste – recycling, incineration or landfilling? A review of existing life cycle assessments. *Waste Management* 27 (8), S29–S46.

Vogt, W. (1949). *Road to Survival*, London: Victor Gollancz.

Volk T. (2003). Natural selection, Gaia, and inadvertent by-products – A reply to Lenton and Wilkinson's response. *Climatic Change* 58(1–2), 13–19.

Wackernagel M., Schulz N. B., Deumling D. *et al.* (2002). Tracking the ecological overshoot of the human economy. *Proceedings of the National Academy of Sciences of the United States of America* 99(14), 9266–9271.

Wackernagel M., Monfreda C., Schulz N. B. *et al.* (2004). Calculating national and global ecological footprint time series: resolving conceptual challenges. *Land Use Policy* 21(3), 271–278.

Wackernagel, M. and Rees, W. E. (1996). *Our Ecological Footprint: Reducing Human Impact on the Earth*, Gabriola Island: New Society Publishers.

Wagner M. (2008). The carbon Kuznets curve: A cloudy picture emitted by bad econometrics? *Resource and Energy Economics* 30(3), 388–408.

Wall G. (Lead Author) and Cleveland C. J. (Topic Ed.) (2008). Exergy. In: *Encyclopedia of Earth*, Ed. C. J. Cleveland, Washington, D.C.: Environmental Information Coalition, National Council for Science and the Environment. [First published in the *Encyclopedia of Earth* August 29, 2006; last revised February 21, 2008; letrieved July 1, 2009]. www.eoearth.org/article/Exergy.

Walsh C., O'Regan B. and Moles R. (2009). Incorporating methane into ecological footprint analysis: A case study of Ireland. *Ecological Economics* 68(7), 1952–1962.

Waltham D. (2007). Half a billion years of good weather: Gaia or good luck? *Astronomy & Geophysics* 48(3), 22–24.

Watson A. M. (1974). Arab agricultural revolution and its diffusion, 700–1100. *Journal of Economic History* 34(1), 8–35.

Watson A. M. (1981). A medieval Green Revolution: New crops and farming techniques in the Early Islamic World. In *The Islamic Middle East, 700–1900: Studies in Economic and Social History*, ed. A. L. Udovitch Princeton NJ: The Darwin Press, 29–58.

Watson A. M. (1983), *Agricultural Innovation in the Early Islamic World*, Cambridge: Cambridge University Press.

Watson R. and Pauly D. (2001). Systematic distortions in world fisheries catch trends. *Nature* 414(6863), 534–536.

Weber C. L. and Matthews H. S. (2008). Food-miles and the relative climate impacts of food choices in the United States. *Environmental Science & Technology* 42(10), 3508–3513.

Welp M., de la Vega-Leinert A., Stoll-Kleemann S. and Jaeger C. C. (2006). Science-based stakeholder dialogues: Theories and tools. *Global Environmental Change-Human and Policy Dimensions* 16(2), 170–181.

Weyzig F. (2009). Political and Economic Arguments for Corporate Social Responsibility: Analysis and a Proposition Regarding the CSR Agenda. *Journal of Business Ethics* 86(4), 417–428.

White T. J. (2007). Sharing resources: The global distribution of the Ecological Footprint. *Ecological Economics* 64(2), 402–410.

Williams G. (2004). Evaluating participatory development, power and (re)politicisation. *Third World Quarterly* 25(3), 557–578.

Willis H. H., DeKay M. L., Morgan M. G., Florig H. K. and Fischbeck P. S. (2004). Ecological risk ranking: Development and evaluation of a method for improving public participation in environmental decision making. *Risk Analysis* 24(2), 363–378.

Willmann R. (2000). Integration of sustainability indicators: the contribution of integrated economic and environmental accounting. *Marine and Freshwater Research* 51(5), 501–511.

Wilson G. A. and Rigg J. (2003). 'Post-productivist' agricultural regimes and the South: Discordant concepts? *Progress in Human Geography* 27(6), 681–707.

Wilson J., Tyedmers P., and Pelot R. (2007). Contrasting and comparing sustainable development indicator metrics. *Ecological Indicators* 7(2), 299–314.

Winkler R. (2006a). Valuation of ecosystem goods and services Part 1: An integrated dynamic approach. *Ecological Economics* 59(1), 82–93.

Winkler R. (2006b). Valuation of ecosystem goods and services Part 2: Implications of unpredictable novel change. *Ecological Economics* 59(1), 94–105.

Wood A. J., Ackland G. J., Dyke J. G., Williams H. T. P. and Lenton T. M. (2008). Daisyworld: A review. *Reviews of Geophysics* 46(1), Article Number: RG1001.

York R., Rosa E. A. and Dietz T. (2003). Footprints on the earth: The environmental consequences of modernity. *American Sociological Review* 68(2), 279–300.

York R., Rosa E. A. and Dietz T. (2004). The ecological footprint intensity of national economies. *Journal of Industrial Ecology* 8(4), 139–154.

Young A. (1989). *Agroforestry for soil conservation*, Wallingford, Oxfordshire, UK: International Council for Research in Agroforestry, CAB International.

Young O. R. (1998). Institutional uncertainties in international fisheries management. *Fisheries Research* 37(1–3), 211–224.

Yunlong C. and Smit B. (1994). Sustainability in agriculture: a general review. *Agriculture, Ecosystems and Environment* 49, 299–307.

Zarate H., Antonio N., Vieira M. *et al.* (2007a). Yield and gross income of taro culture in monocrop system and intercropped with parsley and coriander cultures. *Acta Scientiarum Agronomy* 29(1), 83–89.

Zarate N. A. H, Vieira M. D. C., Giuliani A. R. *et al.* (2007b). 'Macaquinho' taro in monocrop system and intercropped with 'Salad Bowl' lettuce in soil with chicken manure mulching. *Semina-Ciencias Agrarias* 28(4), 563–570.

Zarate N. A. H., Vicira M. D. C., Rech J. *et al.* (2008). Yield and gross income of arracacha in monocrop and intercropping with the Japanese bunching onion and parsley. *Horticultura Brasileira* 26(2), 287–291.

Zhao S., Wu C. W., Hong H. S. and Zhang L. P. (2009). Linking the concept of ecological footprint and valuation of ecosystem services – a case study of economic growth and natural carrying capacity. *International Journal of Sustainable Development and World Ecology* 16(2), 137–142.

Zhu X.-G., Long S. P. and Ort D. R. (2008). What is the maximum efficiency with which photosynthesis can convert solar energy into biomass? *Current Opinion in Biotechnology* 19(2), 153–159.

Zimdahl R. L. (2005). Extending Ethics. *Journal of Extension* 43(5), Article No. 5COM1 October 2005. Available on-line at www.joe.org. (accessed 26 January 2010).

Zimmerman A. and Kibert C. J. (2007). Informing LEED's next generation with the natural step. *Building Research and Information* 35(6), 681–689.

Index